Particulars and Universals in Clinical and Developmental Psychology

A volume in
Perspectives on Human Development
Dieter Ferring, Jaan Valsiner, and Conchita D'Ambrosio, *Series Editors*

Particulars and Universals in Clinical and Developmental Psychology

Critical Reflections

edited by

Meike Watzlawik

Sigmund Freud Privat Universität Berlin

Alina Kriebel

Universität Osnabrück

Jaan Valsiner

Aalborg Universitet

IAP

INFORMATION AGE PUBLISHING, INC.
Charlotte, NC • www.infoagepub.com

Library of Congress Cataloging-in-Publication Data

A CIP record for this book is available from the Library of Congress
http://www.loc.gov

ISBN: 978-1-68123-359-8 (Paperback)
978-1-68123-360-4 (Hardcover)
978-1-68123-361-1 (ebook)

Printed in the United States of America

CONTENTS

PREFACE

SUBJECTIVITY AND KNOWLEDGE CONSTRUCTION

Particular Perspectives and Universal Principles

Psychology as a science requires concepts that create order. In developmental psychology various concepts—such as stages, phases, or levels of organization—have been used to create order, consistencies, or homogeneity across individuals. However, developmental psychology must also account for heterogeneity or inconsistencies within individuals.

—Bibace, Sagarin, & Dyl, 1998, p. 153

Psychologists are thus faced with a dilemma, it seems. They are supposed to simplify to generate universal principles (homogeneity), but at the same time not lose the individual out of sight, accounting for inconsistencies and heterogeneity. How can this be accomplished? Even Goethe already believed that "every rational construction should start from the personal experience of being in contact with the phenomenon of interest" (Cornejo, 2015, p. 9)—human experiences in this case.

This volume will start off from the perspective of the researcher. Bibace, Sagarin, and Dyl's quote (1998) above continues on with, "How developmental psychologists deal with individual differences depends on the assumptions being made regarding development as a theoretical concept"

Particulars and Universals in Clinical and Developmental Psychology, pages ix–xii

(p. 153). These assumptions again differ between individuals, between schools (paradigms), and have changed and keep changing over time.

In the first section of this book, Roger Bibace will show how certain theorists, in his case Heinz Werner, have influenced his own work (Chapter 1). Hroar Klempe will—with reference to Bibace and Werner—continue the discussion on how "psychology is to be regarded as a science that from the very beginning has been forced to take these dynamic and fleeting aspects of life into account." He will demonstrate the influence of several known theorists on the understanding of what psychology is and can be and how this understanding—and with it the understanding of human development—has changed over time (Chapter 2). Jim Laird, in the final chapter of this section (Chapter 3), again starts with personal encounters influencing his own research, but then shows how "all people, including professional philosophers, make sense of new phenomena by applying metaphors from old, well understood phenomena." All three authors stress that every individual working in the practical and scientific field can only understand phenomena from his or her own very personal and subjective perspective. This is not a disadvantage and can even be *erkenntnisproduktiv* [knowledge productive] (Kühner, 2012). An idea that others have also stressed when demonstrating how subjectivity can foster insight is the understanding of interpersonal fields in which self and other emerge and become known (e.g., Groark, 2011).

In the second section, we will take a closer look on how subjectivity, or as Bibace puts it how our own egocentricity influences interactions in the practical field with a focus on conceptions of illness. In Chapter 4, Bibace and Mary Walsh demonstrate how children's conceptions of illness differ from those of adults. Starting with individual statements, they arrive at generalizations of how a child's concept of illness changes in certain specifiable directions with age and development. While developmental progress can influence our view on things, culture can as well, as AeJa Jung describes in Chapter 5. The South Korean concept of *maum*, the "core" of human beings, will be introduced to highlight this observation and to "demonstrate that there are no proper terms in other languages to allow for an adequate direct translation." In Chapters 6 and 7, the focus will switch from the concept of illness to the therapeutic process itself. Again, the expectations of the therapist and patient depend on certain presumptions—vividly demonstrated and discussed by Bibace and Philip Rosenbaum. By drawing attention to "psychological defenses" coming from the patient that can impact "field dynamics," Rosenbaum highlights "the reciprocal process between interpsychic and intrapsychic processes" in the therapeutic situation.

In the third section, the question of whose agent one is—as a practitioner and researcher —will be posed and answered from different perspectives. Bibace will ask the question from the position of a family physician

(Chapter 8). Alina Kriebel and Saskia Stöckigt report on an empirical study in which they confronted physicians and medical students from Germany and the United States with different dilemmas to show how the different groups justify their moral decisions, thereby giving insight into "whose agents they are." In addition, cultural differences are examined (Chapter 9). In Chapter 10, Bibace illustrates that establishing informed consent is not as easy as it may seem, since giving general information does not equal understanding on the individual level. The author stresses that scientific approaches need to reflect the level they are approaching a certain phenomenon at: Is it universalistic striving to articulate processes or is it particular striving to understand how "this instant of the universal process is manifested?" In Chapter 11, Michael Bamberg and Nancy Budwig follow Bibace's suggestion to focus on the patient-doctor or participant-researcher *relationship*, but instead of examining the different (institutional) orientations the individuals bring to the communicative setting, they focus on different orientations or voices within the individuals involved.

In the fourth section, the focus on the researcher–participant relationship continues. After an introduction of the partnership in a research approach by Bibace (Chapter 12), different authors will discuss these and similar ideas from different perspectives. While Nikita Kharlamov, Aleksandra Kaszowska, and Bibace (Chapter 13) argue that the researcher-participant relationship involves a complex constellation of changing and newly emerging, potentially unpredicted goals and interests embedded in multiple values, they also take the broad institutional framing of research, i.e., the influence of ethics regulation and review practices into account. While Kharlamov, Kaszowska, and Bibace arrive at the conclusion that denying

> the existence of change and development in focused researcher-participant interactions and unfolding relationships between them... dehumanizes research... [and] undermines epistemic values of research by blocking possibilities of knowledge creation through making invisible the inevitable change of research participants, researcher, and their mutual relationships,

The authors of the other chapters (Chapters 14 and 15) apply these theoretical assumptions and demonstrate the impact of researcher-participant relationships in different settings. Ana Cecilia Bastos reframes the researcher-participant relationship by adopting an auto-ethnographical approach refusing "to consider the reality of the *other* as something exotic," not estranged but part of human reality. After a brief introduction of basic ideas anchored in semiotic-cultural constructivism, Lívia Mathias Simão, Danilo Silva Guimarães, Djalma Francisco Costa Lisboa de Freitas, Suara Bastos, and Hernán Sánchez Rios discuss theoretical and methodological implications for understanding the meaning of partnership within the framework of semiotic-cultural constructivism in psychology by presenting three very different research projects.

The book ends with a chapter on a specific person, Roger Bibace himself, who as a person, practitioner, and researcher has influenced many others—patients, students, colleagues, and friends. With this volume, we would like to honor the person he is and his work because he always managed to, as we Germans would say, "Pick up the other from where he stands," meaning that one should always take into consideration the individual's standing. It was and is of major importance to Roger Bibace that we should do our best to understand the situation of those we work with and be aware of the dynamics of our interactions. Otherwise, we will not be as successful in what we do, or will at least not have managed to establish rapport even though we might have fixed what was broken (e.g., in the case of the physician) or have gathered extensive data (e.g., in the case of the researcher).

With this book, we also want to stress that understanding someone else is never possible without understanding where oneself is coming from. Our attempt to "pick up the other where he or she stands" is guided by our own experiences, knowledge, and environment as well as situational circumstances. That is why we used Bibace's different "selves" as leitmotif for this book: Starting from particular experiences that lead to the universal principle that understanding our interaction partners and ourselves is an on-going process that will never be fully accomplished, which is not discouraging, but human in its nature.

Meike Watzlawik and **Alina Kriebel**

REFERENCES

Bibace, R., Sagarin, J. D., & Dyl, J. (1998). The heuristic value of Werner's co-existence concept of development. *Journal of Applied Developmental Psychology, 19*(1), 153–163.

Cornejo, C. (2015). *From fantasy to imagination: A cultural history and a moral for cultural psychology.* Retrieved May 2015 from http://www.ccp.aau.dk/digitalAssets/98/98719_from-20fantasy-20to-20imagination.pdf

Groark, K. (2011, March/April). *Devereux's paradox: Disciplined subjectivity as the royal road to objectivity.* Paper presented at the biennial meeting of the Society for Psychological Anthropology, Santa Monica, CA.

Kühner, A. (2012). Subjektivität und reflexivität im erkenntnisprozess. Drei thesen zur vermittlung einer adäquaten forschungshaltung in der qualitativen methodenlehre [Subjectivity and reflexivity in the process of knowledge construction. Three theses for the establishment of an adequate research position in qualitative research methodologies]. *Freie Assoziation, 15*(1), 71–74.

SECTION I

THE THEORIST:
BUILDING ON KNOWLEDGE AND EXPERIENCE(S)

CHAPTER 1

RELATING TO DR. WERNER

Past and Present

Roger Bibace
Clark University

The verb in the title "Relating to Dr. Werner" was selected because *relating* is the continuous present. It is an appropriate choice because Dr. Werner's framework has stimulated me in the past as well as in the present. I refer to Heinz Werner as "Dr. Werner" because I was never part of the scholarly research "inner circles" at work during the 1950s at Clark University. While Werner and Wapner worked on the sensory-tonic theory of perception (see Wapner, 2005) and while Werner and Kaplan (1963) explored the area of symbol formation, I was an outsider with respect to my activities as a clinician, teacher, and researcher.

Dr. Werner was never "Heinz" to me for a number of reasons. Culturally, my use of Dr. Werner's last name was a way of forging a respectful distance between me and a dominant authority in my intellectual life. Even now when I think and engage him in my *private* mental life, it is never Heinz but always Dr. Werner. The *public* counterpart for my inner speech is Werner's framework. In the following, I will describe the ways in which the private is to the personal as the public is to the impersonal.

Particulars and Universals in Clinical and Developmental Psychology, pages 3–29

RELATING TO WERNER

You must always remember the stupidity of professors.

—Heinz Werner

Dr. Werner was my advisor during my years as a graduate student at Clark. In those days, graduate students were *required* to attend colloquia. In fact, if I was absent from such a talk, Dr. Werner would ask me where I had been! After one such talk, Werner asked me to drive him home. I agreed, of course. It was natural that he would ask me what I thought about the talk. By that point in my graduate work, I had learned how to avoid some of the more obvious ways of sounding "stupid," such as not making clear evaluative criticisms or even direct questions related to the talk. So I responded to Dr. Werner by saying, "I am not clear regarding what the speaker meant by . . . " Dr. Werner's response astonished me. "I thought it was stupid," he said. I guess my jaw dropped, and possibly some other nonverbal accompaniments to my astonishment led him to say, "You must always remember the stupidity of professors!" He went on to explain that many professors have "tunnel vision." As "specialists," professors often overlook issues that are obvious to other professionals and lay people. On another occasion, Werner expressed a similar idea. I was standing next to him, and as we talked he was skimming the table of contents to a textbook he had received. This table of contents included headings such as "Learning," "Memory," "Motivation," and so on. Dr. Werner pointed to these words, looked at me, and shook his head. In order to understand Werner's objections, compare such titles with the chapter headings in his book "Comparative Psychology of Mental Development" (referred subsequently as CPMD)—"The Syncretic Character of Primitive Organization," (Chapter 2, pp. 59–103), for example. Many specialists begin with their own focus on a circumscribed topic—like "memory." In contrast, Dr. Werner's framework requires an investigator to study the *development* and *analysis* of such a traditional category. The genesis of any one category, in Werner's structure of ideas, is rooted in the undifferentiatedness from other, abstract categories favored by mainstream psychologists in any one historical era. Beginnings are global and diffuse, as in initial naturalistic observations of a particular that exemplify a phenomenon familiar to laypersons.

THE LANGUAGE REQUIREMENT AS A PREREQUISITE TO THE COMPREHENSIVE DOCTORAL PRELIMINARY EXAMINATION

In the 1950s, all graduate students were required to pass two languages: a Romance language and German. I had no difficulty with French, since that was the first language I spoke. In contrast, passing German was the most difficult barrier to my goal of obtaining a doctorate.

Germany, Germans, and Nazis were all fused in my mind *at that time* in my life. I was born in Alexandria, Egypt, and lived there from 1926 to 1946. Thus I lived in Alexandria during World War II, a time when England and its allies were fighting against the Germans and the Italians. At one point Rommel was less than an hour away from Alexandria, at El Alaimein, and from the British Armed Forces stationed in Alexandria and Cairo. The protection of the Suez Canal was vital to the allies. During this time, I was enrolled in an English private school that was very dedicated to the "war effort."

Even more importantly, my family background reinforced my negative feelings about Germany, Germans, and Nazis. I am a Jew, and I am Jewish in a way that Americans have difficulty understanding. In America, to be a Jew is one's religion, period. But in Egypt at that time, a Jew had a *civil* status as well as a religious orientation recognized by the courts, with a separate judicial system for Europeans in adjudicating civil and criminal proceedings. As a Jew, I had a special animus towards Germany/Germans/Nazis.

Every time the word "Germans" was mentioned, my paternal grandmother, the relative to whom I felt closest, would say *schlecht.* She did not merely say schlecht, she spat the word out. It was only many years later, when I was a patient in psychotherapy, that I was made aware of this unconscious "blind spot" (a *scotoma,* as Freud labeled it). My blind spot for Germany/Germans/Nazis was a good example of "syncresis," (Werner, 1948, pp. 59ff) the fusion of a single word with a category, which I as a graduate student learned meant *bad,* an undifferentiated category of Germany/Germans/Nazis!

So the reader now has some idea of what is vaguely referred to in our psychological jargon as an "emotional block" and why I had a tremendous "problem" every time I sat down to learn to translate from German into English! I tried everything I could think of, including psychotherapy. I even tried to learn by playing an audiotape containing German vocabulary while I slept. Unfortunately, this technological innovation did not work for me!

At that time, the Clark University German language requirement was much harder than that at other universities, where the requirement could be met by passing a national examination limited to the student's particular field. But at Clark, in order to demonstrate proficiency, a student was required to translate not only a psychological experiment, but also a selection from a German literary work, a much more difficult task. My difficulties and failures had attuned me both to these easier requirements at other universities and to the difficulties in passing German at Clark. One graduate student had flunked the exam eight times! Of course, as a result, this student was not eligible to take the doctoral prelims in psychology.

Prior to my fourth attempt, I had been given a written notice by the department stating that my status as a graduate student was in jeopardy. At that time, I felt it was do or die. Dying may sound too dramatic, but consider these consequences. If I failed German, my status as a graduate student in psychology would have been terminated, and given that foreign students were allowed to remain in the country only as long as they were full time graduate students, I feared that I might be forced to leave the country. No other option was attractive. I could not go back to Egypt, and although I had a Spanish passport, I did not speak Spanish and had never been to Spain. I have articulated this sequence because it highlights how a single outcome—one part—can have a drastic effect on the whole of a person's life.

Dr. Werner was the faculty member who accompanied me to the examination. The psychological selection Dr. Werner made was an experiment in the area of perception, which turned out to be easy. Even I, by that time, could translate *perzeption* into *perception*! We walked down three flights of stairs in Jonas Clark Hall to the office of the German professor who administered the examination. This examiner leaned back in his chair and pulled a volume of Goethe from his bookshelf. Goethe had been praised as a stylist whose meandering, convoluted sentences were admirable to German scholars! Even as I write this nearly five decades later, my heart is pounding. I stumbled and fumbled in my translation. Dr. Werner added a word here and there to get me back on track. And Dr. Werner even argued with this German professor, his neighbor, regarding the acceptability of my translation, based on what Goethe might have meant and the various ways each sentence could be translated. The entire session was, and still is, one interminable and tense blur. What I now remember is the outcome, standing outside the office, Dr. Werner patting me on the back. It was over; I had passed!

RELATING TO WERNER'S FRAMEWORK

Werner's Reminder: Mendel Flunked Biology

Faculty in the Department of Psychology at Clark evaluated graduate students twice a year. Graduate students who were evaluated negatively were in danger of being asked to terminate their studies. Faculty discussion would move, slowly, toward a final group decision. At such a time, so the story goes, Dr. Werner would remind the faculty that "Mendel flunked biology." Mendel, who flunked biology, later became the creator of a biological science—genetics. The implication is that one should consider, with respect to every individual, the range of "entirely different levels of development" *within* that person. Dr. Werner's coexistence concept of development was not just a "concept," it was a maxim he implemented in his "world of action" as a psychologist and chair of the department. This is an example of how Dr. Werner particularized the coexistence concept of development.

WERNER'S COEXISTENCE CONCEPT OF DEVELOPMENT

In the opening pages of *Comparative Psychology of Mental Development,* Werner states,

> The genetic approach is of essential importance even in the study of the mental life of the adult normal man, for the following reason. The normal man does not always function on the same level of mental activity. The same normal individual, depending upon inner or outer circumstances, may be characterized by *entirely different levels of development.*" (Werner, 1948, p. 4, emphasis added)

Werner here is pointing to issues that have been neglected for decades. In making this statement Werner is not merely claiming that there is variability observable across different levels of development among groups of people, compared with respect to chronological age, for instance. Another example is the designation of different ethnic groups as being "lower or higher" with respect to their developmental status by psychologists who focus on a socio-cultural level of analysis, but who never address individual differences within a culture. The example of individual differences, the focus of differential psychology, leads to conclusions that individual A is more intelligent or has greater ability than individual B.

None of these orientations addresses Werner's focus, which is intra-individual variability. As Werner stated, the range of "entirely different levels of development or intra-individual variability... can be brought about by "inner or outer circumstances" (p. 4). He adds, "An adult normal person is not the same when he is utterly distracted." Some seven decades later, many contemporary Americans would agree that no individual is "the same" when he or she is "stressed." A person is not at the same level of mental development when stressed compared to when that same person is in a "state of sober scientific or practical work" (p. 4). Note especially that Werner includes "practical work"—the everyday world, the activities of normal adults—not only the abstract world of the scientist. Again, "entirely different levels of development" are posited for a normal adult person who is in a state of "emotional surrender to people or things" (p. 4).

RELIANCE ON WERNER'S COEXISTENCE CONCEPT OF DEVELOPMENT

Werner's coexistence concept of development (CCD) has been utilized empirically to account for intra-individual variability, in addition to expectable differences among groups of research participants. Intra-individual variability is the causal reasoning of children, adolescents, and normal adults when they are asked to account for the causes and cure of diverse diseases.

Reliance on such a concept requires one to account for the range of psychological processes that coexist within each person, regardless of the age or category (e.g., immature/mature) to which that person is assigned (Bibace, Schmidt, & Walsh, 1994; Bibace, Sagarin, & Dyl, 1998; Bibace, Dillon, & Sagarin, 1999). The clinical implications of Werner's CCD for the education of children with asthma has also been explored (Bibace & Leeman, 1999). Or in a critique of the research by a number of other investigators (Bibace, Wiehe, & Leeman, 2001). Lastly, this concept constitutes an important aspect of my partnership approach to clinical, research, and teaching activities (Bibace, 1999). Werner's CCD also has very general implications for appreciating phenomena in everyday life.

The emotional surrender of more than 1 billion people who watched the World Cup soccer games on television illustrates Werner's point here. *Participating* emotionally in the game, wearing the same shirts as the players, yelling, screaming when "they" scored a goal. The national significance of these events was central to countries as disparate as Brazil, South Korea, and Germany. The political leaders of the countries also "participated" in these emotional displays, welcoming heroes such as Ronaldo, who scored two goals for Brazil against Germany.

My interpretation of this type of "emotional involvement" in an event is that it is "enjoyable" precisely because "I am there" for the duration of the match. I am there in the sense that I am not thinking or feeling anything else about my past, my future, or me. I am cheering with those groups of people who are "with me" and against the opponents, the opposite team and their followers. In sports, the pleasures and pain experienced through participation as a mere spectator are universal for a fan of that sport.

What is the relationship of the self as spectator to these players on the television screen? My formal proximal analytical interpretation is that, momentarily, there is a lack of differentiation between the self and the players on the screen. The yells of pleasure; the groans of pain; the flares of anger at a player on an opposing team who "fouls" one of my heroes is shared with other viewers who are on "my side." Many of these people were not merely watching television—they were there! Such a proximal formal analysis focuses on the "here and now." A formal analysis does not seek to understand the history of each of the viewers and the reasons for their feelings. It is clear that events, such as sports are treasured precisely because there is, momentarily, an emotional surrender of the self. There are, of course, numerous other classes of such events, in politics, religion, and so on, which share some of these same characteristics.

But how is one to categorize the disproportionate emotional reactions of some spectators? Clearly, "early versus later levels of development" is not a good fit for the hooligans in England who were deprived of their passports by their own government because of the disturbances they had created in other countries. Nor is "early versus later levels of development" a good fit for the categorization of the leaders and the nationals of two South American countries who went to war over a contested soccer match!

Even the "immature compared to mature" designation for "entirely different levels of development" does not convey the potency of these qualitatively different ways of being in the world. Constrained by my egocentricities, as in my socialization as a psychoanalytically trained clinician, I prefer the categorization of such entirely different levels of development as "irrational compared to rational." What should be added is that both Werner and Freud recognize such irrationality as enjoyable! Such experiences are enjoyable because the emotionality is, for most television viewers, safe.

Psychologists who think that this may be true but trite are reminded that some contemporary cognitive scientists consistently reject such a differentiation between self and the world, between internal and external circumstances. Rather, they insist that such conceptual distinctions are unnecessary "spatial metaphors." The simultaneous orchestration of private, internal psychological states and external expressive behaviors is coherently integrated for that viewer on that occasion. The contents of their behavior, the diversity of means relied upon by that viewer are congruent with that person's ends for that event. There is, *simultaneously*, the enactment of all these organismic activities in a holistic ensemble for the person who is emotionally engaged—who is there! A Wernerian formal analytical approach allows me to create links between the behavior of particular persons and universals, the forms of organization related to a lack of differentiation between self and other, a temporary form of a non-serious condition. Or the blurring of psychological states and the external world as the basis for "poor reality testing" and severe psychopathology. Or for the multiple ways in which people deceive themselves. Common psychological defenses (identification, projection, reaction-formation, and so on) have been analyzed through the differentiation and transformation of actor/action/object propositions (Bibace, Marcus, Thomson, & Litt, 1987).

Analyses that focus on "forms of organization" are generalizations that can be particularized through categorizations, such as "early versus late" and "immature versus mature levels of development." These categorizations make sense to specialists who are devoted primarily to one or another developmental series, such as ontogenesis. I would like to underscore the importance of the shift between such formal analytical statements for these "entirely different levels of development" and the labels or the categorizations by which Werner designates these different levels within the "same normal adult man." The reader is reminded that it was only in 1994 that the APA (American Psychological Association) introduced nonsexist language!

Werner underscores the range of levels of mental development because "at one time man behaves primitively" and at another he becomes relatively "cultured" and "civilized" (Werner, 1948). Werner—while writing in English—puts these words "primitive," "cultured," and "civilized" in quotes. There is no invidious comparison here between individuals, or between groups characterized in diverse ways. Rather, Werner is referring to the same person, a normal adult who at one time behaves "primitively" and at another in a relatively "cultured" and "civilized" manner.

There is a shift here from the conceptual referent, stated in the formal language of lack of differentiation between the self and the other, which is the basis for "entirely different levels of development" or what is generally recognized epistemologically as different levels of organization, to the *categorization* of these different levels of organization. It is precisely this shift of focus from "form" to a "label" for the "contents" that has proved to be difficult and controversial.

Werner's concept of development (Werner, 1957) is stated, most generally, through the abstract formal language of the orthogenetic principle. But this principle, because of Werner's generality, is utilized to *categorize* very different individuals who belong to disparate groups. The "labels" or categories that are commonly used vary with the kinds of individuals who are being compared. For instance, studies in ontogenesis often categorize these different levels of development as "earlier or later" or as "less or more mature" or as "less or more advanced" in development. Such categorizations have a number of advantages and disadvantages. One advantage of relying on the "early versus late" characterization of development when comparing younger and older children is "transparency" This distinction is considered acceptable among mainstream developmental psychologist. Yet from a Wernerian perspective, this distinction does not acknowledge what most parents and every teacher knows, namely that children of the same age tend to behave at "entirely different levels of development."

Freud, of course, repeatedly demonstrated the existence of "entirely different levels of development" in people, not only through our different states of consciousness, as in our dreams but also through behaviors judged as normal or neurotic. Werner acknowledges and brackets such an "obvious" difference so that "even if such states of consciousness as the dream are disregarded, the normal man does not always function on the same level of activity" (Werner, 1948, p. 4). Freud would completely agree—a normal adult makes unintentional slips of the tongue and parapraxes in actions. But Freud's designation or categorization of such behaviors is different. The general categorization for Freud for such different levels of development within the same person is referenced by the title of one of his books, *The Psychopathology of Everyday Life.* On the same page Werner summarizes:

> In general, then, developmental psychology attempts to demonstrate that primitive modes of behavior in the normal man not only appear under cer-

> tain extraordinary conditions, but are *continually present as the basis of all mental being,* and are of *vital* importance in supporting the highest forms of mentality." (Werner, 1948, p. 4, emphasis added)

The definition of vital, provided in the *Oxford English Dictionary* (Oxford University Press, 2015), is as follows: "Consisting in, constituted by, that immaterial force or principle, which is present in living beings or organisms and by which they are animated and their functions maintained." Thus, by the use of the term *vital,* I have interpreted Werner so as to make clear that primitive thinking is not merely an unfortunate occurrence, but rather is indispensable in that it helps to support and maintain higher forms of thinking.

It is clear that Gordon W. Allport understood and supported Werner's assumption that all people, even those considered to be particularly sophisticated will make use of primitive concepts at times. Allport, in his foreword to *Comparative Psychology of Mental Development* (Werner, 1948), provides an eloquent summary of Werner's position:

> [Werner's] vivid accounts of syncretic perception and thought give the reader aid in understanding the ordinary mental operations of himself and his fellow men. No matter how confidently we pride ourselves on our logical acumen and capacity for scientific inference, our thought too turns out to be primitive much of the time. While tactfully confining himself to children, primitives, and psychotics, the author tells us in a sly way more than a little about our own mental lives. (pp. xi–xii)

Allport acknowledged Dr. Werner's self-reference to "understand the mental operations of himself" (p. xii). By stating that "no matter how confidently we pride ourselves on our logical acumen and capacity for scientific inference, our *thought turns out to be primitive much of the time*" (p. xii; italics added). Allport made clear that everyone at times demonstrates less sophisticated thinking. Similarly, David Rapaport's review of CPMD in 1941 acknowledges this same idea. According to Rapaport, Werner "shows us that the different functional levels are not possessed exclusively by a group of living creatures, but that even in the civilized human being of our times, *the different lower functional levels are coexistent with the highest ones* (Rapaport, 1941; emphasis added).

PERSONAL AND FAMILIAL MAGICAL BELIEFS AND BEHAVIOR

The following examples from my personal and familial life will illustrate the reasons why I resonate to Werner's notion of primitive ideas. I was born and raised in Alexandria, Egypt, and lived there for the first 20 years of my life.

Most Europeans, as well as native Egyptians in Egypt, subscribed to numerous magical practices, rituals, as well as magical beliefs. For instance, many people believed in the evil eye, which must be guarded against and warded off. Children and adults wore a *chamsa*—a charm in the form of a "hand" to shield oneself from the gaze of the evil eye. Compliments were avoided as dangerous. Many people believed that conspicuous consumption was an invitation to disaster.

As a youngster I became infected with a "furuncle," which is defined by Webster as a "boil." More descriptively and specifically, this boil was a purplish looking, round mound with a yellow center, i.e., the pus of the infection. The familial conviction was that someone had put the "evil eye" on me. There it was, the evil eye as a concrete unambiguous manifestation. No doubts about it!

To cite a further example, my father's company had moved to a newer, fancier office. Such a "dangerous" move required the performance of a magical ritual, namely an animal sacrifice to ward off evil spirits. A ritual accompanied by prayers so as to insure success. It was common to display an evergreen plant at the top of the entrance door to a house or apartment. Such green plants insured well-being. A complement to this green plant was my mother's statement of good wishes every Friday evening, "May your week be green," a magical belief aimed at bringing about good things during the week ahead.

The following example maximizes the range of beliefs and "cognitive levels of development" for me personally. The person I was closest to during my early years was my paternal grandmother, the family matriarch. Fast forward in time to Worcester, Massachusetts. I am a graduate student at Clark University about to take my doctoral preliminary exams. The preparations for this exam had included 2 years of weekly meetings with a group of four other graduate students. The results of these exams answered a most important question, *if* you were going to get a PhD. But it left open the secondary question, *when* you would get a PhD.

My grandmother's concern and wishes for a "good result" were expressed through magic. She sent me something through the mail to "ensure" my success. This magically potent thing was some "sand" taken from the grave of a scholarly rabbi. When I telephoned Alexandria to tell my family I had passed, my grandmother interpreted that as verification of the efficacy, the power of what she had done. As Werner recognizes, "magic achieves systematic expression only when it is on a social, and not an individual, phenomenon" (Werner, 1948, p. 29).

The discrepancies between the *public* "psychologist-in-training" and my *private* experiences could not have been greater, and it is only now, late in life, that I am willing to make public these private personal experiences. Werner's CPMD transformed such personal experiences for me by making them general, impersonal psychological processes common to everyone. To use a contemporary cliché, Werner's general assumptions "normalized" such experiences for me. Even the medical jargon (there is a lot of it around) does not match the generality of Werner's assumptions or the evidence for primitivism that I was able to observe, both then and now, in others and myself.

Examples from my peers who were also taking doctoral exams included a graduate student who, since he felt he did well on the first day of the examination "therefore" did not change his shirt for the rest of the week. Why risk changing your luck by changing your shirt? Recently during the World Cup soccer games, the television commentators mentioned that the German coach, whose team had succeeded in reaching the finals did not change his shirt for the same reason. Even more explicitly, was the colorful magician, with all his magical wands and paraphernalia, who came to the soccer matches from Senegal.

Despite these personal experiences, dreams of reason in my professional life as a researcher persisted. The idea that surely a "mature" person, in their "knowledge domain and their everyday world of activities" would be "consistently" rational. Especially if deviance from socially prescribed behaviors of professionals in a particular context entailed serious consequences for that person's own health. In my research with Mary Walsh (see Bibace & Walsh, 1981), dealing with conceptions of illness from childhood to adulthood, we had adopted the mainstream criterion for determining an individual's developmental level. We relied upon a social cognitive developmental criterion, articulated by Damon, that the two highest developmental levels in a person's protocol with regard to the definition, cause, and cure of an illness would determine "the" developmental level to which that person was assigned. We were able to empirically demonstrate that the average developmental level varied with chronological age for normal children. This "categorization" was widely used and "replicated," to the tune of roughly 130 science citations in 80 different journals.

It was not until the late 1990s that I explicitly argued for a coexistence concept of development (Bibace, Sagarin, & Dyl, 1998; Bibace, Dillon, & Sagarin, 1999). In the papers, we provided examples of the range of development level from the least to the most mature concept of illness for normal adults and how a normal child could, on the same day for the same concept of illness, demonstrate a wide range of levels of development. The less mature spontaneous answers coexisted with the most mature levels of that particular child's understanding of the definition, cause, and cure of an illness. Coexistence emerged when the children were asked to evaluate responses provided by other children, which acted as concrete exemplars of the categories for every level of development, in the language of other children. Our approach to understanding concepts of illness led us to create "categories," which linked abstract developmental principles to concrete answers from groups of all research participants, irrespective of age.

IRRATIONAL BEHAVIORS BY PHYSICIANS IN MEDICINE

The coexistence concept of development has been further substantiated by my weekly experiences with faculty family physicians and also as a direct observer of doctor–patient interactions involving residents and faculty family physicians for 15 years. For instance, I had heard the "mantra" regarding the taking of antibiotics for an infected bacterial "sore throat or cold, a streptococcus infection" numerous times. "You will probably feel better after two or three days, but you *must* take *all* the pills." This was accompanied by the doctor's emphasis on the negative effects of terminating the antibiotic prematurely. You can imagine my surprise when some physicians told me that they personally did not take the antibiotics for the entire prescribed period, an example of the expression, "Do as I say, not as I do." But surely in medicine, physicians would be more rational!

A close faculty colleague in obstetrics carried out a study in the early 1990s on the implementation of universal precautions during childbirth. There is often, contrary to the layperson's idea of what happens during birth, a lot of blood during a delivery. Because of the risk of AIDS and hepatitis, obstetricians had been required to "adhere to universal precautions in a delivery." Universal precautions are designed to protect the obstetrician from being exposed, through cuts on their own body, to HIV. Such precautions include plastic shields worn over the face to protect the eyes; plastic gowns to prevent the physicians from becoming "soaked to their skins" with blood. Especially important are the universal precautions related to the way that surgical instruments grouped as "sharps" (such as a scalpel) should be handled.

What led to this study were observations by faculty that some residents in obstetrics and gynecology did not "adhere to universal precautions during deliveries." This faculty obstetrician conducted a classic "before and after" study with an intervening lecture given by a national expert on infectious diseases who emphasized the importance of observing universal precautions in the operating room. The results, based on observations of residents before and after the lecture, showed no effect for many residents. This faculty obstetrician reported her findings during one of our weekly sessions with other faculty obstetricians. I had great difficulty in accepting the results that physicians would expose themselves to such severe consequences for their own health. Why? My experience from weekly meetings with third-year residents in family medicine, who also delivered babies, had made me aware that deliveries may occur in the middle of the night when the physician has had very little sleep. It was understandable, I told the group, that such a physician would not want to put on the special booties and take the time to carry out all these universal precautions when they were tired, when an immediate intervention was necessary and so on. In other words, my research on concepts of illness was based on the assumption that if you really understood, if you have a mature concept, then your behavior would change. Physicians, in this specific context, exemplified an ideal of understanding, which could rarely be reached by lay people.

In contrast to the previous antibiotic example, no adherence to "universal precautions" in the operating room entailed possible severe consequences for the physical well-being of the doctor and other personnel. Bibace and Walsh (in this volume) had demonstrated that there were differences in the maturity of a person's concepts of the definition, the cause and cure of common episodic illnesses, such as a cold, or severe illnesses, such as heart attacks, cancer and AIDS. The scoring system and the assumptions were based primarily on a medical concept of disease. My hope was that if one could educate, make ordinary people more mature, with respect to their understanding of illness, then they would act in a more rational way. That was why Bibace "the researcher" was now raising objections to this faculty obstetrician's study. I had gone on for some time with these objections when the director of the residency program interjected with this example in support of the findings from this study. It was early afternoon when an experienced obstetrician had come into the operating room to deliver his patient. This faculty obstetrician and the residents were also in the operating room as participants and observers. This middle-aged physician walked into the operating room prepared to begin the delivery. The residency director very clearly, directly, and bluntly told him: "You are not observing universal precautions." The director of the residency was concerned, he now told the group, that this physician was a "poor model for our residents," to which this obstetrician replied, "Somebody's got to be immune!" He then proceeded with the delivery without having observed universal precautions. This was not just an immature *belief* but a *behavior* considered irrational by the other faculty. That observation had a major effect on me.

CONCEPTUAL RECONCILIATION OF MATURE/IMMATURE: BELIEFS THROUGH WERNER'S COEXISTENCE CONCEPT OF DEVELOPMENT

I had previously rationalized the difference between the "do as I say, not as I do" behaviors of some physicians regarding antibiotics. I told myself that such deviations are not that serious, the consequential effects are not immediate, and so they are not as likely to lead to adherence. But nonadherence to universal precautions in the operating room can lead to contamination and HIV. To be HIV positive has serious consequences related to morbidity and mortality, for a physician personally and professionally. Nevertheless, a number of obstetricians (experienced and inexperienced) were failing to observe universal precautions. I use the past tense because faculty tell me that nowadays medical students are indoctrinated to respect universal precautions.

Parenthetically, I also asked myself another question in a "get over it" moment. How would I, and possibly other psychologists, have reacted if the person who was not observing necessary precautions, such as wearing a helmet when bicycling, was an adolescent. It is a common belief among many social scientists that adolescents behave in dangerous ways because they have a "sense of invulnerability." Werner to the rescue! This is yet another example of the way in which many of us implicitly rely on chronological age regarding our interpretations of the maturity or developmental level of an individual.

Werner's coexistence concept of development, the vitality of the so-called primitive levels of development, can also be illustrated through the *positive* effects of magic. In contrast to many psychologists and scientists who regard magical beliefs as negative, Werner understood the positive aspects of magic. Nowadays, many clinicians and research psychologists have come to respect the positive aspects of magical beliefs. Hope, even when it is irrational according to biomedical standards, is not dismissed by many clinicians in diverse helping professions when they are relating to a person who is dying, or for whom all medical avenues have been exhausted.

Werner's multifaceted analysis of magic includes magic by "analogy or imitation," based on the lack of differentiation between internal psychological processes and events in the environment. Werner states, "When form is given to an image, reality itself is given form and direction. The new attribute, in accordance with the syncretism of this mode of thought, spontaneously *becomes* [italics added] the attribute of the real object" (*CMPD*, p. 350). Werner adds,

> In a deeper sense the magical procedure creates not alone an image from out of which the attribute is taken and intermediately transposed; but in creating the attribute in an image, the procedure likewise creates it *simultaneously* [italics added] in the things showing identity with this image. This desired quality, therefore, belongs not to the image alone, but equally to the objects of everyday life involved in the procedure. (Werner, 1948, p. 350)

Werner characterizes this transformation, as "creative magic" because "the desired attribute or event is not imitated or copied, but is actually brought into *immediate* [italics added] being and formed objectively through the magical activity" (Werner, 1948, p. 350–351). This last quotation also illustrates how Werner empathically adopted the perspective of the person whom the psychologist is analyzing. The magician is "creative" not derogated as a result of their beliefs that the desired attribute actually came about. No other psychological processes as "mediation" are required; the effects for the creative magician are *immediate.* This immediacy is again indicative of a lack of differentiation between the person and their environments. It is the lack of differentiation that permits the transformation of external reality. This is just another example of how Werner explores sympathetically both the "positive" as well as the "primitive" aspects of these different levels of mental development, a lack of differentiation between the *subjectivities* of psychological processes of an "image" and the *objectivity* attributed to *perception.*

THE COGNITION OF MAGNITUDE: A COMPARATIVE STUDY OF NORMAL AND SCHIZOPHRENICS

In retrospect, this was my first research study which relied on Werner's genetic parallels, namely, that there are *formal parallels* among various developmental sequences (Bibace, 1956). Although the ontogenetic sequence for the concept of number had been articulated by Piaget, he had not sought to encompass the behavior of a variety of populations within his theory. In contrast, Werner's psychology of mental comparative development posits formal parallels among ontogenetic, phylogenetic, microgenetic, and pathological (organic and functional) processes underlying behavior. Both Werner and Piaget assumed that the development of the category of number—of which the concept of magnitude is one aspect—is one of the basic categories of cognition for the patterning of objectified experience.

The question was not whether schizophrenics are different from normal adults. Rather, the question focused on the *forms of organization* relied on by normal adults and schizophrenics in their concept of magnitude. More specifically, the study focused on a formal part/whole analysis of what the subjects' responses entailed. The schizophrenics who were selected for this study demonstrated "formal thought disturbances" *at the time of testing.* It was hypothesized that the forms of organization, posited by the orthogenetic principle, would parallel the ontogenetic forms of thinking Piaget had constructed for his studies on number with children. Such parallel forms of organization have been referred to and categorized by various authors as variations in maturity, earlier-versus-later development or, as in this study, indicative of normal-compared-to-abnormal populations.

The results were interpreted as substantiating the hypothesis. In one part of the study, different versions of the following question were asked of normal adults and schizophrenics:

There are 60 wooden beads in a box.
ALL (emphatic tone) the beads are made of wood (Whole).
Of these wooden beads, 40 are white (P1).
Another 10 are brown (P2).
Are there more wooden beads or more white beads?
Are there more wooden beads or more brown beads?

Both children, in Piaget's study, and schizophrenics, in contrast to normal adults, answer that because P1 (40) is > than P2 (10), then P1 is > than the Whole. Some schizophrenics also reduced the whole to P3, the 10 beads with no color, so P1 is bigger than the Whole because P1 is > than P3.

Another major similarity between Freud, Piaget, and Werner is their positive valuation of errors. The detailed analysis of how a person reasons so as to produce a "wrong answer" illuminates how the mind works. Errors can show doubts and vacillations in a person's answers and in the ways they correct themselves.

Public disclosures of their private mental representations are a worthwhile focus from this perspective. In contrast, a "correct" response, without knowledge of the underlying psychological processes, yields little understanding of how that person "achieved" that answer. This issue persists today. Should one focus on outcomes, evaluations, achievements, and manifest behavior? Or should one also take into account the processes, at all levels of organization (biological, psychological, and socio-cultural), that determine *how* the former comes about? Werner, Piaget, and Freud all agree that the former is necessary to understand the latter.

Current Interpretation

Included in the following are my current interpretations of the study on the cognition of magnitude. Rereading this study in 2003, the following "self-critical" comments come to mind. First, my study was limited to schizophrenics with formal thought disturbances. Secondly, the study was limited to male participants only. I did not state in my dissertation, publicly, the reasons behind this decision, namely that female schizophrenics were believed to be more "variable" than males. In retrospect, this is interesting because of the following incongruities. My clinical experiences in descriptive psychiatry did not provide *any* basis for gender differences in formal thought disturbances. For both my descriptive psychiatry teacher, Dr. David Rothschild[1] and his mentor Eugene Bleuler, a formal thought disturbance (such as a loose association) was a judgment to be made irrespective of gender! For Freud, the distinction between primary and secondary processes transcended gender, SES, and ethnicity. Similarly, Werner did not relate forms of organization regarding "entirely different levels of development" to gender.

So why was my sample of schizophrenics limited to males? I now think that one reason was because of the major programmatic research conducted by Leslie Phillips in the psychology department at Worcester State Hospital. The aim of the research project was related to the creation of a scale based on a schizophrenic patients' "pre-morbid" social attainment. One component of this instrument, which came to be known as the Worcester Social Attainment Scale, was an assessment of the respondent's occupational status. The official *United States Dictionary of Occupational Titles* assigned different degrees of "complexity" to different occupations. For example, a janitor's occupation was less complex than that of a mechanic. These differences in "complexity" were interpreted as indices of lower or higher levels of development. The Worcester Social Attainment Scale was limited to males because in the 1940s and 1950s there were relatively few females in the workforce, and accordingly, the range of occupations open to women in American society, at that time, was limited.

Historical Eras as a Factor

It was only much later that I began to appreciate the importance of the historical era as a factor in science. It was only in the 1970s and 1980s that I became familiar with Foucault's thesis that the "episteme is rooted in time" (Foucault, 1970). Epistemologically, there are, at any one time, paradigms that reflect mainstream science. Of course, as a scientist I could have had the courage to argue that a "representative sample" of schizophrenics should include females as well as male patients with formal thought disorders. But I did not. That would, practically, have had the consequence of doubling the statistical comparisons required in the study—normal (both male and female) compared to schizophrenics (both females and males). Note also how "complexity" is evaluated in antithetical ways. In experimental design I avoided it as impractical, yet as a researcher I subscribed to "complexity" as an indicator of a higher developmental occupational status!

There was yet another very practical reason for limiting myself to males. I needed patients for my study who had severe, "obvious" formal thought disturbances, and there were not enough such patients at Worcester State Hospital. Herb Lipton, a fellow student and friend, invited me to come to the hospital where he worked, a Veterans Administration hospital. Again, in that historical era, the veterans from World War II and previous wars were almost without exception males.

I have dwelt on the "historical era" as an influential factor because others as well as I may not be sufficiently sensitive to the ways in which interpretations are impacted by our contemporary zeitgeist. Sexism and feminism in the 1950s were not prepotent in the consciousness for lay people, scientists, or psychologists. Similarly, such oversights are evident in Werner's *Comparative Psychology of Mental Development*, written in the 1920s in Europe, and even in Allport's foreword to the 1948 version, written in the United States. Similarly, our current historical era has made terms such as "primitive" or "native" politically incorrect. Yet, paradoxically, it is still quite acceptable to refer to countries as Third World, compared to postindustrial nations such as the United States or some nations in Europe.

Oftentimes the valence of a particular word is highly reflective of a particular culture and/or historical era. A given term may have both positive and negative connotations as well. For instance, consider the terms "consistency" and "variability" Each may have positive and negative connotations for the interpreter. Consistency can be interpreted positively as *stability* and negatively as *rigidity*. Similarly, variability can be interpreted positively as *flexibility* and negatively as *labile*. The choices of the interpreter are pervasive and unavoidable.

Werner's *CPMD* also demonstrates another relationship between what is to be explained and the explanation. In this early comprehensive work, he relies on a "one:many" relationship between the forms of organization and the phenomena to be explained. So, for instance, the lack of differentiation between the self and the other is explored in multiple sociocultural contexts in organic pathology and psychopathology, in microgenesis as well as in ontogenesis. One characterization of the forms of organization between the self and the other, namely the lack of differentiation between self and other or between self and the inanimate world, is relied upon to explain many different phenomena. Werner, in this respect, is quite different from Piaget, who limited himself to science as the domain to be explained. This Wernerian reliance on the "one:many" kind of relationships parallels Freud's perspectives. For Freud, the forms of mental life and their psychological representation were characterized as "primary versus secondary processes." Diverse psychological processes were used to explain levels of consciousness, levels of maturity (normal/neurotic/psychotic), and the "psychopathology of everyday 1ife"—slips of the tongue and other parapraxes. For Werner, Piaget, and Freud, the relationship between *form* and *content* is that of abstract to concrete—abstract forms of organization referring to concrete phenomena. Form is the abstract generalization that transcends the particular, which is to be explained.

COEXISTENCE IDEA: FROM PERIPHERAL TO CENTRAL IN THIS AUTHOR'S UNDERSTANDING OF DEVELOPMENT AS CONCEPT

The 1956 empirical results indicated that normal adults as well as schizophrenics were relying on immature psychological processes, which were formally similar to those forms of organization in this schizophrenic group. But this was acknowledged at that time merely as a footnote: "Some normal adults, although they do not show the primitivity of schizophrenics, also rely to some extent on primitive operations in thinking" (Bibace, 1956, p. 81).

In sharp contrast, as the previous attempts to demonstrate, I now think that Werner's coexistence concept of development is central to a comprehensive concept of development—a concept for such diverse domains as science, art, and religion, but also a concept which has implications for how people behave toward one another in their everyday activities.

I have interpreted the approach of John Rawls's (1985) value orientation to "justice as fairness" as one such possible positive and meaningful consequence of not making any differentiations with respect to other human beings. Rawls's thought experiment and his orientation to values requires one to posit no differentiations whatsoever among any human beings. Justice as fairness is the emergent from dialogs based on such a premise. Initial reactions to such an idea will be to dismiss the idea as absurd. Indeed, Judith Rick Harris, a developmental psychologist, has more empathically voiced the dilemma in such a proposal, when she asks, "How can we reconcile our desire for fairness and equity with the brutal fact that people are not all alike?" (Quoted from the *New York Times*, January 6, 1998; see Ellis, 1998).

There are at least two historical examples that underscore the value of the proposal by Rawls. First, the Bill of Rights in the Constitution, which for every American was, and many would say still is, counter to the facts of racism, sexism, and ageism of everyday life. Second, the Universal Rights adopted by the United Nations, initiated by Eleanor Roosevelt, are even more blatantly violated with respect to millions of people worldwide.

Three important assumptions are part of my heritage: ideals have to be "posited" not abstracted from empirical facts or the sensory manifold; positing ideals will lead to the search for means to implement the ideals. Such ideals enable us to overcome the barriers and inevitable conflicts we will encounter as one spirals from past to future.

INTEGRATION AS ORCHESTRATION

I was talking to Dr. Werner about the concept of "integration." Going beyond the mantra and the clichés commonly relied on by me and some of my peers, Werner restated the formal abstraction of "integration" through a concrete idea: orchestration. There are advantages to construing "integration" as orchestration.

Orchestration is a concrete analogy for this writer, which helps me to clarify the concept of multilinearity. Ordinarily, multilinearity addresses the distal ends, or *teloi,* for divergent domains such as science or aesthetics. But these domains are so varied, in and of themselves, that comparability is difficult. A common critique is that cross-cultural comparisons that rely on mainstream Western methods of assessment and evaluations to reach conclusions regarding other groups or cultures are not taking into account the actualities of this other culture. Such comparisons are not only epistemologically invalid, but they disregard the world of everyday activities for people living in these other cultures. What those people in other cultures, according to *their* standards, find acceptable or not acceptable is disregarded.

Orchestration as integration is also constrained to a coherence theory of truth rather than a correspondence theory of truth. The music or products considered beautiful in one culture violate the canons of what is culturally acceptable as beautiful in another culture. Leonard Bernstein asks whose musical notations should be relied upon in making an evaluation of music: "The twelve notes of our Western chromatic scale, or the five notes of the Chinese pentatonic scale?" (Bernstein, 1973, p. 57). Indeed music within one culture, or a particular historical era within a culture, suffers the same fate—novelty is often not accepted. The idea of relying on orchestration as an analogy for integration should be recognized as subject to such a limitation.

However, reliance on orchestration as a way of thinking about integration has some advantages. Orchestration clearly relies on a "relational" concept, not a substantive focus on one part or a musical note. A musical note only gains its meaning from its relationship to other musical notes, musical chords, and themes. This musical analogy also makes it clear that one part, a musician or an instrument, can play an infinite variety of sounds, songs, or symphonies. That is, a one-to-many abstract formal relationship is stated concretely in a way that is readily understandable. Conversely, many parts, many instruments, many musicians can all play in unison—united by a musical theme. This, in turn, exemplifies the abstract many-to-one relationship of analogous processes—so familiar to Wernerian developmental psychologists—that serve the same function.

Most important, the many-to-many relationships, between means and ends, between musician and orchestra, are easily conveyed, such as when an orchestra plays a particular song or symphony. Orchestration allows the abstract notion of integration to be flexibly enacted in that various parts (instruments, musicians) are central and/or peripheral in diverse segments of the "same" piece of music. This orchestration metaphor can be extended further to include the concepts of sequence and simultaneity. Sequence is essential to melody, just as simultaneity; the immediacy of all of the music is essential to the "experience" of music. This is surely a simplification, but it may have implications that are worth pursuing. To concretize the idea of orchestration further with respect to sequence and simultaneity: Sequence is essential to melody, just as simultaneity, the immediacy of all of the music, is essential to the "experience" of music.

Werner distinguishes the immediacies of the world of action and perception by a participant compared to an appreciative observer. Many would agree that there are major differences between a person who can "only appreciate music experientially" and a person who is a musician, who plays music.

There is another aspect of this orchestra analogy to be considered, namely, the audience as a group, or a particular listener. The orchestra analogy takes into account the significant differences, for both groups and individuals: *who* is the player, the conductor, or the orchestra. The same symphony is often played by different orchestras, conductors, and players, but a particular listener likes one version and dislikes others. One potential explanation for this phenomenon is the notion of *style*. Style here means an integration or putting together of all the notes in a distinctive way, which differentiates one rendition of a song or symphony from all other renditions of the "same" piece. A particular *style* can unite both player and listener as "partners," who are not equal but who complement one another (the musician needs the audience just as the audience needs the musician). Further, there are reciprocities between the audience and the performer, such that the performer may acknowledge that this audience, or even a particular person in the audience, enhances his or her performance (Bibace, 1999, pp. 284–285).

This orientation toward integration also permits a Wernerian framework to go beyond a formal proximal analysis. How so? The musicians' instruments are all there, all of the time. They are all present from start to finish. The formal cause is thereby connected to the predisposing cause. The characteristics of the instruments, in and of themselves, hinder or facilitate certain sounds and the particular type of participation in the musical composition as a whole. The material cause, to pursue Aristotle's four causes, is also represented in the "sounds" made by the orchestra. As is well known, sounds have specificities in meaning *physiognomically*. A high, tinny sound cannot represent either a fat person or a sensuous musical passage. Orchestration addresses the precipitating cause, the sequences that herald the figure/ground relationships between the players, their instruments, and a passage in the musical score. A radical cause can also be represented musically, by a discordant note negatively or by an unexpected positive note or theme. The saliency of a note or a series of notes or passage can often be represented musically.

Orchestration can also be construed to address two distinctive abstractions in Werner's domains of scholarly work: perception and symbol formation, namely, simultaneity and sequence. Just as the orthogenetic principle requires the criterion of *sequence*, a coexistence concept of development posits *simultaneity*.

An orchestration analogy facilitates my interpretation of Werner's *CPMD* as being based on two contrapuntal themes. Sequence, the basis for one theme, culminated in the orthogenetic principle of development, and the lesser recognized theme, *coexistence*, was posited by Werner as "vital."

The vitality of these themes in Werner's work is manifest in one of his earlier publications: *Unity of the Senses* (Werner, 1934). The orchestration of such contrapuntal themes in the immediacies and the coexistence of emotion and perception in physiognomic perception in normal development are followed by a geometrical-technical perceptual orientation to the world. On a related note, in his more general exploration of the ways in which the senses are unified, Werner referred to the phenomenon of synesthesia. For Werner, synesthesia "mean[s] that one specific stimulus may arouse not only the specifically corresponding sensation, but a second sensation united with the first" (p. 86; A common instance is color-tone synesthesia, as when the perceiving individual sees color while listening to tone.) Werner's *CPMD* makes it clear that both physiognomic perception and synesthesias are phenomena demonstrable in children, schizophrenics, brain-damaged individuals, and creative people, as well as in normal adults.

The contrapuntal theme in Werner's work is also manifest in a theoretical and methodological approach that analyzed the forms of organization attributed to phenomena and that avoided distal, material, and causal explanations. Werner insisted on "probing" for the latent, multiple psychological processes that underlie a behavioral product.

The reconciliation of this counterpoint requires the psychologist to pay strict attention to the *description* of the content of the phenomenon, that is the "particular" on which the "formal analysis" is carried out. The form is the generalization for diverse contents. I am relying on the musical term contrapuntal in a variety of ways. Contrapuntal is defined as "the nature of counterpoint" (*Oxford English Dictionary* [OED], 2015), and counterpoint is defined as the "opposite point" (OED). Musical examples predominate in the examples for these terms provided in the OED. For instance, the example cited for counterpoint is "the song or music pointed against... (by the) plain song indicated by the notes or points of the original melody" (OED). Or T. S. Eliot's reliance on the term contrapuntal in his *Music of Poetry*: "There are possibilities for verse which bear some *analogy* [my italics] to the development of a theme by different groups of instruments... there are possibilities of contrapuntal arrangement of subject matter" (quoted in OED).

Gunther Schuller has written a scholarly book entitled *The Swing Era,* which is valuable because it contains a glossary of musical terms that exemplify "simultaneity" in the orchestration analogy. For instance, swing swings because of rhythms, and Schuller defines a *polyrhythm* as "the use of three or more rhythms simultaneously in different parts" (Schuller, 1989, p. 866). Similarly, polyphony "can be applied to the simultaneous use of several melodies or contrapuntal lines" (p. 866).

In everyday life, some would assume that simultaneity is more likely to occur within the "here and now" of horizontal events, rather than in the "then and there" of events organized vertically. But in music, Schuller states that horizontal relationships refer to "the melodic, or linear, aspects of a musical structure as differentiated from the harmonic, or chordal. Relationships are notated and read horizontally, i.e., across the page from left to right, in musical notation" (Schuller, 1989, p. 864). In contrast, vertical relationships in music are defined as

> relationships notated and read vertically, i.e., up and down the page, in musical notation. Also, in the rhythmic aspects of a musical structure, a rhythmic simultaneity, i.e., a chord, will appear vertically aligned in musical notation, whereas nonsimultaneous rhythmic elements will appear vertically unaligned." (p. 868)

In my quotations of Werner, I have noted the importance of *intra-individual variability* as integral to his coexistence concept of development. The orchestra analogy facilitates references to the "consistency" of a musical performance through an individual musician's style, but also refers to "variations" in the quality of a musical performance by a particular musician playing the same or different pieces of music. The evaluation of Gene Krupa, a drummer for Benny Goodman, by Schuller is illustrative of such an antithesis. The specific occasion was the historical inaugural of swing as sufficiently important to American culture to warrant an appearance at Carnegie Hall in 1938. Goodman's orchestra featured Krupa in "Sing, Sing, Sing." Schuller evaluates Krupa as follows: "One is hard put to also explain Krupa's often deplorable monotonous drumming . . . or the horrors of 'Sing, Sing, Sing,' or the countless other examples of Krupa's rigidly relentless pounding." (p. 29). Parenthetically, I have to note that I disagree completely with Schuller, who also characterizes Krupa's playing as vulgar. But then Schuller also evaluates Krupa's drumming in very laudatory ways, to wit, "Throughout this performance (of "Swingtime in the Rockies") Krupa displays consummate dynamic control, and through his dynamics helps to delineate perfectly the form and structure of Mundy's fine arrangement" (p. 29).

Antithetical evaluations of the same person by another individual are common. Indeed, so are antithetical self-evaluations. In the former, the mutuality of infatuation and derogation can lead to marriage and divorce; just as in the latter, the roller coaster of self-evaluations in mania and depression can also be noted in how "normal" people feel about themselves in the course of a single day.

SEQUENCE AS AN IMPORTANT PRINCIPLE IN PSYCHOLOGY

Sequence as a principle has played an important role in psychological frameworks and attempts to construct order. Stages, phases, steps in developmental psychology, all rely on sequence for generating order in cognitive development. Controversies abound over the rate of development and the consistency or variability of the sequence utilized by a particular developmental theory. But sequence is an invariant criterion as a guideline for creating order. It is rare to be able to cite a consensually validated criterion in psychology, but there is one criterion that psychologists rely on when they utilize psychophysical methods: sequence. Thus, in the psychophysical measurement of perception, a researcher is required to "control" for sequence. Sequence as an abstraction may be a heuristic link between cognition and perception. Currently, for instance, Werner and Piaget each have two theories, one for the genesis of thought as interiorized action and the other for perceptual activities.

SIMULTANEITY AS AN IMPORTANT PRINCIPLE IN PSYCHOLOGY

Simultaneity as a principle is less evident in psychological theories. Even when it does appear, the label for the concept is not clearly labeled as simultaneity. So, simultaneity, I will argue, may be referred to as synchrony or as coexistence in diverse disciplines. Other terms that can be interpreted as representations of this idea include "spontaneous intuitions" (Myers, 2002, p. 4); the immediacies of "aha" experiences of insight discussed by psychologists from the Berlin Gestalt group; and "saliency" and "vividness," both in perception and in experiences that "transform" a person's life. A major transformation may be experienced as a conversion, such transformations may be a "discontinuity" in life or be brought about by what Gladwell (2002) has titled a "tipping point," or "how little things can make a big difference."

In contrast to the references in psychology, simultaneity and synchrony are frequently acknowledged in music. In the following examples I have relied heavily on musicians who "hear" and write about the music that I enjoy listening to, music that I enjoy but that I can only refer to through vague phrases like "Benny Goodman is fabulous!" or "I like Mozart!" Bernstein explains Mozart's G-minor symphony through three distinct forms of representation: a linguistic narrative, a corresponding musical notation, and the music itself that can be heard on CDs. Bernstein states that this symphony demonstrates

> that classical balance we were talking about—chromatic wandering on top but firmly supported by the inverted tonic-dominant. Do you see now what I mean by the structure underneath. Do you see now what I mean by the beauty of ambiguity? *It's the combination of those two contradictory forces, chromaticism and diatonicism, operating at the same time* [italics added], that makes this passage so expressive. (Bernstein, 1973, p. 43)

The contrapuntal themes discussed previously can also be interpreted as manifesting itself through the antitheses within the Wernerian concept of development. Global, undifferentiated forms of organization, "vital" and valued positively, are, on the one hand, the source of all forms of genesis (onto-/phylo-/microgenesis). On the other hand, differentiation can be valued negatively as a "specialization" that hinders further development. The latter differentiations, however, are the antithesis of the sequence and forms of organization that are posited as constituting development in Werner's orthogenetic principle. Analogically, the forms of organization in a coexistence concept of development are antithetical to the forms of organization posited by the orthogenetic principle of development, as is the idea of simultaneity in the former to the idea of sequence in the latter. In thinking about integration through the orchestration analogue, Werner was possibly speaking not only as a psychologist, but was relying on his *anlage* as a musician. Perhaps others may find it worthwhile to articulate this suggestion by Werner.

ACKNOWLEDGMENT

Originally published as: Bibace, R. (2005). Relating to Dr. Werner: Past and Present. In J. Valsiner (Ed.), *Heinz Werner and Developmental Science* (pp. 235–258). New York: Kluwer Academic/Plenum Publishers. Republished in this volume with kind permission of Springer Science+Business Media.

NOTE

1. Dr. David Rothschild, director of Clinical Psychiatry at Worcester State Hospital while I was an intern, studied with Eugen Bleuler in Switzerland.

REFERENCES

Bernstein, L. (1973). *The unanswered question: Six talks at Harvard.* Cambridge, MA: Harvard University Press.

Bibace, R. (1956). *The cognition of magnitude: A comparative study of normals and schizophrenics.* (Doctoral dissertation). Clark University, Worcester, MA.

Bibace, R. (1999). A partnership ideal. In R. Bibace, J. J. Dillon, & B. Dowds (Eds.) *Partnerships in research, clinical and educational settings.* Norwood, NJ: Ablex.

Bibace, R., Dillon, J. J., & Saragin, J. (1999). Toward coexistence concept of casual reasoning about illness in children and adults. In R. Bibace, J. J. Dillon, & B. Dowds (Eds.), *Partnerships in research, clinical and educational settings.* Norwood, NJ: Ablex.

Bibace, R., & Leeman, R. (1999). Some psychological processes involved in managing pediatric asthma. ln R. Bibace, J. J. Dillon, & B. Dowds (Eds.), *Partnerships in research, clinical and educational settings.* Norwood, NJ: Ablex.

Bibace, R., Marcus, D., Thomason, D., & Litt, E. A. (1987). Teaching psychological defenses: An interactive computerized program. *Teaching of Psychology, 14*(1), 35–37.

Bibace, R., Sagarin, J. D., & Dyl, J. (1998). The heuristic value of Werner's coexistence concept of development. *Journal of Applied Developmental Psychology, 19,* 153–163.

Bibace, R., Schmidt, L., & Walsh, M. E. (1994). Children's perceptions of illness. In G. N. Penny, P. Bennett, & M. Herbert (Ed.), *Health psychology: A lifespan perspective* (pp. 13–30). Chur, Switzerland: Harwood Academic Publishers.

Bibace, R. & Walsh, M. E. (1981). Children's conceptions of illness. In R. Bibace & M. E. Walsh (Eds.), *Children's conceptions of health, illness, and bodily functions* [Vol. 14 of *New directions for child development*]. San Francisco, CA: Jossey-Bass.

Bibace, R., Wiehe, K., & Leeman, R. (2001). Children's understanding of biology and health. *Applied Developmental Psychology, 22,* 543–551.

Ellis, D. E. (1998, January 6). Finding some answers. *The New York Times.* Retrieved from http://www.nytimes.com/1998/01/06/science/l-finding-some-answers-932388.html.

Foucault, M. (1970). *The order of things: An archaeology of the human sciences.* New York, NY: Random House.

Gladwell, M. (2002). *The tipping point: How little things can make a big difference.* Boston, MA: Little, Brown.

Myers, D. G. (2002). *Intuition: Its powers and perils.* New Haven, CT: Yale University Press.

Oxford University Press (Eds.).(2015). Oxford English Dictionary. Retrieved from http://www.oed.com/ [Access date: November 2015].

Rapaport, D. (1941). Review of H. Werner "Comparative psychology of mental development." *Journal of Genetic Psychology, 58–59,* 429–434.

Rawls, J. (1985). Justice as fairness: Political not metaphysical. *Philosophy & Public Affairs, 14*(3), 223–251.

Schuller, G. (1989). *The swing era: The development of jazz.* New York, NY: Oxford University Press.

Wapner, S. (2005). The sensory-tonic field theory of perception. In J. Valsiner (Ed.), *Heinz Werner and developmental science* (pp. 155–177). Berlin, Germany: Springer.

Werner. H. (1934). Unity of the senses. In S. S. Barren & M. B. Franklin (Eds.), *Developmental processes: Heinz Werner's selected writings* (p. 153). New York, NY: International Universities Press.

Werner, H. (1948). *Comparative psychology of mental development* (Rev. ed.). Chicago, IL: Follet.

Werner, H. (1957). The concept of development from a comparative and organismic point of view. In D. B. Harris (Ed.), *The concept of development: An issue in the study of human behavior* (pp. 125–148). Minneapolis, MN: University of Minnesota Press.

Werner, H. & Kaplan, B. (1963). *Symbol formation: An organismic developmental approach to language and the expression of thought.* New York, NY: Wiley.

CHAPTER 2

THE BIG DIFFERENCE

The Explanatory Power of the Undifferentiated and Differentiated

Sven Hroar Klempe
Norwegian University of Science and Technology

One challenge in a globalized world is to deal with the great variety of names given to individuals. Names are not just a personal thing, they are also, or maybe even more, an expression of group identity. That is why we have family names, which point out the group to which we belong. Yet, the names may also quite easily reveal a national belonging, and in some cases even the village or the place where the ancestors originally came from. The names may thus give away a lot of information about the individual in terms of group identity and regional belonging in the world.

NAMES LINKING PEOPLE

When I came to Clark University for a sabbatical in 2010, I would use my middle name Hroar as my first name, which I had been doing for more

Particulars and Universals in Clinical and Developmental Psychology, pages 31–49

or less my whole life. However, this caused problems: first of all because the combination of the H and the R confuses the reader from the very beginning, but also because a double dose of the Norwegian rolling Rs are hard to pronounce for an English-speaking person. Interestingly, I got the chance to collaborate with the legendary American psychologist and former Heinz Werner assistant Roger Bibace during my stay, and he was no exception when it came to pronouncing my name. Although we got along well from the start and spent a lot of productive hours together, my name represented a minor obstacle in our relationship. It was a big surprise for both of us when we realized that "Roger" and "Hroar" actually are the same name by origin.

The reason is the close relationship between the two languages, English and Norwegian, which were almost the same language 1,500 years ago. The root for the two names is *Hrogar*, which also was the name of the king of Denmark around the year 500 AD. Yet, language and names changed over time, as reflected by the place King Hrogar took great pride in: *Roskilde* in Denmark—an abbreviation for Hrogar's fount. The two languages, English and Norwegian, also changed over time, but they both share many common roots. Hrogar is one of them: It became Roger in English, and the most common version in Norwegian today is *Roar*. In the Norwegian version, the H is normally quite simply deleted; it has not been pronounced for several hundred years.

This example tells us something about how differences and boundaries may turn into the opposite by disappearing completely when the same phenomenon is regarded from another perspective. This is easy to trace in language, but we can experience the same effect in other situations, for example, when two people meet for the first time and they suddenly discover that they have a common friend or share the same interest. In such situations, the boundaries dissolve and the conversation may flow as if the two had been pals for years. These changes—from almost insurmountable boundaries and differences to nearly the opposite—may easily make us conclude that differences and distinctions are just feigned and do not count at all. However, they also lead to another conclusion: These changes of perspective on distinctions and differences make the borders still fundamental and crucial in each individual's actual life. They tell us something about the individual's development, and that development is a result of crossing borders (Marsico, Cabel, Valsiner, & Kharlamov, 2013). Yet, this brings in a conflict between the static aspects of borders and the dynamic aspects of development. The aim of solving this contradiction was something the Austrian-American psychologist Heinz Werner (1890–1964) focused on.

DIFFERENTIATION AS A MULTI-LINEAR PROCESS

Usually, we think of development as linear growth in just one direction, from the primitive to the more complex. Heinz Werner suggested a different approach, since, for example, we may also trace primitive traits like the imprecise use of words or even "childish" behavior in more highly developed adults. Werner (1948) saw development as interplay between the two terms *undifferentiation* and *differentiation*. He focused on this dynamic interplay from the very beginning, when he investigated how children dealt with different forms of melodic singing. "It is likely that the genuine melodic germ is a diffuse descending glissando, out of which the so-called 'ur-motif" (primary motif) may have developed as a descending two-toned pattern with the interval of a minor third" (Werner, 1948, pp. 124–125). The diffuse descending glissando is also characteristic of the first type of communication between mother and child in the first few weeks after birth. The point here is not that communication stems from singing, but rather that this descending glissando is an example of undifferentiated types of communication. This undifferentiation can also be observed in a child's first use of language: "Immature language behavior... lacks the distinctiveness in the relation of word to context that characterizes, at least in our culture sphere, mature verbal activity" (Werner & Kaplan, 1952, p. 14). This "immature language behavior" represents a "lower degree of differentiation." (Werner & Kaplan, 1952, p. 14). Yet, there are fleeting boundaries between the lower and higher degrees of differentiation, and therefore there is a "co-existence" between the different levels (Bibace, Sagarin, & Dyl, 1998; Bibace, 2005). Intonation is a factor in all languages, although it is reminiscent of the preverbal stage of the baby's communication.

Thus, in this paper, I will first demonstrate how psychology is to be regarded as a science that from the very beginning has been forced to take these dynamic and fleeting aspects of life into account. (This was certainly not easy, especially as psychology struggled to be seen as an independent discipline.) An examination of the rudimentary understanding of the term "psychology" will form the point of departure, and, not least, how Wilhelm Wundt summarized the main aspects of the term later on in the 19th century, which formed the basis for a structuralistic approach in psychology. Yet, a structuralist approach was not completed by Edward B. Titchener, but rather followed up by the Swiss linguist Ferdinand de Saussure, and brought back to psychology by Jean Piaget. In this respect, there is a common understanding of psychology in the first half of the 20th century, and this understanding is reflected in Werner's terms and developed further by Roger Bibace, who made a synthesis of Heinz Werner, Jean Piaget, and Sigmund Freud's elaborations by emphasizing the ego as a dynamic entity that transcends stages conceptualized as rigid and generic phases of an individual's life (Bibace, 1961, 2005).

DIFFERENTIATION AS SPECIALIZATION

Man is often regarded as the most complex creature in this world. If this is true, it obviously does not contradict its need for development. This has caused a lot of paradoxes in describing man. From a biological perspective, man is described as the less specialized compared to other creatures. Man is able to run, climb, swim, jump, work hard, etc., but, compared to animals, we are losers. But even if we cannot move as quickly as animals, we are equipped with the potential to build cars, planes, and other devices that help us out. Hence, our rather primitive abilities still provide the greatest potential for development (Betzig, 1997; Damasio, 2000). These contradictions stress Werner's point that development includes both: going from the undifferentiated to the differentiated and vice versa.

An example to illustrate this can, yet again, be taken from language. My Norwegian name causes even more trouble for East Asians. A good Chinese colleague of mine had an 8-year-old daughter when I first met her. The mother was neither able to perceive nor to pronounce the two Rs in my name. Her attempts to pronounce my name ended up as sounding something like "loal" or "doad." However, the daughter was able to almost pronounce the name correctly. Hence, the adult Chinese appeared as more specialized in her competence in Chinese, which excludes the rolling Rs, whereas the 8-year-old child demonstrated openness to linguistic sounds that are strange to Chinese.

This is the same for a Westerner coming to learn Chinese Mandarin. The four different pitch accents in Mandarin (see Figure 2.1) are almost impossible to discern from each other for Westerners. In other words, when we are used to certain sounds in the language, it is hard to even imagine other linguistic sounds.

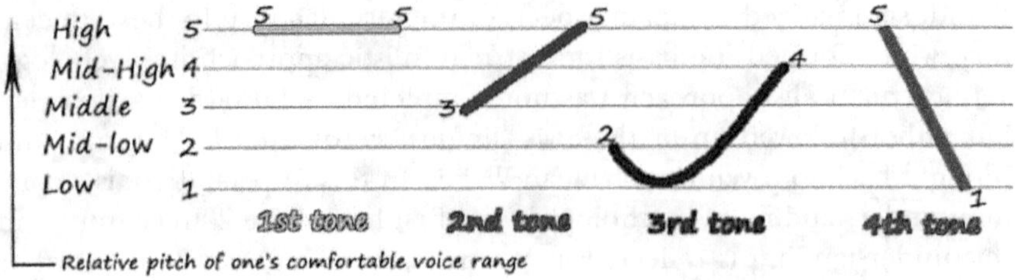

Figure 2.1 The four pitch accents in Mandarin. *Source:* chinesestep.com.

Based on these observations, we may say that there are more distinctions in sounds than an individual is able to perceive as an adult. The rolling R in Scandinavian and other languages, like Arabic for example, is difficult to pronounce not only for East Asians, but also for a native English–speaking person. The four different pitch accents in Mandarin are hard to perceive and discern for a Westerner. But the *potentiality* is there for every human being, and one can learn. The Chinese ability to differentiate pitches in language is one of the reasons for some psychologists to suggest that every child has the potential for having perfect pitch from the very beginning (Mithen, 2006), and that the occurrences of absolute pitch are more frequent among the Chinese than among other populations (Deutsch, Henthorn, Marvin, & Xu, 2006). Consequently, a good musical ear is a good illustration of how development also goes from the differentiated to the undifferentiated. Absolute pitch is the undifferentiated potential. In language it is useful to retain just some few aspects of it, as we have best illustrated in Chinese. Yet, for a musician, it is useful to retain more of this ability. Thus, a musician goes through a process from the undifferentiated to the differentiated by learning a certain language. However, through musical training, the same person has to acquire the more generic skill of recognizing all types of pitches. For a musician, some aspects of the differentiated and the undifferentiated thus have to coexist.

PSYCHOLOGY AS UNDIFFERENTIATED TERM

Although psychology is regarded as a young science, its origin can, nevertheless, be traced back to the early 16th century (Mengal, 2005; Vidal, 2011). At first, an undifferentiated understanding of the field emerged because it was difficult to distinguish from other fields. One important element was, nevertheless, quite distinct: During the Middle Ages, the term *soul* or *anima* pointed in two directions—to the human soul seen from a theological perspective representing the eternal aspect or part of an individual,[1] and to the soul as the bearer of the individual's knowledge. The latter represents a tradition going back to Aristotle and his book "De Anima." Primarily, this book is about how man acquires knowledge, either through sensation or by thinking (Aristotle, 1976). These two perspectives did not disappear when *psychology* was introduced in the 16th century. However, the scope became considerably broadened. Also physiology was included, simply because it is impossible to talk about the acquisition of knowledge through the senses without examining the nature of these senses. By then, physiology was not regarded as an independent science or as a cause able to explain all aspects of sensation and knowledge itself—it had to be combined with another discipline. This was also true for medicine and physiology, so all three sciences represented a nondiscernible science about actual life, or what we would call "life science" today. Psychology thus became a somewhat holistic perspective on life standing in opposition to the science of the soul, because the latter was not about actual life, but about the eternal aspects of an individual (Vidal, 2011).

Psychology as a life science was just one of those factors that made psychology holistic. In medieval times and early modernity, another important factor was metaphysics. This was also a rather undifferentiated term before the 18th century. Although Aristotle, who had introduced the term, defined metaphysics as the basis for scientific knowledge, the term itself was just a technical term without any deeper meaning. *Meta* means after, and originally referred to the order of the books. Specifically, *Metaphysics* was the book that came after the book about physics (Aristotle, 1995). Ancient Greek psychology or the thesis on the soul was not included in metaphysics. Yet, this changed radically during medieval times. If we look at Thomas Aquinas's writings, for example, we see that the principles Aristotle discussed in his metaphysics are not differentiated from, but rather combined with topics from *On the Soul* (Aquinas, 2001). Thus, what we would call a rudimentary psychology today was by then deeply interwoven with metaphysics.

Metaphysics was thus an undifferentiated and unspecified term until the late 17th and early 18th centuries. Although, by then almost all scholars provided some sort of systematization of the term, Christian Wolff (1679–1754) probably provided the most influential contribution. He divided metaphysics into (a) ontology, (b) cosmology, (c) psychology, and (d) natural theology and dedicated at least one volume to each part (published from 1730–1737). By then, psychology appeared as an explicit part of metaphysics, although it consisted of two parts presented in separate volumes: *Psychologia Empirica* (1732) and *Psychologia Rationalis* (1734). The order of the two volumes was not chosen randomly: Psychology was primarily about sensation (*empirica*), whereas the rational psychology focused on the soul from an eternal perspective including inner perceptions. This systematization of metaphysics had a tremendous influence on intellectual life for a short period, not only because metaphysics by then, did not target things beyond scientific activities, but also because it provided the basis for them. The most adequate perspective on the role of metaphysics in early modernity is to compare it with today's methodology (Varzi, 2011). It defined the constraining principles for assessing statements as acceptable or not from a scientific point of view.

IN THE ETERNAL SHADOW OF KANT

The relationship between metaphysics and empirical psychology forms a kind of neglected core of Kant's philosophy. On the one hand, he regards empirical psychology as important, but on the other hand he "banished" it from metaphysics. This was motivated by his understanding of metaphysics. Specifically, he defined it as the science of the general principles for acquiring knowledge: "Metaphysic is the science of the first principles of human cognition" (Kant, 1781/1899, p. 298). However, this definition does not entail a clear demarcation for what is or what is not general. In other words, it does not tell us how the general is different from the empirical. This distinction is just a question of degree, and Kant even says that it is hard to make that distinction at all, a reason for why empirical psychology ended up as part of metaphysics:

> I ask: Does the conception of extension belong to metaphysics?
> You answer, "Yes."
> Well, that of body too? "Yes."
> And that of a fluid body?
> You stop, you are unprepared to admit this; for if you do, everything will belong to metaphysics. (Kant, 1781/1899, p. 298)

Against this background, empirical psychology became a part of metaphysics. But according to Kant, it does not belong to metaphysics more than physics because both are not about general principles, but rather about particular events in man's lives and in nature, respectively.

Thus, the specification Kant made was to restrict metaphysics to solely concern general principles. These are given by our rational understanding of the world and they are not derived from the world given as an empirical entity. On this basis, Kant also suggested that metaphysics should be divided into four, but, compared to Wolff, differently labelled subdisciplines in which psychology is apparently excluded: (a) ontology, (b) rational physiology, (c) rational cosmology, and (d) rational theology. Psychology is replaced by rational physiology. This is interesting in itself, because it exemplifies how close those two sciences were regarded to be. The term reflects the rudimentary idea of a life science, but from a very unique perspective defined by Kant. Yet, at the same time, he suggested that rational physiology should be subdivided into rational physics and rational psychology. This implies that he did not want to promote the idea of a "life science," but rather stress what should be the target of observations. On the one hand, rational physics refers to the nature of external observations we make of the world. Rational psychology, on the other hand, refers to the internal observations we make of ourselves in terms of cognition. This distinction appears to be crucial for how psychology was later conceptualized. Focusing on observation was just a consequence of the general understanding of psychology as the science of sensation. From a scientific perspective, the introduction of observations as scientific approach was one of the most radical turning points that became generally accepted and widespread during the 18th century. The challenge was, of course, to balance this with the classic requirement of general validity of scientific statements. Kant's most important contribution to science was that he apparently arrived at this balance by introducing the idea of pure sciences. This idea permeates almost all scientific discourses today when proclaiming that all sciences should be based on the universality of mathematics. This is also why Kant only included the rational and not the empirical aspects of the different parts of metaphysics. However, his emphasis on rationality related to psychology, at the same time, promoted *cognition*—a more or less commonly used term for the German word *Erkenntnis* since Meiklijohn's translation from 1899 (Kant, 1781/1899). This translation combined with Kant's emphasis on physiology makes it tempting to conclude that Kant not only subverted the spiritual aspects of the soul, but in addition provided the basis for cognitive psychology as well as neuroscience. In other words, psychology went through a radical change during the 18th century: from something unspecified and undifferentiated to a more specified and differentiated psychology.

AN ABUNDANCE OF PSYCHOLOGIES

Although Kant apparently arranged for some sort of demarcation between the sciences, this was yet not set in stone. The idea of highlighting purity in science generated a fundamental paradox: Because of their empirical basis, neither psychology nor physics satisfied the criteria for being a pure science, although both generated scientific knowledge. Therefore, attempts to continue Kant's project veered in different directions. One of his successors, Johann Friedrich Herbart, followed up Kant's ideals by using the means of mathematics and music to make psychology "pure" (Leary, 1982; Klempe, 2008). Instead, Kant's student Johann Gottfried Herder opened up to language and culture, the so-called *Volkstümlichkeit* [popularities], assuming that these form the basis for thinking. Another scholar who tried to follow up on Kant, Johann Gottlieb Fichte, ended up with some sort of philosophical subjectivism, which did not leave any space for psychology at all (Klempe, 2014). And one of Kant's resistors, Ernst Platner, occupied the term *anthropology* and reserved it for physiology in his 1772 publication entitled *Anthropology for Physicians and Philosophers* (Vidal, 2011). In addition, Alexander Baumgarten's two volumes on aesthetics from the 1750s paved the way for the German tradition to connect psychology with aesthetics (Allesch, 2006). Thus, psychology, at the beginning of the 19th century, was not just one thing, but at least six, if not seven or even more different disciplines: anthropology, a mathematical science, the science of subjectivity, a cultural science, physiology, and aesthetics. At the same time, psychology was, to some extent, still included in metaphysics and regarded as methodology in terms of *ars observandi*—and sometimes it was even closely connected with ethics (Klempe, 2008). What we see is that all these disciplines were established as independent disciplines at the same time. Thus, there is a continuous process of differentiation. Although the term psychology still appeared as quite undifferentiated, its subdisciplines appeared to be more and more profiled and easy to identify.

THE EMERGENCE OF THE SCIENCE OF SUBJECTIVITY

The previously described differentiation of the disciplines had been taking place when Wundt established his psychological laboratory in Leipzig in 1879. However, his background reflected the diversity of the term psychology and the great variety of its subdisciplines. He had studied medicine, but was primarily interested in physiology. He worked as the assistant of the physicist Hermann Helmholtz for several years, and at the same time he was highly involved and interested in the emerging *Völkerpsychologie* (folk psychology) founded by Moritz Lazarus and Heymann Steinthal, who established the journal *Zeitschrift für Völkerpsychologie und Sprachwissenschaft* (Journal of Folk Psychology and Linguistics) in 1860. His first professorship was in anthropology and medical psychology, but his second was in inductive philosophy, a position he filled for only a year before he became professor in philosophy of science in Leipzig in 1875. Wundt's approach to deal with the still unspecified field of psychology at that time was to take just one step at a time. This formed the background for the elementaristic approach Wundt represented. When we look at his activities until his death in 1920, we may trace recurrences of all the diverse elements that characterised his professional efforts up until the laboratory was established in 1879. The psychological laboratory was furnished with almost the same equipment found in Helmholtz' physical laboratory that Wundt had worked in 20 years earlier. Thus, what exactly differentiates physics from experimental psychology is difficult to grasp. Wundt himself, nevertheless, provides an answer to this question in his *Outlines of Psychology* written in the late 1890s. There are two directions for the treatment of experience: "One is that of the natural sciences, which concern themselves with the objects of experience, thought of as independent from the subject. The other is that of psychology, which investigates the whole content of experience in its relations to the subject and also in regard to the attributes which this content derives directly from the subject" (Wundt, 1896/1897/1902, p. 3, original italics).

Therefore, psychology has much in common with physics, but there is one crucial difference: While psychology includes the subjective experience of an object, physics is about the object itself detached from subjective experiences.

Experimental psychology was primarily about the immediate experience of the physical objects. This involved the whole transformational process from the peripheral, physiological system of senses to the inner, mental production of ideas and representations. This, of course, included the whole nervous system and other physiological aspects, which required knowledge in those areas as well. Seemingly, physiology was Wundt's main interest. However, if so, it is remarkable that he ended up publishing the thesis of psychophysical parallelism (Wundt, 1894). Through this principle, Wundt wanted to avoid materialism by saying that mental functions are not a result of physiology. Yet, physiology is still a constraining factor "in the sense that different kinds of stimulation always correspond to different sensations" (Wundt 1896/1897/1902, p. 45), but "it is impossible to explain the character of sensations from the character of physical and physiological stimuli" (Wundt 1896/1897/1902, p. 45). Another aspect to highlight in this regard is that one of the positions Wundt had was a professorship in inductive philosophy. One may ask how this topic could fill a full position, but the role of inductions was of course a crucial problem in philosophy at the time, and it was primarily related to psychology. Psychology focused on sense-impressions, which is about the particular, but at the same time psychology was also focusing on mental ideas and representations, which are about the general. In other words, it is not only a physiological transformation that takes place in psychology, but also a logical transformation in the sense that the particular experiences are immediately transformed into a general understanding. Thus, the problem of induction summarized the main challenges in psychology, specifically the physical and logical transformations of particular sense impressions into more general mental representations.

THE CENTRALITY OF FEELING

In addition to sensations and mental representations, feelings should be considered as well. The English verb *to feel* reflects the intimate connection between the physiological act of touching and some unspecified emotional reactions. Also the term *touching* is an example of a similar double meaning, but maybe in the opposite direction. Therefore, they both refer to the act of sensing, but also to some emotional reactions—not necessarily at the same time. We know very well from the context whether they are referring to an emotional state or a sensational act. Yet, the close connection reflects that sensation and emotion have, historically speaking, not always been fully differentiated. In addition, the emotional state and the sensational act were regarded as undivided and undifferentiated experiences in daily life. Wundt put a lot of effort in both, pointing at the close connection between the physiological act of sensation and the emotional experiences of it, but also differentiating between them. His argument for making a distinction is that sensation is related to sense qualities, which implies that each impression of objects in the world is different. Thus, as sensational, the world appears to be disparate and various. The emotional reactions as a whole, however, go in another direction. They may be varied as well, but the differences are rather based on the mental reaction, which may include putting them into words, and therefore making them point in a general direction, whereas sense impressions are connected to a particular experience. Wundt thus applies the term *differences* when it comes to sensations, and *oppositions* with regards to feelings in the sense that "the former (sensation) range between maximal differences, the latter (feelings) between maximal opposites" (Wundt, 1896/1897/1902, p. 37).

The distinction Wundt made between sensational differences and emotional opposites is crucial. Yet it is necessary to clarify the three tricky terms applied here, specifically *feelings*, *affects*, and *emotions*. In this context feeling refers to the bodily reaction related to a sense impression. A feeling is unspecified and impossible to put into words. Affect, on the other hand refers to the more specified and general aspects of a feeling. Hence an affect can be put into words. Emotion is used as a generic term, which refers to both feelings and affects. The distinction Wundt makes between the emotional and the sensational is, at the same time, the distinction between language and physiology, or culture and nature. The example given in the beginning about the use of the Rs in different languages may tell us why. The acoustic differences between the rolling and the guttural Rs are definitely there, but they may not have any affective meaning, especially, when the focus lies on the content of the word. As long as the pronunciation indicates that it is my name that is articulated, I will act due to the fact that my name is called up. Yet, if my focus is on other types of information, like for example, the geographical region the person that calls my name is from, the opposition between the rolling and the guttural R is crucial. The difference indicates which part of Norway the one who calls my name is from. In other words, meaning is produced on different levels at the same time, and this meaning is first of all produced in terms of the system of oppositions that is established. Thus, there are different systems that operate at the same time. The opposition between a guttural and a rolling R does not influence the general understanding of Norwegian, but it becomes important when one wants to find out which part of Norway the person is from. Sometimes, we are interested in both types of information, and we are obviously able to identify them at the same time. If so, the rolling and the guttural Rs form two oppositions, if the distinction does not matter, the two Rs are just different.

Hence, oppositions are characterized by the affective meaning I experience when I—in this example—am interested in regional belongings, whereas the acoustic differences do not require and are not related to these kinds of experiences. From this perspective, emotions appear to be a kind of mediator between pure sense impressions and meaning. They even seem to have the role of transforming the sense impressions into meaning. However, this is not a mechanical process with a causality that goes in just one direction. It is rather a type of process, in which cognition and bodily reactions are jointly interacting. Wundt's understanding of emotions can be regarded as an elaboration of the theory of emotions that goes back to Immanuel Kant. He talked about emotions as the bodily reaction to something of which the mind does not have a full understanding (Kant, 1790/1972). Emotions were regarded as related to cognition, but at the same time standing in opposition to cognition. In Wundt's terms, the emotions are rather to be regarded as being closely related to mental processes in the sense that they reflect not only the preunderstanding, but also the active cognitive interest and focus a person may have. Thus, meaning-making is a result of how sense impressions are transformed into a general cognitive understanding by means of constructing oppositions in terms of their differences in triggered emotions.

There are reasons to say that, in this way, Wundt presented an advanced theory of emotions. The aspect that makes it advanced is the reciprocity between the body and the mind, which is explained in such a way that it forms the basis for human meaning making. For a better understanding of emotions, Wundt spoke of an *indifference-zone* (Wundt, 1896/1897/1902, p. 35), a neutral zone that appears as a turning point inbetween the two extremes of affective qualities called *maximal opposites* (Wundt, 1896/1897/1902, p. 34). The reason for introducing this is to emphasize that emotions and feelings are not a part of the physiological nervous system. The sense impressions have to be neutralized, so to speak, before they become affectively "loaded." With regard to these concepts, Wundt cautioned against two misunderstandings that may occur when looking at emotions: "[T]wo false views may easily arise, either that sensations are the *causes* of feelings, or that feelings are a particular species of sensations" (Wundt, 1896/1897/1902, p. 37). The affective aspect can never be derived from sensations, but "only from the attitude of the subject" (Wundt, 1896/1897/1902, p. 37), and feelings and sensations are two different spheres, of which the former is related to the subject and the latter to the object. Thus, Wundt makes some distinctions that are not included in Kant's theory of emotions, but that are able to form a better basis for how to understand the process of human meaning-making.

FOLK PSYCHOLOGY

The experimental psychology of Wundt represented a starting point, which quite soon transcended itself. However, a statement like this depends very much on how experimental psychology is to be defined. The physical approach was transcended by focusing on subjects instead of objects, the physiological perspective was surpassed by focusing on feelings instead of sensation, and the scientific perspective changed from detecting mental laws to emphasizing the unpredictable free will as the basis for meaning making. This is highlighted by the fact that the outcome of experimental psychology was the superior mental principle of the creative synthesis (Wundt, 1896/1997/1902). This principle tells us that the human mind is governed by a free will, which contradicts the assumptions implied in conducting experiments. Thus, Wundt had to transcend the experimental design, which he did by developing aspects of a folk psychology.

Although folk psychology is focusing on language, myths, and habits (Wundt, 1896/1897/1902), these categories are to be understood as broadly as possible. When Wundt talked about language, for example, he started with gestures (Wundt, 1973). In the small book *The Language of Gestures* he exemplifies how meaning is processed in its most basic form (Wundt, 1973). Again, this represents his elementaristic approach, but it also demonstrates that elementarism is not necessarily a reductionistic approach. Language can never be reduced to gestures, but the use of gestures demonstrates some principles that can also be applied to language. One of them is the principle of affective loading as a factor for talking about oppositions, as described previously. Wundt presents different traditions for applying gestures in different cultures, and his conclusion is quite clear: "It is not the degree of education but rather the degree of emotion or the constant affective tendency, the temperament that is important for the formation of gesture" (Wundt, 1973, p. 66). In other words, the gesture is the best example for demonstrating the importance of affective loadings in the process of making distinctions, oppositions, and differentiations.

Gestures very easily demonstrate the need for creativity as well. It is this spontaneous form of communication we immediately apply when we communicate with people speaking languages we do not understand. The language of gestures may well be standardized, as it was done when developing sign systems for deaf mutes for example. The fact that we also find well-developed systems of gestures in different cultures indicates that they are not only a substitute for language, but are often felt as a necessary compensation for deficits in the ordinary language. This is still very noticeable among south Italians today, who apply a certain repertoire of gestures almost consistently in a conversation. Although these sign systems of communication are well established, their compensatory role to language is related to their ability to facilitate what Wundt calls "arbitrary neologisms" (Wundt, 1973, p. 59). This term refers to two aspects of the gesture. One is the invitation to invent neologisms, which requires a creative effort. The other is that the new invented gesture is, in part, chosen arbitrarily, but acquires its meaning by standing in opposition to the other gestures. As long as the newly invented gesture is able to provoke and mobilize the same type of affect given by the oppositional context, the outcome would still be a common understanding of meaning. This demonstrates the arbitrariness of the gesture, because it is not the gesture itself, but its relationship to other gestures in terms of differences in affective loadings that constitute the gesture's meaning.

THE ARBITRARY SIGN AND STRUCTURALISM

Arthur Blumenthal highlights that Wilhelm Wundt was the most influential theorist in the late 19th century in several areas, one of them being linguistics: "His lectures on the psychology of language were the most heavily attended in the world, and those who heard him included de Saussure, Paul, Delbrück, and Bloomfield" (Blumenthal, 1973, pp. 12–13). In contrast to Wundt, de Saussure tried to avoid psychological explanations of language as such to escape a certain type of reductionism saying that every science could be explained by psychological categories, the so-called *psychologism* (Knobloch, 1988). This was also what Edmund Husserl fought against in the field of logic. Although his two volumes of *Logical Investigations* (Husserl, 2001) are dedicated to the psychologist Carl Stumpf, it is first of all an attack on psychologism in logic, i.e., he wanted to define logic as an independent scientific area. It was the same battle de Saussure fought, specifically by establishing linguistics as an independent science standing on its own based on the thesis of the arbitrary sign. This is why the distinction between the signifier and the signified (signifiant versus signifié) became so important. The sign as arbitrary implies that there are no inner connections between the sign and its reference. The connections are not only conventionally established, but the oppositions of the signifiers themselves generate them.

The aspect of arbitrariness is the basis for French structuralism. Yet, what we see is that this is a latent factor in Wundt's structuralism as well. It is not the external references or objects that generate meaning and our understanding, but rather the differences in their affective loadings. The organism provides those differences, and, in that sense, they represent a type of independency from the external world as such. The external world exists, of course, as a potential and constraint and by this provides the Gibsonian affordance needed to derive meaning from the external world (Gibson, 1977). The guttural Rs are there along with the rolling Rs, but the differences between them do not represent oppositions in the Norwegian language. They have the same affective loading and therefore the same meaning although they are quite different, seen from an acoustic point of view.

Thus, the distinction Wundt made between differences and oppositions is crucial, as the differences represent the affordances in the external world from which the oppositions are independent.

Against this background, structuralism is not an unambiguous term. When Eduard Titchener applied this term at the end of the 19th century (Titchener, 1898, 1899), he did not include the aspect of arbitrariness: "Introspection, from the structural standpoint, is observation of an Is" (Titchener 1899, p. 291). This sentence defines structuralism in terms of reflecting what there is and it highlights the neutrality of structuralism. This is also a certain understanding of the elementaristic approach, which builds up the whole by means of its stable elements. This does not provide any space for development and changes, and, in this sense, is a form of structuralism, which contradicts the structure to which Wundt referred. The Titchenerian understanding of structuralism has had a great influence on the American tradition. This was not only established by Titchener, but also by one of the American linguists who also studied in Leipzig and listened to Wundt's lectures on psychology and language, Leonard Bloomfield (1887–1949). Although he declared his adherence to Wundt in his earlier work, he changed and instead developed a distributional grammar, which aimed at isolating syntax from semantics, and, because of this, is regarded as belonging to a positivistic movement in linguistics (Lyons, 1977).

In opposition to both Titchener and Bloomfield, Jean Piaget called for a type of structuralism that was based very much on the Saussurian understanding, opposing the American understanding of structuralism (Piaget, 1968/1971). Although he is primarily referring to Jerome Bruner as "the American," he meant that the American structuralism let "the subject's strategies remain isolated instead of becoming integrated into systems" (Piaget, 1968/1971, p. 72). For Piaget, "a structure is a system of transformation" (Piaget, 1968/1971, p. 5), and the structuralistic systems are characterized by being "self-sufficient and that, to grasp them, we do not have to make reference to all sorts of extraneous elements" (Piaget, 1968/1971, p. 5). This is another way to formulate the aspect of arbitrariness specifically in terms of a self-sufficient system of oppositions. The fact that the system regulates itself allows for transformation, changes, and development. In opposition to Titchener, Piaget does not make a sharp distinction between structure and function, which is also obvious from a Saussurian perspective. The elements that form the oppositions stand in a functional relationship to each other, in the sense that their function *is* to be in opposition to each other. Wundt explained this in terms of affective loadings, whereas the explanatory terms for Piaget are assimilation and accommodation, with a certain emphasis on the former.

SOME CONCLUSIONS ABOUT THE EXPLANATORY POWER OF DIFFERENTIATION

One of the biggest challenges in psychology has been to unite stable scientific knowledge with the aspects of changes and development in the actual human life. Hence, even the term *development* is normally understood as linear movement from a starting point to an end. However, what Heinz Werner and his followers have emphasized, and what is being focused on here, is that neither an individual nor its artifacts can be understood in terms of one-dimensional growth. The development of language and other human artifacts change in different directions at the same time. In this respect, we talk about a movement from the undifferentiated to the differentiated, and back again. This does not only have consequences for psychology, but also for historiography, which is demonstrated by the development of the term *psychology*. Thus, the general value of the undifferentiated and the differentiated appears to have a broad scope, and therefore also an extraordinarily strong explanatory power.

Yet, strong explanatory power does not necessarily represent a good theory. It might be too general. This is also what characterizes these terms. One may even say that the theory of the movement from the undifferentiated to the differentiated and back again is in itself an example of something undifferentiated. Yet, what has been brought up here are some examples, which specify how the theory has some differentiated aspects as well. The best example of this is the theory of the arbitrary sign, which is a specified theory about how language develops and changes due to specified and nonspecified terms. The same could be said about Wundt's experimental psychology. He started with sensation because sensation is about the rudimentary awareness of the unspecified differences out there, which is at the same time the undifferentiated. The sensational impressions do not become differentiated before there is a subject that creates oppositions. Simultaneously, this is the transition from experimental to folk psychology. In line with this, Wundt considered experimental psychology as a supporting discipline (Wundt, 1920). However, oppositions represent a double communication in the sense that they both provide distinctions, but at the same time refer to a whole they both belong to, specifically the system of which they are elements. Our ability to unite by means of distinctions is the creative synthesis, which according to Wundt was the main outcome of experimental psychology (Wundt, 1896/1897/1902).

The creative synthesis is, at the same time, the basis for the gestalt. When Piaget thus investigates the *structuralism*, he highlights the gestalt psychologists (Piaget, 1968/1971). Yet, he does not refer to Heinz Werner although Werner is probably the most interesting gestalt psychologist that brings in the distinction between the undifferentiated and the differentiated in terms of development:

> The more perfect the creature becomes, the less similar become the [morphological] parts to one another. On the one genetic pole, the whole is more or less similar to the parts, and on the other the whole is dissimilar to its parts. The more nearly equal parts, the less are they subordinated one to another. Subordination of the parts indicates a perfect creature. (Werner, 1948, pp. 40–41)

This is a quotation Werner took from Goethe and presented as a general statement that counts for all types of organic development, from the most primitive bacteria to the subtlest discourse, as exemplified here with the development of psychology and use of language. The point is that the elements that constitute a system are organized, so that they have a certain position; they form a hierarchical order, and this presupposes a differentiation. To go back to the introductory example, the distinction between the R and the other letters is more important than the distinction between the guttural and the rolling Rs to catch the meaning of a word in Norwegian. And the more we are able to differentiate between words, the better our understanding. However, this is an endless process going back and forth, and the same term, like structuralism for example, may have very different meanings in different contexts.

Another important point from this exploration is that the elements go beyond the word or the sign; they are rather founded by means of their forms. This is the basis for Ernst Cassirer's[2] understanding of culture in general. He relates culture to form and structure, and form is first of all an Aristotelian term closely related to Plato's ideas (Cassirer, 1961). Yet during history, the term *form* was related to a vitalistic perspective, which also formed the basis for the previous quotation from Goethe. Culture, therefore, is related to the vitalistic principle that permeates human activities, not least the use and development of a symbolic language. Language must be regarded as a representational system, which is completely different from what it represents. Thus, it must be organized in a way that the oppositions are "reciprocally conditioned" (Cassirer, 1961, p. 107). This is the same as underlining the arbitrariness, the independency between the signifier and the signified, because signification is produced by "reciprocally conditioning." According to Cassirer, it is not just language that is built on this principle: "Civilization is itself the most striking expression and incontrovertible proof of this reciprocal conditioning" (Cassirer, 1961, p. 107f). Against this background, culture in general is to be understood in terms of symbols, communication, exchange, and change, which has been natural for the last five decades (Geertz, 1973). In other words, the aspect of self-constituting systems in terms of affectively loaded differentiations forms the basis for understanding the organic coherence in both human development and its products. Aiming to combine different schools in psychology, like Bibace has done, one manages to highlight the composite aspects of both. Yet, we have seen that there is still a great and unexploited potential in following this pathway, which implies that the theory of differentiation may appear as a sustainable strong theory in psychology.

NOTE

1. A value added to the term by Christianity.
2. Ernst Cassirer was Heinz Werner's colleague in Hamburg. Both left Nazi Germany in 1933.

REFERENCES

Allesch, C. G. (2006). *Einführung in die psychologische Ästhetik* [Introduction to psychological aesthetics]. Wien, Austria: UTB.

Aquinas, T. (2001). *Summa contra gentiles* [The sum against the heathen]. Darmstadt, Germany: Wissenschaftliche Buchgesellschaft.

Aristotle. (1976). *De anima.* New York, NY: Arno Press.

Aristotle. (1995). *Philosophische schriften 5. Metaphysik* [Philosophical writings 5. Metaphysics]. Darmstadt, Germany: Wissenschaftliche Buchgesellschaft.

Betzig, L. (1997). *Human nature. A critical reader.* New York, NY: Oxford University Press.

Bibace, R. (1961). Piaget and analysis: A synthetic attempt. *Contemporary Psychology, 6*(10), 351–352.

Bibace, R. (2005). Relating to Dr. Werner: Past and present. In J. Valsiner (Ed.), *Heinz Werner and developmental science. Path in psychology* (pp. 235–258). New York, NY: Kluwer Academic/Plenum.

Bibace, R., Sagarin, J. D., & Dyl, J. (1998). The heuristic value of Werner's co-existence concept of development. *Journal of Applied Developmental Psychology, 19*(1), 153–163.

Blumenthal, A. L. (1973). Introduction. In W. Wundt (Ed.), *The language of gestures* (pp. 11–19). The Haag, The Netherlands: Mouton.

Cassirer, E. (1961). *The logic of the humanities.* London, England: Yale University Press.

Damasio, A. R. (2000). *Descartes' error: Emotion, reason, and the human brain.* New York, NY: Quill.

De Saussure, F. (2011). *Course in general linguistics.* New York, NY: Columbia University Press.

Deutsch, D., Henthorn, T., Marvin, E., & Xu, H.-S. (2006). Absolute pitch among American and Chinese conservatory students: Prevalence differences, and evidence for a speech-related critical period. *Journal of Acoustical Society of America, 119*(2), 719–722.

Geertz, C. (1973). *The interpretation of cultures: Selected essays.* New York, NY: Basic Books.

Gibson, J. J. (1977). The theory of affordances. In R. Shaw & J. Bransford (Eds.), *Perceiving, acting, and knowing: Toward an ecological psychology* (pp. 67–82). Hillsdale, N.J.: Erlbaum.

Husserl, E. (2001). *Logical investigations.* London, England: Routledge.

Kant, I. (1781/1899). *Critique of pure reason.* New York, NY: Willey.
Kant, I. (1790/1972). *The critique of judgment.* New York, NY: Hafner.
Klempe, S. H. (2008). *Fra opplysning til eksperiment: Om psykologiens oppkomst fra Wolff til Wundt* [From enlightenment to experiment: The rise of psychology from Wolff to Wundt]. Bergen, Norway: Fagbokforlaget.
Klempe, S. H. (2014). *Kierkegaard and the rise of modern psychology.* London, England: Transaction.
Knobloch, C. (1988). *Geschichte der psychologischen sprachauffassung in Deutschland von 1850 bis 1920* [History of the psychological language conceptions in Germany between 1850 and 1920]. Tübingen, Germany: Max Niemeier.
Leary, D. (1982). Immanuel Kant and the development of modern psychology. In G. R. Woodward & G. Ash (Eds.), *The problematic science: Psychology in the nineteenth century* (pp. 17–42). New York, NY: Praeger.
Lyons, J. (1977). *Chomsky.* London, England: Fontana/Collins.
Marsico, G., Cabell, K. R., Valsiner, J., & Kharlamov, N. A. (2013). Interobjectivity as a border. The fluid dynamics of "betweenness." In G. Sammut, P. Daanen, & F. Moghaddam (Eds.), *Understanding the self and others: Explorations in intersubjectivity and interobjectivity* (pp. 51–65). London, England: Routledge.
Mengal, P. (2005). *La naissance de la psychologie* [The emergence of psychology]. Paris, France: L'Harmattan.
Mithen, S. (2006). *The singing Neanderthals. The origins of music, language, mind, and body.* London, England: Phoenix.
Piaget, J. (1968/1971). *Structuralism.* London, England: Routledge & Kegan Paul.
Titchener, E. B. (1898). The postulates of a structural psychology. *Philosophical Review, 7,* 449–465.
Titchener, E. B. (1899). Structural and functional psychology, *Philosophical Review, 8,* 290–299.
Varzi, A. C. (2011). Boundaries, conventions, and realism. In J. K. Campbell, M. O'Rourke, & M. H. Slater (Eds.), *Carving nature at its joints: Natural kinds in metaphysics and science* (pp. 129–153). Cambridge, MA: MIT Press.
Vidal, F. (2011). *The sciences of the soul: The early modern origins of psychology.* Chicago, IL: University of Chicago Press.
Werner, H. (1948). *Comparative psychology of mental development.* New York, NY: International Universities Press.
Werner, H., & Kaplan, E. (1952). The acquisition of word meanings: A developmental study. *Monographs of the Society for Research in Child Development, 15*(1), i–iii, v–vii, 1, 3–120.
Wundt, W. (1894). Über psychische causalität and das PRINCIP des psychophysischen parallelismus [About mental causality and the principle of psychophysical parallelism]. In W. Wundt (Ed.), *Ausgewählte psychologische schriften, abhandlungen, aufsätze, reden (1891–1913)* (Band II) [Selected psychological writings, essays, papers, talks (1891–1913)] (pp. 133–256). Leipzig, Germany: Zentralantiquariat der Deutschen Demokratische Republik.
Wundt, W. (1896/1897/1902). *Outlines of psychology.* Leipzig, Germany: Engelmann.
Wundt, W. (1920). *Erlebtes und erkanntes* [The experienced and recognized]. Stuttgart, Germany: Alfred Kröner.
Wundt, W. (1973). *The language of gestures.* The Hague, The Netherlands: Mouton.

CHAPTER 3

WORLD HYPOTHESES AND THEIR IMPACT ON EVERYDAY LIFE

James D. Laird
Clark University

PEPPER'S CONCEPT OF WORLD HYPOTHESES

The concept of World Hypotheses was first developed by the philosopher Steven Pepper (1942). He was puzzled by the difficulties philosophers had in reaching agreement and proposed that the difficultly arose because different philosophers used different and irreconcilable explanatory systems or epistemologies.

Pepper argued that all people, including professional philosophers, make sense of new phenomena by applying metaphors from old, well understood phenomena. Pepper argued that there were four relatively adequate *root* metaphors in general use and from which the four World Hypotheses were derived. Most people probably use all four kinds of World Hypotheses, but most people "specialized" and use one or two most of the time. Pepper's proposal was that two people who used different World Hypotheses might not be aware of their differences, but would be unable to find broad agreement.

Particulars and Universals in Clinical and Developmental Psychology, pages 51–61

The four World Hypotheses Pepper identified were Formism, Mechanism, Organicism, and Contextualism, each with a distinctive root metaphor and explanatory style. The root metaphor of Formism was the everyday experience that the world consists of entities, some of which are similar, some different. The basic epistemological task was to identify similarities and differences and to develop classifications to bring order to the array of objects and things. A psychological example would be trait theories.

The root metaphor of Mechanism is the causal relationship between cause and effect, epitomized by one billiard ball striking another and causing it to move. Mechanists see the world as a great machine, and understanding consists in identifying causes of events. Behaviorism is one such kind of thinking.

Organicists view the world as an organism, in which the parts and their interactions are organized to produce more complex wholes and accomplish ends or goals. Piaget's developmental psychology is an example of this kind of thinking.

Finally, Contextualists recognize organized, goal oriented systems like Organicists do, but also recognize that the organizations are different at different times and depend on the perspective of the observer. The same elements may be part of more than one organized whole. Cultural psychology is one such theoretical example.

Table 3.1 gives an overview of the four hypotheses and their ideas as well as examples for potential representatives.

WORLD HYPOTHESES IN EVERYDAY LIFE

Pepper had focused his attention on the explanatory styles of professional thinkers, but it seemed that the same World Hypotheses might be found among ordinary people. To discover philosophers' World Hypotheses, Pepper had examined their formal writings, but of course most ordinary people do not have such a body of material available for scoring, so a different kind of measurement method was required. Initial attempts to get people to write samples to be analyzed proved difficult and confusing to most people, so the next step was a much simpler task. Participants were shown a series of items that consisted of a very skeletal description of a person doing something, followed by four alternative explanations for their actions. Each of these alternatives embodied a very simple version of one of the four World Hypotheses. This approach and the final scale were developed by Maxine Harris (Harris, Fontana, & Dowds, 1977)[1]

TABLE 3.1 Stephen Pepper's World Hypotheses (Pepper, 1942)

	Dispersive	Integrative
Analytic	FORMISM Classification of Similarities Focus on the Concrete Description *Root Metaphor:* similarity/artifact *Associated with:* Realism, Platonic Idealism *Representatives:* Plato, Aristotle	MECHANISM Cause and Effect Focus on the Quantitative Focus on Principles *Root Metaphor:* machine *Associated with:* Naturalism, Materialism, (Realism) *Representatives:* Galileo, Locke
Synthetic	CONTEXTUALISM Focus on Contexts in which Phenomena Occur (Dependence) *Root Metaphor:* historic event *Associated with:* Pragmatism *Representatives:* Peirce, James, Mead	ORGANICISM Holistic Focus on Relationships *Root Metaphor:* integration/organism *Associated with:* Absolute Idealism, Objective Idealism *Representatives:* Hegel, Green, Royce
	• Knowledge is not systematic • World is not orderly • Unpredictable	• Knowledge is orderly & systematic • World is orderly • Predictable

Here is an example of these items:

Frank is getting a divorce.

1. There are a number of ways of looking at Frank's getting a divorce. Emotionally he feels one way about it, and morally he feels another way about it. There is no one way Frank understands it (Contextualist).
2. Frank is getting a divorce, because he and his wife fight constantly. Thus there is a specific reason for the divorce (Mechanist).
3. Frank's getting a divorce is the current stage in the development of his emotional detachment. This development began several years ago and has passed through many previous stages (Organicist).
4. Frank is an immature person. He is the kind of person who has never been able to maintain a stable relationship (Formist).

Participants ranked each of the four alternatives in each item. There were 12 similar items, and on each item, the underlined parts of each alternative were the same. The final scores consisted of sums of ranks for each of the four World Hypotheses (WHS scores). So for each person, there were separate scores for each of the four World Hypotheses. In the original by Harris, Fontana, and Dowds (1977), final scores of each alternative were ranked, so that the scores for any one World Hypothesis could range between 12 and 48. An alternative scoring method allowed a response of 0 for any alternative and permitted a maximum score of 5 for an item, making the potential totals for each hypothesis range from 0 to 60. The results with the two scoring systems are very similar. The items seem remarkably schematic and even primitive. However, as we will see, these items "work" in the sense that WHS scores relate to other theory-defined phenomena and measures. Furthermore, attempts to produce more sophisticated-appearing measures have not been successful. The best results come from this simple scale. Perhaps the reason is that people are not aware of their own World Hypotheses, nor that others might have different epistemologies. A clear example of how unaware people are of their World Hypotheses occurred early in this research. I gave the WHS to a class on methodology with about 25 students. After they had completed the scale, they scored their own scales, and then we explained the general rationale for developing the scale and the nature of World Hypotheses. One of the students immediately challenged me saying that the scale could not be any good, because in each item there was only one alternative that made any sense, and it was the same alternative in almost every item. A second student agreed enthusiastically, and the two had a good time teasing their professor and his measure that consisted of identical items. The rest of the class seemed to agree. I was a bit embarrassed, but luckily at the end of this discussion I asked the two challengers which choice was the only possibility. The two critics did not agree! One thought the only reasonable choice was one involving specific causes (Mechanism), while the other thought only the ones that described the actor as a certain sort of person (Formism) made sense. And needless to say, each thought the other's choice was irrational.

Not all people are as single-mindedly confident as these two were, but the usual pattern in all later studies was for participants to choose one alternative in preference to all the others, or sometimes to exhibit a preference for two World Hypotheses. In general, each participant in subsequent studies did tend to think that their way of responding was the only reasonable one. It is relatively rare for a respondent to choose the same alternative for each item, but most people exhibit a strong preference.

Once the measure of World Hypothesis preference was constructed, some of its properties could be explored. For example, scores were reasonably stable over short periods of time, like a few days, and also for longer spans, like two months. The item scores for each of the four Hypotheses were internally consistent as well (Harris, Fontana, & Dowds, 1977).

What difference do World Hypotheses variances make? One place to look was in career choices. Some World Hypotheses seem to be more appropriate for some careers than others. For example, a Formist might be attracted to professions that emphasize classification and grouping, such as being an accountant, or a librarian, or in biology, a taxonomist. Mechanists would be attracted to professions that emphasize causal analyses and using principles developed by others to accomplish specific ends. Obvious examples would be an engineer and also a manager. The Organicist would be seeking to understand the role of parts within complex wholes and to look for development and growth. Teachers are the clearest example. Finally, Contextualists are attracted to complex analyses that depend on one's perspective, like historical analyses. The perspective aspect of Contextualism would be particularly attractive to artists and humorists.

In a series of studies, college student participants were asked to select the career they thought they would pursue. No relationship with World Hypothesis preference was found. That was a bit disappointing. The students also were asked what occupations they would prefer, if there were no practical constraints on their choice. In this case, there were quite consistent relationships between WHS and the desired profession (Harris, Fontana, & Dowds, 1977).

Preferred majors in college also were related to World Hypotheses. For example, Formists were attracted to chemistry and some parts of biology; Mechanists to physics and some aspects of psychology; Organicists to teaching, sociology and art; and Contextualists to history and literature. In these studies, different professions or majors did not differ in their attractiveness overall, but rather choice was determined by compatibility or fit between World Hypothesis and career or major choices.

In all these earlier studies, some of the World Hypotheses were more incompatible than others. For example, a physics major might prefer Mechanism, but find Organicism acceptable and Contextualism unacceptable. Pepper (1942) attributed these differences in compatibility to two dimensions on which the Hypotheses varied: analytic versus synthetic, and integrative versus dispersive. By his analysis, four pairs should be less incompatible, Formism and Mechanism, Mechanism and Organicism, Mechanism and Contextualism, and Contextualism and Formism (see Table 3.1 for a summary of these relations.)

The first test of this prediction was to correlate scores on the four World Hypotheses across samples. As Pepper predicted, the correlations between Formism and Mechanism, and between Mechanism and Organism were high. That is, people who were attracted to the Formist explanations also liked Mechanist choices. The correlation between Organicism and Contextualism was also significant, although not as high. There was one exception to Pepper's predicted order, and it was a substantial exception. This was the relationship between Formism and Contextualism. Pepper expected this pairing to be no more incompatible than the others, but instead this was the least compatible pairing. Preferences for Formism correlated $r = -.63$

with scores for Contextualism indicating that Formists were particularly unattracted to Contextualist choices, and the reverse.

This pattern does not fit Pepper's views, but fits perfectly if one assumed that the various World Hypotheses were arrayed in linear fashion, with the end points being Formism and Contextualism, with Mechanism and Organicism between. In this organization, World Hypotheses that were adjacent in the lineup would be compatible, those with two steps between, Formism and Organicism, and Mechansim and Contextualism would be somewhat more incompatible, and the least compatible would be Formism and Contextualism (see Figure 3.1). The correlations between WHS scores and preferred occupations and majors all fit this pattern, in almost all kinds of comparison.

Why would the hypotheses be ordered in this way? Formism and the comparable scientific practice begin with the recognition of events in the world (physical or intellectual) and the basic elements of phenomena. The periodic table of elements and Linnaean identification of species, etc. are good examples. In real life, too, we need to know first of all what the "things" of everyday existence are. Once we know the objects of the world, we can begin to identify the ways in which the objects affect each other. The basic example of objects affecting each other is, of course, causation, the business of Mechanism. Clearly, identifying billiard balls comes first before we can recognize causal impacts among them. So Formism is in some sense simpler than Mechanism, but essential in order to move on to Mechanism. First, we need to have objects before they can affect each other. Once these mechanistic encounters are occurring, we can identify their role within the game of billiards, where some causal connections might be good shots and bad shots, but all part of a game. Other movements, like the ball thrown by a bad sport, are not. Only after we have mastered games of billiards and other less obvious games, such as social roles and structured interactions, can we then see them as part of a social system. Organicisim is only possible when the causes and effects are identified, so that a patterning among them can be recognized. Finally, one can only recognize the origins of the variety of organized systems and identify higher level wholes if they have recognized some systems that might then vary and interweave.

This pattern is quite similar to one that was described by Whitehead (1925) as the progression of scientific perspectives. Whitehead marked the

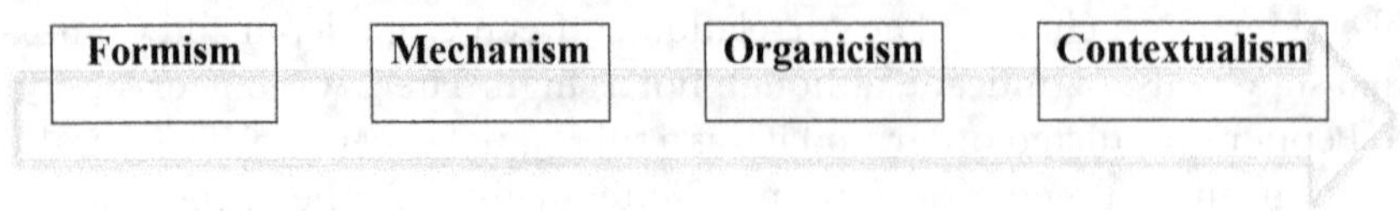

Figure 3.1 "Developmental" order of world hypotheses.

beginning of modern science with the activities of alchemists and taxonomists in the pre-15th century who were preoccupied with identifying and naming the objects of the world. Newtonian physics marked the beginning of an era of Mechanist exploration of cause and effect. This was followed in the later 19th century by a kind of physics that viewed the world as a complex organism, or a field. Finally in the early 20th century with relativity theory and quantum mechanics, in which different kinds of complex patterns were related, the prevailing view of physics was Contextualist. Each perspective did a kind of intellectual work, and the varieties of perspective were ordered because each "higher one" depended on the accomplishments of the lower level.

Applying this view to World Hypotheses, the order of the Hypotheses and their appearance begins with the intellectual task of Formism, of identifying and organizing the objects and types of things to be recognized. Once the Formist thought has been reasonably well mastered, the next step is the comprehending of the relations between objects, the prototypical relation being cause and effect. Notice that until objects have been identified, their relationship must be obscure. Once cause and effect relations are identified, the next step is to discover patterns and sequences of causes that lead to development and integration of the network of types of objects, interacting in causes and their connections. Finally, Contextualism recognizes that the networks and developments of Organicism are not the only such complex systems and focuses on the role of lower level elements in a variety of organizations.

In Whitehead's view, the changing world view of physical science was definitely a developmental progression, a view that seems to contradict Pepper's assertion that each of the World Hypotheses was equally adequate. One resolution is to recognize that each of the World Hypotheses and Whitehead's levels of science have different and essential roles and that the differences are ordered in some way. This is where the insight I got through Roger comes in.

Roger has often discussed stage theories in his developmental work and the contrast between replacement stage theories and additive stage theories. Replacement theories assume that early stages are dropped or lost and are replaced with later stages. Additive theories assume that early stages are preserved and have an important role in later activities. The early stages are like building blocks for the later stages. In Pepper's view, the World Hypotheses are not stages at all and not ordered in a developmental sense. However, the data strongly suggest an ordered progression, and one in which the contribution of the early stages is retained and in fact is essential to higher level functioning.

The linear, developmental model of World Hypotheses relations suggests three types of relations. The most straight forward one is when two people share a preference for the same hypothesis. If two people prefer hypotheses that are adjacent in the linear sequence, they may be said to have compatible hypotheses. Finally, if their World Hypotheses are two or more apart in the linear sequence, they will be incompatible.

FURTHER OBSERVATIONS OF WORLD HYPOTHESES IN EVERYDAY LIFE

Pepper saw conflict between the different hypotheses as the explanation for enduring disagreements. To explore conflict, what is needed is a situation that requires confronting another. Moral dilemmas seemed to be a good context for conflict resolution.

In one study, participants responded to the WHS, and then a week or so later, pairs of participants were created in which the pair had identical WHS preferences (i.e., two Mechanists or two Organicists) or compatible pairs whose WHS preferences were for hypotheses that were adjacent in the linear scheme (for example, a Formist with a Mechanist, or a Mechanist with an Organicist), and the incompatible pairings such as a Mechanist with a Contextualist or a Formist with an Organicist.

The pairs were then asked to discuss one of Kohlberg's (1969) moral dilemmas and to reach agreement about how to solve it. After discussion, they rated the other pair member on various dimensions. In general, the identical and compatible pairs agreed and felt positive about their pair-member. The incompatible pairs, however, found their pair-member to be significantly more stubborn, domineering, frustrating, and as less likable and agreeable. They also judged that their pair was less successful at reaching agreement. WHS scores were impressively good predictors of how well people would work together.

This was of course a highly artificial and brief situation to explore the impact of World Hypotheses. Another approach was much longer and did not just *affect* real life. It *was* real life, or at least the participants' reports of real friendship. In the first study, participants were instructed to bring a friend to the research session, and both responded to the WHS and various measures of affection for each other. Incompatible pairs reported significantly less interest in staying friends or working together (Harris, Fontana, & Dowds, 1977).

In a second, similar study, participants were asked to respond to the WHS, and then pairs of roommates answered a series of questions about their relationship. In general, identical and compatible pairs did not differ much in contrast to the incompatible pairs. Incompatible pairs reported lower scores on Rubin's Loving and Liking scales which measure affection, felt they knew their roommate less well and reached agreement less easily. They found it more difficult to work with their roommate and were less willing to room together in the future. However, all of these results applied only to men. Men with roommates who had incompatible WHS scores were significantly less happy about their relationship than women in the same situation.

Women were generally more comfortable in their roommate relationships than were men, a common and unsurprising finding. Furthermore, women's feelings about their roommates were not affected by WHS scores, and this is more puzzling. Perhaps, women base friendships less on agreement about how to explain things, but more on some other factors that are unrelated to World Hypotheses.

Romantic relationships are, of course, even more intense than friendships and roommate relations, and hence might be expected to also be affected by World Hypotheses compatibility. To test this possibility, 50 pairs of students who reported being in a relationship were asked to respond to the WHS and to a questionnaire about their relationship. More compatible pairs reported that their relationship had lasted significantly longer. The causal direction is uncertain, but it seems that either people who have more compatible World Hypotheses avoid breaking up, or people seek out partners with more compatible World Hypotheses.

WORLD HYPOTHESES AND THERAPEUTIC INTERVENTIONS

If World Hypothesis preferences can affect roommate satisfaction, friendship strength, and romantic attraction, it seems probable that World Hypotheses would affect the success of an even more intense relationship, psychotherapy. Maxine Harris and her associates (Fontana, Dowds, & Bethel, 1976; Harris, Fontana, & Dowds, 1977) explored this possibility. A particularly interesting finding was that among alcoholic clients, those who were Formists on the WHS did much better at participation and outcome if their treatment was attendance at the Anonymous Alcoholics meetings. Clients whose World Hypotheses were compatible with therapists' also reported greater satisfaction with their therapist, and most insightful, they stayed in treatment longer. A second study (Bresler, Laird, & Bibace, 1984) produced very similar results: When clients and therapists had identical or compatible World Hypotheses, therapy proceeded significantly better. In an exploration of doctor-patient relations and therapeutic impact of World Hypotheses, the patients were all suffering from high blood pressure. Among the doctor-patient pairs, some were incompatible on the WHS, while others were compatible or shared identical views. The incompatible pairs showed poorer response to treatment, including a smaller reduction in systolic pressure. The patients in the incompatible pairs were also less satisfied with their treatment and liked their physician less.

CULTURE AND WORLD HYPOTHESES

All of the observations outlined previously were based on data gathered from American participants, and the most common WHS preference was Mechanism. This seems to reflect a general inclination toward Mechanism in the American culture. However, our American clockwork world view is clearly not the only one possible. At the very least, many Asian cultures appear to be more Organicist and Contextual. To explore this possibility, Yen Hung Lo generated a Chinese version of the WHS test and administered it to a number of Asian groups. As expected, among Chinese people Organicism was most common, with Contextualism coming a distant second place, and Mechanism and Formism essentially being rejected (Lo & Laird, 1992). Yen Hung attributed the differences at least in part to religions. Buddhism and Taoism both emphasized the larger whole and view the universe as a single entity.

To ensure that the Chinese results were not due simply to the presence or absence of religion, Yen Hung Lo (1996) administered the WHS survey to Indian and Japanese samples as well as mainland Chinese and Taiwanese. The Indian, Japanese, and Taiwanese samples were similar to the U.S. samples in being predominantly Mechanist, although not as strong as were Americans.

Generalizing about whole cultures is obviously hazardous, but at the least, these results are consistent with our expectations and support the overall World Hypothesis scheme.

CONCLUSION

We have seen differences in World Hypotheses that affect (or at least are related to) choices of major and career, how well roommates and lovers relate to each other, and how well random strangers can resolve disagreements. The research indicates that World Hypotheses vary with cultural background and even predict success in psychotherapeutic and medical treatments. These effects seem to be hidden from our everyday conscious awareness, so we are unaware of the role that World Hypotheses may play in our everyday interactions. Probably in most everyday situations, we use any of the World Hypotheses that seem appropriate in the situation. Only when the issues are unclear or complex, like a theory of human behavior, personal preferences for World Hypotheses are activated.

Through all this research, Roger has been a regular participant in our endeavors and a source of encouragement. Maybe, back to the beginning and my job interview, Roger perceived that each of us following their own WHS, we could do some fun things together—not perceiving the different World Hypotheses as a handicap, but as a source for vivid discussions and exchange.

NOTE

1. Maxine Harris was the first to study World Hypotheses experimentally, beginning with her excellent dissertation. She did a prodigious amount of work and found a number of intriguing relationships. In describing the overall research array, I have tried to be very clear which of these results she was responsible for. Some of the other studies were performed by different individuals. The unattributed remainder of these experiments was performed by members of our research group whose identities are no longer recoverable.

REFERENCES

Bresler, C., Laird, J. D., & Bibace, R. (1984, May). *Compatibility of understanding and the doctor-patient relationship.* Paper presented at annual meeting of National Association of Primary Care Research Group, Orlando, FL.

Fontana, A. F., Dowds, B. N., & Bethel, M. H. (1976). A. A. and group therapy for alcoholics: An application of the world hypotheses scale. *Journal of Studies on Alcohol, 37*(5), 675–682.

Harris, M., Fontana, A. F., & Dowds, B. N. (1977). The world hypotheses scale: Rationale, reliability and validity. *Journal of Personality Assessment, 41*(5), 537–547.

Kohlberg, L. (1969). Stages and sequences: The cognitive development approach to socialization. In D. A. Goslin (Ed.), *Handbook of socialization theory of research* (pp. 347–480). Chicago, IL: Rand McNally.

Lo, Y. H. (1996). *The role of culture and subculture in world views: The impact of western influence and profession in Taiwan.* [Doctoral thesis]. Clark University, Worcester, MA.

Lo, Y. H. & Laird, J. D. (1992, April). *Chinese/American differences in world hypotheses.* Paper presented at the Eastern Psychological Association meeting, Boston, MA.

Pepper, S. C. (1942). *World hypotheses: A study in evidence.* Berkeley, CA: University of California Press.

Whitehead, A. (1925). *Science and the modern world.* New York, NY: Free Press.

SECTION II

THE PRACTITIONER: PSYCHOANALYTIC DEFENSES AND CONCEPTIONS OF ILLNESS

CHAPTER 4

CHILDREN'S CONCEPTIONS OF ILLNESS

Roger Bibace
Clark University

Mary E. Walsh
Boston College

In psychological, psychiatric, and pediatric literature of the past several decades, there has been considerable attention given to the psychological needs of the ill child. Until very recently, the major theoretical format for understanding and intervening in the behavior of sick children has been psychoanalysis. A number of studies, both clinical and empirical, have addressed children's responses to illness and/or hospitalization in terms of the feelings of the child. The psychic and physical trauma experienced by the sick child were seen to result in feelings of fear, anger, anxiety, withdrawal, and depression. Thus, therapeutic interventions were best directed to the affective level—toward acknowledging and modifying these negative feelings.

But, even within the psychoanalytic orientation, it became obvious that the feelings of the sick child or adult were related to beliefs or concepts about illness—that is, to the way the patient understood illness at a

Particulars and Universals in Clinical and Developmental Psychology, pages 65–82

cognitive level. For example, much of the depression and withdrawal of the hospitalized child was presumed to be related to the child's belief that he or she was being punished for wrongdoing or was to blame—was at fault—for the illness being contracted. The negative effect or feeling was in some way seen to be related to the child's cognition or understanding of the causes of the illness.

This awareness among clinicians of the importance of the child's beliefs about illness, along with the academic psychologist's interest in cognition, has in the last two decades provoked a considerable amount of research about the child's concepts or ideas or illness. A number of different beliefs or concepts of illness have emerged in the research.

One of the early studies in this area confirmed the psychoanalytic interpretation that children believe that illness is a punishment for wrongdoing or that they are to blame for the illness. Brodie (1974), in a study of children, found this notion to be particularly prevalent among hospitalized children, but even among healthy children a full quarter of the sample thought that "boys and girls who misbehave get sick more often than those who are good" (p. 1157). More recently, Cook (1975) found this moral explanation to be characteristic only of the spontaneous accounts of illness offered by children. When children were challenged in a directive interview to explain to the best of their ability the cause of illness, the so-called moral explanation was far less frequent and under these circumstances occurred more frequently among sick than among healthy children.

But, in spite of the seeming predominance of this moral explanation, other beliefs, or concepts of illness as they came to be called in the literature of cognitive development, have surfaced in the research. The belief that illness is caused by germs and/or contact with sick people was noted in several studies (Palmer & Lewis, 1975; Perrin & Gerrity, 1979). Being in the mere presence of a sick person was assumed by many children to be a potential cause of their becoming ill.

Palmer and Lewis (1975) observed in a number of children the concept of prevention—that is, the belief that illness can be avoided by certain activities of the person, for example, eating the appropriate foods or getting adequate rest.

A number of studies have pointed to a concept of illness in which psychological as well as physical processes are used to describe and/or explain the illness (Campbell, 1975; Natapoff, 1978; Palmer & Lewis, 1975).

An aspect of the child's belief system that has received considerable attention in the literature is the extent to which the child believes he or she is likely to get ill—that is, perceived vulnerability to illness (Gochman, 1971; Palmer & Lewis, 1975). Children have been found to differ from one another consistently in the degree to which they believe they will be victims of sickness or accidents.

Perceived vulnerability appears to be linked to another dimension of the belief system (Gochman, 1971)—locus of control—regarding the onset or healing of illness. Children differ from one another in terms of how much control they feel they can exert over events that cause or cure illness (Neuhauser, Amsterdam, Hines, & Steward, 1978).

In brief, the research of the past decade has demonstrated that the range of children's concepts about illness is broader than the original psychoanalytic notion that children understand illness predominantly in terms of punishment. Children also conceptualize illness in terms of catching germs, as an experience that they can avoid through certain behaviors, as having both psychological as well as physical aspects, and as an event to which they are to varying degrees vulnerable.

But as significant as the variety or range of explanations of illness offered by children is the order in which these explanations are manifest. The empirical evidence clearly suggests that the child's concept of illness changes in certain specifiable directions with age and/or development.

In contrast to those of the younger, immature child, the concepts of illness of the older, mature child evidence increased conceptual sophistication (Campbell, 1975), greater complexity (Natapoff, 1978; Perrin & Gerrity, 1979), more frequent reference to internal body cues (Natapoff, 1978; Neuhauser et al., 1978; Palmer & Lewis, 1975), more realism (Palmer & Lewis, 1975), more restricted definitions and focus (specificity) on specific diseases (Campbell, 1975), greater generalization based on principle (Perrin & Gerrity, 1979), greater differentiation and abstractness (Carandang, Folkins, Hines, & Steward, 1979; Simeonssori, Buckley, & Monson, 1979), greater integration of parts and wholes (Natapoff, 1978), more organized description of process and cause (Perrin & Gerrity, 1979), and increased number of categories to define health or cause of illness (Carandang et al., 1979; Natapoff, 1978).

It is evident from these studies that the child's conception of illness is clearly related to the child's developmental status. However, a number of situational variables have been found to affect the developmental level of the child's expressed concept. It has been demonstrated that the developmental level of the concept is related to the nature of the inquiry—that is, whether the interview is spontaneous, or structured (Cook, 1975); whether the disease under discussion is visible or invisible (Neuhauser et al., 1978); and the content of the question asked—for example, whether the question concerns the cause or cure of the illness or the function of medicine (Simeonsson, Buckley, & Monson, 1979). Surprisingly, there is no evidence to suggest that sex differences affect the concept of illness. Similarly, while effect on developmental level has not been the specific focus of several studies, they have shown that the influence of the mother's concept of illness has no significant effect on the child's concept (Campbell, 1975; Mechanic, 1964).

The data then converge around a single theme—that there are manifest age differences in the type of explanation of illness offered by children.

How have these age differences been interpreted in the literature? In general, studies have varied in the extent to which they integrate the empirical finding of age differences with theoretical explanations of development. A number of studies, predominantly early studies in this area, examine concepts of illness in children of differing ages with no reference to developmental theory. Such studies either categorize various explanations on themes offered by children and determine the frequency of each type of response at each age level, or across all age levels (Brodie, 1974; Campbell, 1975; Mechanic, 1964); or dimensionalize an aspect of the child's explanation (for example, degree of perceived vulnerability to illness) and relate this dimension with age (Gochman, 1971). Only the empirical marker of age is utilized and no attempt is made to understand or explain age differences in terms of a theoretical framework, especially from the perspective of cognitive-developmental theory.

A second group of studies, done predominantly in or after the mid 1970s, address themselves specifically to examination of age-related changes in the concept of illness, but any explanation of these age changes in terms of cognitive-developmental theory occurs only in post hoc discussions of the findings. Thus we see, for example, Palmer and Lewis (1975) suggesting that young children's accounts of the cause of illness reflect "the syncretic thinking identified by Piaget" (p. 2), or Natapoff (1978) indicating that the quantitative and qualitative age-related changes in children's concept of health "are consistent with theories of concept development" (p. 995).

A third group of studies make much more explicit use of cognitive-developmental theory. Investigators in this group use developmental theory to make predictions about the types of differences in concepts to be expected at different ages (Campbell, 1975; Carandang et al., 1979; Neuhauser et al., 1978; Perrin & Gerrity, 1979; Simeonsson, Buckley, & Monson, 1979; Steward & Regalbuto, 1975). Usually, the differences consist of one or a few characteristics of the general and abstract developmental stages of Piaget (1930) or Werner (1948), such as global and undifferentiated thinking versus differentiated thinking, or magical thinking versus concrete logical thinking.

However, even though they specify the developmental dimensions along which the child's concept changes, none of these analyses of differences explicates the novel or unique way in which Piaget and Werner's general stages of cognitive development are expressed in the particular content area being investigated. Thus, these analyses provide no appreciation for the way in which the child assimilates a particular phenomenon or aspect of reality—that is, illness—to the general schemata that reflects the evolution of

TABLE 4.1 Developmental Conceptions of Illness

I. Prelogical Explanations:
   Category 1: Phenomenism
   Category 2: Contagion
II. Concrete-Logical Explanations
   Category 3: Contamination
   Category 4: Internalization
III. Formal-Logical Explanations:
   Category 5: Physiological
   Category 6: Psychophysiological

cognition. These studies merely reassert categories of the middle range—the existence of the general stages of cognitive development.

In our recent research (Bibace & Walsh, 1980), we spell out six qualitatively different categories of explanations of illness that are developmentally ordered. These categories are derived from a study of an initial sample of 180 children aged 4 to 14 years and validated in two subsequent studies (Bibace & Walsh, 1977, 1979). A description of these developmental categories of explanation of illness follows.

In general we derived three major types of explanations consonant with Piagetian stages of cognitive development: prelogical, concrete logical, and formal logical. Within each of these major categories we were further able to distinguish two subtypes of explanation. Thus, in addition to the category Incomprehension, which characterized a few of the very youngest subjects in our pilot study, we delineated six types of explanations of illness that were then developmentally ordered with chronological age used as the gross index of developmental status.

The categories are briefly described and illustrated in Table 4.1. The illustrations used refer to responses about a single type of illness—that is, a cold. The complete scoring system, available from the authors, provides numerous examples with regard to the range of illnesses sampled by the protocol.

PRELOGICAL EXPLANATIONS

According to Piaget (1930), prelogical thinking is typical of children between 2 and 6 years of age. It is characterized by children's inability to distance themselves from their environment and results in explanations accounting for the cause-effect relationship in terms of the immediate spatial and/or temporal cues that dominate their experience. In both types of prelogical explanations of illness—phenomenism and contagion—we see children being overly swayed by the immediacy of some aspects of their perceptual experiences.

Phenomenism represents the most developmentally immature explanation of illness. The cause of illness is an external concrete phenomenon that may co-occur with the illness but that is spatially and/or temporally remote. Children at this stage are unable to explain the manner in which these events cause the illness:

> How do people get colds? "From the sun." How does the sun give you a cold? "It just does, that's all." How do people get colds? "From trees." How do people get measles? "From God." How does God give people measles? "God does it in the sky."

Contagion is the most common explanation of illness offered by the more mature children in the prelogical stage. The cause of illness is located in objects or people that are proximate to, but not touching, the child. The link between the cause and the illness is accounted for only in terms of mere proximity or magic:

> How do people get colds? "From outside." How do they get them from outside? "They just do, that's all. They come when someone else gets near you." How? "I don't know—by magic I think." How do people get colds? "When someone else gets near them."

CONCRETE-LOGICAL EXPLANATIONS

Concrete-logical reasoning is manifest by children roughly between 7 and 10 years of age. In this stage, according to Piaget (1930), the major developmental shift is in accentuation of the differentiation between self and other, so that the child clearly distinguishes between what is internal and what is external to the self. This distinction is manifest in the two explanations of illness characteristic of this age group—contamination and internalization.

Contamination characterizes the explanations of younger children in the concrete-logical stage. The child now distinguishes between the cause of the illness and the manner in which it is effected. The cause is viewed as a person, object, or action that is external to the child and that has an aspect or quality that is bad or harmful for the body. Such a cause effects illness in the child either through the child's body physically contacting the person or object (for example, through touching or rubbing) or through the child's physically engaging in the harmful action and thus becoming contaminated:

> What is a cold? "It's like in the wintertime." How do people get them? "You're outside without a hat and you start sneezing. Your head would get cold, the cold would touch it, and then it would go all over your body."

Internalization is a type of illness explanation typically offered by older children in the concrete-logical stage. Illness is now located inside the body, while its ultimate cause may be external. The external cause, usually a person or object, is linked to the internal effect of illness through a process of internalization—for example, swallowing or inhaling. Even though the illness is now located within the body, it is described in only vague terms, evidencing confusion about internal organs and functions:

> What is a cold? "You sneeze a lot, you talk funny, and your nose is clogged up." How do people get colds? "In winter, they breathe in too much air into their nose, and it blocks up the nose." How does this cause colds? "The bacteria gets in by breathing. Then the lungs get too soft [child exhales], and it goes to the nose." How does it get better? "Hot fresh air, it gets in the nose and pushes the cold air back."

FORMAL-LOGICAL EXPLANATIONS

According to Piaget (1930), children who are approximately 11 years of age and older manifest formal-logical thinking. At this stage, there is the greatest amount of differentiation between the self and the other; conversely, the organism is least likely to manifest the effects of stimulus-boundedness because of the compensatory character of operational or logical thinking. In both the physiological and psychophysiological explanations of this stage, we note the greatest amount of differentiation between the external and internal world, so that the source of the illness is located within the body even though an external agent is often described as the ultimate cause.

Physiological explanations are usually offered by the younger children in the formal-logical stage. In this explanation, while the cause may be triggered by external events, the source and nature of the illness lie in specific internal physiological structures and functions. The cause is usually described as the nonfunctioning or malfunctioning of an internal organ or process, explained as a step by step internal sequence of events culminating in that illness:

> What is a cold? "It's when you get all stuffed up inside, your sinuses get filled up with mucus. Sometimes your lungs do too, and you get a cough." How do people get colds? "They come from viruses, I guess. Other people have the virus, and it gets into your blood stream and it causes a cold." Have you ever been sick? "Yes." What was wrong? "My platelet count was down." What's that?

> "In the blood stream they are like white blood cells. They help kill germs." Why did you get sick? "There were more germs than platelets. They killed the platelets off." How did you get sick? "From germs outside. They killed off the platelets."

Psychophysiological explanations represent the most mature understanding of illness. As in physiological explanations, the illness is described in terms of internal physiological processes, but the child now perceives an additional or alternative cause of illness—psychological cause. The child is aware that a person's thoughts or feelings can affect the way the body functions:

> What is a heart attack? "It's when your heart stops working right. Sometimes it's pumping too slow or too fast." How do people get a heart attack? "It can come from being all nerve-racked. You worry too much. The tension can affect your heart."

Consistent with the expectations of a cognitive-developmental framework, we found that the type of explanation of illness varied as a function of the developmental status of our subjects (see Table 4.2).

Among the 4-year-olds, 54% gave contagion explanations and 38% contamination explanations. Among 7-year-olds, 63% gave contamination explanations and 29% internalization explanations. Among the 11-year-olds, explanations were classified as 54% internalization and 34% physiological.

The findings of both the pilot study (Bibace & Walsh, 1977), with normal children from 3- to 13-years-old, and this study, with normal children aged 4- to 11-years-old, were clearly congruent with the theoretical expectations regarding the qualitative differences in the cognitive processes relied upon by children. Further, the categories of responses, reflecting these qualitative differences in thinking, could be ordered in a developmental sequence

TABLE 4.2 Percentage of Subjects Manifesting Various Types of Explanations of Health and Illness

Type of Explanation	4 Years Old (*N* = 24)	7 Years Old (*N* = 24)	11 Years Old (*N* = 24)
0 Incomprehension	4	—	—
1 Phenomenistic	—	—	—
2 Contagion	54	—	—
3 Contamination	38	63	4
4 Internalization	4	29	54
5 Physiological	—	8	34
6 Psychophysiological	—	—	8

consonant with the theoretical framework. Lastly, the frequency distributions of normal children who vary in chronological age are congruent with Piagetian theory and constitute empirical grounds for the value of those categories.

As scientists relying on this theoretical perspective, we concluded what the earlier studies in this area (Cook, 1975) had already confirmed that children's conceptions of illness reflect the more general processes (stages) of cognitive development as they have been articulated by Werner and Piaget. Thus, the preschooler's conception of illness as caused magically by clouds, or the sun, reflects the prelogical stage of cognitive development, in which cause and effect are linked by magical association. From the point of view of theoretical significance, therefore, our findings merely add to the list of studies that suggest that the child's concept of illness is related to his or her cognitive-developmental level.

THE SCIENTIFIC AND CLINICAL PERSPECTIVES

These scientific findings and their utilization by clinicians, educators, and parents raise a number of more general issues. These include the different and complementary objectives of the scientist and the clinician. Another way in which this issue has been cast is the relative emphasis and valuation of forms, or the cognitive processes underlying thinking versus content, that is, what is being thought about. Scientists seek to arrive at generalizations that transcend contents and contexts. Clinicians require scientifically based generalizations that are applicable to specific contents and contexts. These issues are elaborated in the following paragraphs.

Many studies relying on a developmental framework in the areas dealt with in this volume appear to have been initiated through an intuition or judgment that such studies were relevant to education, to patients, to the helping professions—that is, to individuals who were not merely interested in knowledge for its own sake. Rather, these audiences wanted to use such knowledge to help children, students, and patients. These differences in aim (the love of abstract knowledge for its own sake versus the utilization of knowledge in diverse settings, or the Kantian distinction between knowledge and judgment) have not been sufficiently acknowledged by many investigators. One purpose of this chapter is to argue that these different aims require more elaborate research strategies so that a classification system with a different end product (what we have called task-relevant categories) may evolve.

Our research accomplished what might be termed its scientific objective, confirmation of the validity of the general theory. The goal of the scientist is to articulate the universals—that is, the similarities among individuals—and to minimize individual differences. As our data demonstrate, general cognitive processes are indeed reflected in the specific contents of illness. Yet the conclusion that the child, dealing with health and illness contents, can also be shown to proceed through preoperational, concrete-operational, and formal-operational stages of causal reasoning would be completely unsatisfactory for clinicians. Those clinical-developmental psychologists who work with children and adults who are ill have an additional objective—to articulate a set of categories that are not only scientifically valid but also clinically useful. Whereas the scientist's search for universals leads to a focus on groups, the clinician focuses on the particulars—that is, the specific person. This is consonant with the clinician's goal of helping that person. For the scientist, the individuals in a group are the means to the end of attaining knowledge. For the clinician, general theoretical principles and findings must be specific to an individual if such theories or findings are to be helpful. The clinician therefore requires a classification system that simultaneously reflects the scientifically based general-formal categories of cognitive-developmental theory and the specific contents of the task. In order for developmental categories of the concept of illness to be useful to clinicians, the categories must reflect the relationship between health and illness questions and cognitive processes in a more intimate manner than research with the purely scientific objective of specifying the cognitive processes relied upon by the subject.

In much of the past research which has attempted to make cognitive-developmental psychology meaningful to clinicians, the difficulty of the relationship between form and content is clearly evident. The majority of these studies appear to have merely reiterated the formal-abstract categories. While such studies may have achieved their scientific objective, the findings are not very useful to clinicians who can better grasp and utilize the forms of organization inherent in the universals when they are concretized with respect to the contents which have relevance to both patient and therapist.

The categories that meet both scientific and clinical aims may be termed task-relevant categories. A methodological strategy that includes these categories is consonant with and exemplifies a central theoretical tenet of the type of theory that both Piaget and Werner espouse epistemologically. That is, both Piaget and Werner adhere to a genetic-interactionist position. Originally, we labeled such categories *categories of the middle range,* but that term has been used by sociologists to refer to categories solely derived from an inductive-empirical analysis of data. In contrast, we recognize explicitly that our categories are concretizations or particularizations of the abstract theoretical framework that we bring to the analysis of the data. Consequently, one could now view studies that merely reassert the validity of the abstract universals as being, from this interactional—theoretical position, reductionistic. They do not capture the specifics of the interaction between the subject and the particular task. Indeed, within a Piagetian framework, such studies reflect an imbalance between the assimilatory and accommodatory processes of the researcher. Here reductionism refers to the researcher's overemphasis on assimilating the subjects' products to an a priori abstract system of categories.

At the other end of the continuum are studies that focus solely on the content of the responses and do not probe the abstract universals or cognitive processes that such responses reflect. In contrast to studies that are reductionistic, this group of studies show the converse imbalance between the researcher's assimilatory and accommodatory processes. That is, the investigator can be criticized as over-accommodating to the specifics of the content of each experimental task. Typically, studies in this group present their findings in the form of tables that merely tabulate the frequency with which a particular content has been verbalized. There is no assimilation of these diverse contents to some more general abstract schema that can be applied consistently to other contents.

METHODS AND PROCEDURES FOR ELABORATING TASK-RELATED CATEGORIES

The process through which we articulated the task-relevant categories with respect to illness provides an illustration of the ongoing dialogue between theory and data. Our beginning point was theory-specifically, the hypothesis that the seemingly infinite variety of explanations of illness could be subsumed by a limited range of categories and that these categories could be developmentally ordered in a manner that reflected both the sequence and structure of the major stages of cognitive development (Piaget, 1930; Werner, 1948).

If one focuses solely on the formal or abstract level, the categories—that is, Piaget's abstract stages of cognitive development—have already been generated and one need only confirm or disconfirm their existence in concrete data. The child's responses are then analyzed in terms of the presence or absence of the characteristics of the different stages—for example, magical thinking in the preoperational stage or hypothetical thinking in the formal-operational stage.

Consistent with our expectation, we initially examined the concepts or explanations of illness offered by subjects representing the entire range of cognitive development. In order to insure subjects representing each of the major stages of cognitive development, we selected children—subjects from a population where cognitive development is most clearly evident. Further, in order to maximize the possibility that there might be explanations offered that would not be covered by the category system, we selected subjects from each and every age along the entire continuum of cognitive development.

This sample of explanations was ordered initially using the criterion of age—youngest to oldest. However, at this point in the theory-data dialogue (that is, in the balance between the assimilatory and accommodatory schemes of the investigators), age was subordinated to sequence and order. Within the ordered data, all the various forms of explanation were categorized empirically according to the most salient feature of content, as, for example, explanations that attributed the cause of illness to a remote external person or object: "A cold is from the sky" or "God gives you a stomachache." Each of the types or forms of explanation that emerged was more clearly evident in one broad age group rather than another. In addition, the general or overall order provided by age was congruent with a developmental sequence within which these various explanations emerge. However, it is crucial to note that age could not in any way be rigidly adhered to as the sole developmental marker, since it was possible, for example, that the explanation of illness offered by a single normal 6- or 7-year-old was more characteristic of that offered by most 4-year-olds. On the other hand, age could be used as a general index of development; for example, no normal 12-year-old offered explanations characteristic of the 4-year-old modal response and vice versa. Thus, while age and stage were not seen, either from a theoretical or an empirical perspective, to be equivalent, they were strongly correlated during the early phases of ontogenesis for normal children.

In spite of the clear argument that can be made for using age as a developmental indicator, there are many who would challenge this assumption, arguing instead for an independent index of developmental status, in particular, a measure of performance on such other cognitive tasks as conservation of weight, causal reasoning regarding the origin of night, and perspective-taking tasks (Perrin & Gerrity, 19979; Simeonsson, Buckley, & Monson, 1979).

It seems to us, however, that there is no index that is, in the real sense of the word, independent. All are embedded in content, and there is abundant evidence that content strongly affects the form of thought—or cognitive stage (Walsh, 1974). Further, we would suggest that the index least embedded in content is age, and as long as one assumes that it is not equivalent to stage, but rather only correlated with stage, as abundant evidence suggests, then age is an appropriate index of developmental status (Wohlwill, 1973). Age and stage are strongly correlated for normal children up to about 13, but the relationship between age and stage is clearly not correlated, in that the six categories do appear to be exhaustive for all people at all ages. Old people, for instance, are distributed among categories that are not among the most mature.

While the theoretical issue of cognitive stage or structure of thought was a central concern in our study, the categories themselves were articulated in terms of content as well as structure or form. Thus we described a category typical of the youngest children, in which

> illness is described in terms of concrete perceptual events with no reference to the inside of the body or even to the body itself. The cause of illness is seen to be remote external objects or persons and the link between the cause and the illness itself can only be explained in terms of magic.

In spite of the predominance of content in this example, the underlying structure of the thought can be discerned, the concrete perceptual-magical thinking characteristic of the preoperational stage of cognitive development. It is this focus on the integration of form and content that requires that the cognitive maturity of the response be the overriding criterion for scoring rather than the presence or absence of the so-called correct answer. Piaget consistently argued against the use of *wrong/right* as a way to classify children's thought.

Once the initial set of categories (six in our case) had been generated, an independent sample of children representing the three major stages was used to validate them. Here again, age was used as the developmental indicator. Our study also showed this grouping of responses in terms of these three age groups: Evidence from innumerable studies had suggested that preoperational thinking is characteristic of most children between 3 and 6 years of age, concrete-operational thinking is characteristic of children between 7 and 10 years of age, and formal-operational thinking is characteristic of children 11 and older. This widely accepted finding supported our selecting 4-, 7-, and 11-year-olds as the age groups that would represent each of the major stages.

The major hypothesis of the validation study was that the type of explanation of illness would vary as a function of the developmental status of the subjects, that explanations emerging earlier in the posited developmental sequences would be more typical of the younger subjects, while most of the older subjects would offer explanations that emerge later in their developmental sequence.

While the categories must clearly reflect the particulars of the content, clinical usefulness argues for some degree of generality so that the clinician will not be required to keep in mind a large number of specific category systems. Consequently, the categories we developed encompassed illness in general and not merely specific illnesses (such as, cold) as was done in some of the earlier studies (Cook, 1975). This kind of clinically oriented research requires that investigators decide on the range of contents and hence the generality of the concepts to be studied. The categories to be articulated in a study must clearly reflect the particulars of the contents and still allow for clinically meaningful generalization. Thus our study investigated specific illnesses such as colds, heart attacks, and so on. However, the inquiry into these specific contents was aimed at articulating the child's general conceptions of illness at the same developmental level across a variety of contents. Piaget described what he termed horizontal decalage—that is, consistently different rates of development across such content areas as conservation of mass, weight, volume (Flavell, 1963). Give the variability across different contents, how does one determine a single stage or category that is most appropriately characteristic of the child? When assessing cognitive development, some investigators (Perrin & Gerrity, 1979) rely on the mean or average score, or developmental category, across a range of contents. Other investigators (Damon, 1977) have argued that the child's level of cognitive development is best described as the highest level of thinking the child consistently manifests. As an empirical measure we have opted for the latter approach and have characterized a subject by the highest category, or level of thinking, at which the subject responds two or more times (consistently).

While some of the variability in level of reasoning across contents can be attributed to varying rates of cognitive development, it is essential to examine the data for any other sources of systematic variation that consistently yield a lower or higher level of response. In the literature on developmental concepts of illness, a number of variables have been systematically examined: the perceptual aspects of the stimulus, the degree of familiarity of the stimulus, mode of presenting the task, and the affective status of the subject.

The perceptual characteristics of the illness result in a systematic variation in response. Illness that can be seen, such as a skin rash, in contrast to illnesses that cannot be seen, such as a stomach ache, facilitate a higher level of causal reasoning (Neuhauser et al., 1978).

The degree of familiarity of the stimulus—in this instance, the type of illness—has an effect on the level at which the child conceptualizes the illness. For example, the conceptualization of some common illnesses such as colds have apparently no developmental trajectory. Simeonsson, Buckley, and Monson (1979) report that subjects at various cognitive stages of development have similar conceptions of a cold. However, Piaget's theory, substantiated by empirical work in a number of domains, in addition to our findings in this content area, would suggest that sufficient probing would reveal the expected differences. For instance, we found repeatedly that, while initial responses often appeared very similar and even identical across the age groups, further probing revealed significant differences in the quality of reasoning underlying the responses.

Researchers, for the past four or five decades, have also speculated and studied whether the type or mode of presentation of the question to the subject (for example, verbal versus pictorial) might affect the level of the response. In an analysis of this issue with respect to illness, Simeonsson, Buckley, and Monson (1979), in keeping with previous findings, found no differences in response between pictorial and verbal modes of presentation.

Still other investigators have questioned whether how the question is asked would affect the child's level of causal reasoning. For instance, Cook (1975), in examining how children respond to spontaneous versus structured modes of questioning, found a consistently higher level of responses for the structured mode of questioning. However, this finding may be due to the higher levels of reasoning that emerge when a child's spontaneous utterances are sufficiently probed. Indeed, this is why Piaget insisted on the use of what he called the clinical method of inquiry, since the spontaneous or initial response may very well not be representative of that child's cognitive level of development.

Another variable presumed to affect the way in which a person thinks about illness is the affective or emotional states of the subject. Brodie (1974), for example, found that anxiety was related to the way in which the child reasoned about illness. The more fundamental issue here from the perspective of developmental psychology is the interrelationship between cognitive and affective processes. Both theoretical conceptualizations and empirical findings have dwelt on the question as to whether or not affective states accelerate or delay cognitive development. But the explanations of many such studies remain ambiguous. If affective variables accelerate the rate of cognitive development, then it can be argued that familiarity with one's illness enhances the level of understanding. If, however, the rate of cognitive development appears to be decelerated when certain affective states are present, it can be argued that the experience of illness has such overwhelming emotional concomitants that the level of conceptualization with respect to the illness is inhibited or regressed. Relying on current cognitive-developmental theories apparently limits the range of relationships that can be posited between cognitive processes and affective states. Outcome measures in such terms as the acceleration or delay of development focus only on the rate of development. They do not speak to the qualitative aspects involved in the organization of cognitive and affective factors: how these factors develop, and how they are related to one another under different affective conditions or at different stages of cognitive development.

CLINICAL IMPLICATIONS

How can these findings be used? We will describe three significant uses. An appreciation of the patient's conceptions of illness (a) fosters empathy, (b) facilitates explanation of illness and medical procedures, and (c) bolsters health education.

These general categories of meaning are useful clinically because, insofar as we zero in on the patient's meaning for his or her illness, we can foster empathy with the patient. And, of course, this sort of understanding could have all sorts of implications for the health professional in terms of where to go and how to get there. Helping patients to feel that their ideas about themselves and their illness are understood, not weird, contributes to workable and rewarding health professional-patient relationships.

The utilization of this category system by health professionals can assist relatives and other staff in dealing with patients who are ill. Fears that the professional may consider irrational can become more understandable through a developmental analysis of the patient's conceptions of illness. Such interpretations can have direct implications for better patient management. We have seen, for example, many 5- or 6-year-old children on a hospital pediatric unit become inexplicably upset and ask to be moved to another room. Their fears were based on their preoccupation with catching the disease of their roommate. It should be helpful for a health professional to appreciate that this is normal for children or immature adults in the contagion stage of cognitive development. Such an appreciation will prevent the health professional from dismissing such fears as irrational and will allay the frustration caused by the patient's lack of understanding. Even if the health professional is unable to make physical changes to alleviate the patient's worry, he or she can at least accept and not dismiss the patient's fear and hence offer genuine reassurance. Further, the health professional can better explain the reason for the patient's upset to the other staff members. Such explanations or remedial actions should increase the patient's sense of control. Patients' fear that they are at the mercy of the diseases they perceive around them can be directly acknowledged and addressed.

In recent years, there has been an enormous emphasis on the importance of communication in the health professional-patient relationship, particularly in the realm of patient education. Doctors and other health professionals are taught to respect patients' requests for an explanation of their illness. But often their intuitive attempts to respond to these requests lead them to rely on scientific explanations, or what we would call *physiological* explanations. The patient's inability to grasp these explanations can lead to the doctor's frustration. Our data will hopefully increase the kind of alternative explanations that doctors can rely on in their attempts to communicate with patients. For instance, our studies (Bibace & Walsh, 1980) show a large number of elderly patients in the category of *internalization.* This would suggest that a concrete analogy might be more effective in explaining a particular illness to some elderly patients than an abstract physiological one. However, even though the largest number of elderly are in this category, it should be remembered that it is important to find out first how the individual patient relates to his or her illness. Determining the particular category of explanation suitable for a particular individual will be less of a problem for family physicians who, through continuity of care, come to know their patients (Stephens, 1975). Providing alternative explanations should also be easier for family physicians, who have the opportunity to deal with people throughout the life cycle.

Live patient education efforts might also incorporate these cognitive-developmental differences in people's understanding of illness. For instance, preoperative teaching with a 5-year-old would focus primarily on external observable events surrounding the surgery, such as the light in the operating room, uniforms of nurses, and so forth. This would be consistent with the young child's experience of illness in terms of external observable events. However, preoperative teaching about the same event with an older child who is at the abstract-logical stage of cognitive development would focus on the details of anatomy—what would be happening to the inside of his or her body. This is consistent with the child in the *physiological* category, who can conceptualize internal parts of the body as well as their functioning.

We have just suggested some answers to the question we are most often asked by clinicians: "How can I use these findings with patients?" But there is another aspect of this approach that we would like to stress because it is what originally got us interested in this research. We are intrigued, fascinated, and invigorated by what children and adults tell us regarding their ideas about how the body functions. And for some of the health professionals with whom we work, our finding that all ideas about illness follow a developmental sequence is not only of empirical interest but also has significant clinical import.

ACKNOWLEDGEMENT

Originally published as: Bibace, R. & Walsh, M.E. (1981). Children's conceptions of illness. In R. Bibace & M.E. Walsh (Eds.), *Children's conceptions of health, illness, and bodily functions* (Vol. 14 of *New directions for child development*). San Francisco, CA: Jossey-Bass. Republished in this volume with kind permission of John Wiley & Sons, Inc.

REFERENCES

Bibace, R., & Walsh, M. E. (1977, August). *The development of children's concepts of health, illness, and medical procedures.* Paper presented at the annual meeting of the American Psychological Association, San Francisco, CA.

Bibace, R., & Walsh, M. E. (1979). Developmental stages of children's conceptions of illness. In G. Stone, F. Cohen, & N. Adler (Eds.), *Health psychology: A handbook.* San Francisco, CA: Jossey-Bass.

Bibace, R., & Walsh, M. E. (1980). Development of children's concepts of illness. *Pediatrics, 66*(6), 912–911.

Brodie, B. (1974). Views of healthy children toward illness. *Annual Journal of Public Health, 64*(12), 1156–1159.

Campbell, D. (1975). Illness is a point of view: The development of children's concepts of illness. *Child Development, 46*(1), 92–100.

Carandang, M., Folkins, C., Hines, P., & Steward, M. (1979). The role of cognitive level and sibling illness. *Annual Journal of Orthopsychiatry, 49*(3), 474–481.

Cook, S. D. (1975). *The development of causal thinking with regard to physical illness among French children.* (Unpublished doctoral dissertation). University of Kansas, Lawrence, KS.

Damon, W. (1977). *The social world of the child.* San Francisco, CA: Jossey-Bass.

Flavell, J. H. (1963). *The developmental psychology of Jean Piaget.* Princeton, NJ: D. Van Nostrand.

Gochman, D. (1971). Some correlates of children's health beliefs and potential health behavior. *Journal of Health and Social Behavior, 12*(2), 148–154.

Mechanic, D. (1964). The influence of mothers on children's health attitudes and behavior. *Pediatrics, 33*(3), 444–453.

Natapoff, J. N. (1978). Children's views of health: A developmental study. *American Journal of Public Health, 68*(10), 995–1000.

Neuhauser, C., Amsterdam, B., Hines, P., & Steward, M. (1978). Children's concepts of healing: Cognitive development and locus of control factors. *American Journal of Orthopsychiatry, 40*(2), 335–341.

Palmer, B. B., & Lewis, C. E. (1975, October). *Development of health attitudes and behaviors.* Paper presented at the American School Health Association Convention, Denver, CO.

Perrin, E. C., & Gerrity, P. S. (1979, May). *The development of concepts regarding illness.* Paper presented at the 19th annual meeting of the Ambulatory Pediatric Association, Atlanta, GA.

Piaget, J. (1930). *The child's conception of physical causality.* London, England: Kegan Paul.

Simeonsson, R. J., Buckley, L., & Manson, L. (1979). Conceptions of illness causality in hospitalized children. *Journal of Pediatric Psychology, 4*(1), 77–84.

Stephens, G. (1975). The intellectual basis of family practice. *Journal of Family Practice, 2*(6), 423–423.

Steward, M., & Regalbuto, B. A. (1975). Do doctors know what children know? *American Journal of Orthopsychiatry, 45*(1), 146–149.

Walsh, M. E. (1974). A developmental analysis of the relationship between perceptual and representational processes. (Unpublished doctoral dissertation). Clark University, Worcester, MA.

Werner, H. (1948). *Comparative psychology of mental development.* New York, NY: Science Editions.

Wohlwill, J. F. (1973). *The study of behavioral development.* New York, NY: Academic Press.

CHAPTER 5

KOREAN UNDERSTANDING OF THE "*MAUM*" (MIND)

Cultural Differences in Explaining the Causes of Illness

AeJa Jung
Jeonbuk National University

When talking about psychological concepts, we often use terms that, assumedly, can be commonly understood by the group we want to address. Sometimes the discussion involves theoretical constructs that can be understood in different ways, so that we need to define them first. For example: What are love, identity, and other concepts, by our understanding? Having provided these definitions, we can then pursue our initial quest. In the case of the Korean concept of *Maum*, it is not that easy (Jung, 2008). In this chapter, I will demonstrate that there are no proper terms in other languages to allow for an adequate direct translation of *Maum*. Even defining *Maum* is difficult, because our general understanding of the "core" of human beings and where this core can be found differs between cultures. Thus, our understanding will differ in the way it influences therapeutic approaches.

Particulars and Universals in Clinical and Developmental Psychology, pages 83–90

THE WORD *MAUM*

Maum is a pure Korean word: 마음. The word consists of different parts: ㅁ is a consonant, ㅏ is a vowel, ㅇ is similar to a consonant, and ㅁ is a consonant. In the Korean alphabet, *Hangul*, words usually consist of a consonant and a vowel and, depending on the word (see previous), more consonants. Before *Hangul* was introduced, it was common to represent *Maum* by the Chinese letter sim (心, hsin). This double representation was—and still is—problematic in many ways, as will be explained (see Sohn, 2001 for a further discussion).

Hangul was created during the Joseon Dynasty in 1443 and was proclaimed the national alphabet of Korea by Sejong the Great in 1446. Previously, Korea had no official alphabet of its own and therefore used Chinese letters. Since the Chinese alphabet is very complex, only a few Koreans, mainly the privileged aristocrats, could actually invest time in learning it. The aim of *Hangul* was (a) to do justice to the Korean language, which according to Sejong the Great is fundamentally different from Chinese, and (b) to enable more people to learn how to read and write—especially women, who often did not have the opportunity for literacy in a society ruled by the aristocratic ideologies of Confucianism.

BUT WHAT IS *MAUM*?

Maum has been translated as "mind" by many scholars. In Confucianism, *Maum* (心, shin) even serves as the central theme and represents the center of the universe. The central concept of the so-called *Maum school* (心學) is to transcend the worldly or human mind to reach the universal or true mind. The true mind would then not be flawed by memories or false images of the world that had cluttered the worldly mind. This is also a central idea in Buddhism: *Maum* is Buddha's mind. It represents the true self. If you are able to see your *Maum*, you should become Buddha. Scholars in both Buddhism and Confucianism have described the mind as *Maum* in their writings.

In addition to these interpretations of the word *Maum*, Korean sayings suggest further possible translations or meanings. Examples include the following:

> "You cannot sell or buy *Maum*, but you can pass it on."
> "Sincerity, even in the slightest way, can warm the *Maum*."
> "It depends on what your *Maum* decides."
> "The *Maum* is the origin of thoughts."
> "The cozy *Maum* creates love and understanding."

> "If your *Maum* allows you to treasure the value of small things, then give that *Maum* to somebody whom you want to give it to."

In some of these examples, *Maum* can be translated as "heart," e.g., "Sincerity warms the heart" or "Do what your heart says!" Even "love" would fit in some of the sayings. Yet in others, the equation of *Maum* with heart would not make sense. Especially in the Western world, the origin of thought is more likely the mind than the heart. *Maum* thus seems to be a broader concept than the words mind or/and heart can encompass.

The broadness of the concept is also depicted in poems and song lyrics. An example is the poem "My *Maum* Is," written by Dong Myoung Kim in 1937 (Kim, 2005).

> My *Maum* is a lake. Please paddle in it. . . .
> My *Maum* is a candle. Please close the door.
> I will be totally burnt out without a single lighted candle.
> My *Maum* is a stranger. Please play the flute for me.
> I will stay up listening by myself at night in the moonlight.
> My *Maum* is a dried leaf. I want to stay in your garden.
> When the wind blows, I will leave you like a stranger.

On the one hand, *Maum* seems to be something delicate, and on the other something very powerful. It is a metaphor that can be everything you want it to be. In everyday life, the most important thing is "to be happy." This common goal is reflected in therapy: to be happy again, to solve problems, and to be more in harmony with oneself. In terms of *Maum*, this can be accomplished by "voiding" the *Maum*, or in other words by not leaving anything in your *Maum*, meaning that you should not focus on anything unnecessary. In the case of facing conflicts with others, the recommendation is to "open the door of the *Maum* wide, as your *Maum* goes through it," meaning that you should not be narrow-minded and be open to the view of others, even if emotions suggest otherwise. And another saying asks you "to look at the world through your true *Maum*'s eye to find a dream and hope!" In a Buddhist temple, the same advice might be given: "Cleanse your *Maum* so as to turn it into a clean mirror." You can then look at yourself and see how your preconceptions or preoccupations have made you deviate from your goals; you are rarely free of all kinds of conflicts. A mirror can also show you your real self, thus providing a goal that you should strive for. It is possible to train or study the *Maum*, but due to its complexity it is not possible to really know it.

MODERN MEDICAL STUDENTS' UNDERSTANDING OF *MAUM*

To better understand the Korean concept of *Maum*, I asked 56 medical students what they think *Maum* is and where they think it is located in their bodies. Examples of how they responded can be found in Table 5.1.

For the students, *Maum* represents many different things: willpower, face, love, themselves—everything in one sense or another. There is no consensus. Everyone seems to have his or her own concept of *Maum*. Nevertheless, nobody denies its existence.

The students' answers to the question of where the *Maum* is located are depicted in Table 5.2. In addition to this general question, I also asked them when they are bothered by something, where in their bodies they would most feel it. The answers are also presented in Table 5.2.

The majority of the students said that the *Maum* is located in the chest, whereas stress is more often felt in the head. Finally, I asked the students whether they would say that the *Maum* ruled the body or that the body ruled the *Maum*. Their replies are shown in Table 5.3.

The majority think that the *Maum* rules over the body, which in some sense makes the *Maum* more powerful. A similar picture is drawn by the *Korean Herbal Medicine Book* (Dong-Eui-Bogam [東醫 寶鑑]. Seong-Rae, 2005). It is written that "if the *Maum* is confused (心亂即病生), illness comes, and if the *Maum* is calm, illness naturally disappears (心定即病自癒)." By definition, *Maum* is thus a necessary and sufficient condition for health. When close friends are ill, a common saying is: "Their *Maum* is ill!" When a woman gets sick and her husband does not understand her, she might complain: "You don't know my *Maum*, do you?" Of course, in the case of illness, *Maum* is not understood as desire, love, or will (Table 5.1); it is depicted as the origin and possible cure of illnesses.

CULTURE-SPECIFIC DISEASES

In Korea, *Hwa-byeong* is known as fire or anger disease. It is also listed as a culture-bound syndrome in the *Diagnostic and Statistical Manual of Mental Disorders IV* by the American Psychiatric Association (2000). *Hwa-byeong* is more frequent in females than in males, and can more often be observed in middle-aged, less-educated patients with a lower socioeconomic status than in better-educated populations from a higher socioeconomic background.

According to Korean traditional herbal medicine, fire (one of the five elements in Confucianism) is a possible cause of the disease. These five elements must always be in balance, and if fire is excessive in the body it results in disease. The patients might describe their condition as having

TABLE 5.1 Medical Students' Answers to the Question of What the *Maum* Is

Define the *Maum*!
1. Connection between me and what surrounds me.
2. What rules over my body.
3. It clears my mind. To love, to see the beauty of things; it causes happiness.
4. Basic thing that makes "me." Represents me.
5. Takes charge of my thoughts and mind.
6. It might be the transmission of the mind.
7. What controls my mind.
8. Recognizing feelings.
9. *Maum* is the origin of it all.
10. Standards guiding my life, the mind guiding all the thoughts.
11. It's the place of thoughts; sensitive, wide, and limitless.
12. Willpower.
13. Accumulation of my thoughts and emotions.
14. Understanding, consideration, and love.
15. Emotionally, physically thinking and feeling everything.
16. People's inner personalities (justice, will, etc.).
17. Emotions depending on the situation.
18. Helps with decision.
19. Psyche.
20. First emotional response.
21. Keeps your body healthy, rules over me, and is an inner motor.
22. The power to move and think.
23. The water.[1]
24. *Maum* is the filter through which I look at the world.
25. Mind. It's bad for the mind, when you get hurt inside.
26. Entails thinking, trust, habits, actions, and destiny.
27. It depends on what you decide with your mind and it comes with action and practice.
28. Basic everyday attitude.
29. Face.
30. My awareness of the mind and what my thoughts are made out of.
31. Love.
32. My mood. If my health is good, my mind is also comfortable: Most important thing in our body.
33. Feelings, thoughts, or my present emotions felt by every fiber of my body: Head to heart.
34. My center, background that explains who I am.
35. My thoughts.
36. Me.
37. It has to be warm all the time.

"fire in their *Maum*, "which would then be located in the chest. They might also experience "boiling, exploding sensations in their chest." According to Western standards, *Hwa-byeong* is caused by the inability of a patient to confront his or her anger that was triggered by unfair conditions. This explanation draws from alternative Korean concepts: *Hwa-byeong* can originate

TABLE 5.2 Body Locations Given for the *Maum* and When Bothered By Something

	Question	Head *N* (%)	Chest *N* (%)	Other *N* (%)	Several Locations *N* (%)
1	Where is your *Maum* located in your body?	19 (33.93%)	33 (58.93%)	0 (0%)	4 (7.14%)
2	When something is bothering you, where do you feel it in your body?	32 (57.14%)	17 (30.36%)	3 (5.36%)	4 (7.14%)

TABLE 5.3 Students' Answers: Does the *Maum* Rule the Body or Does the Body Rule the *Maum*?

Question	*Maum* Rules the Body *N* (%)	Body Rules the *Maum* *N* (%)	No Hierarchy *N* (%)	No Response *N* (%)
What rules over what?	45 (80.36%)	7 (12.50%)	3 (5.36%)	1 (1.78%)

from *Hann* (恨) due to a lack of *Jeong* (情). Indeed, *Hann* is an unexpressed vengeful motive or desire that leads to anger resulting in the previously described symptoms (e.g, pain in the chest). *Jeong* cannot exist without the *Maum. Jeong,* in fact, "contains" aspects (e.g., good and bad emotions that can be ambivalent, Yoon, 2007) of the *Maum* that can be mutually shared with significant others. Significant others are usually family members, including parents, spouses, children, in-laws, and other relations, who in Korea are very dependent on each other. Non family members, such as roommates or neighbors, can also become part of this close inner circle. If *Jeong* is not mutual and/or significant others disappoint the trust placed in them, *Hann* emerges. In this understanding, which is supported by Choi and Choi (1991), *Jeong* (情) must be considered a core concept of Korean clinical psychology in guiding therapy.

WHAT DO WE LEARN FROM THIS?

Maum along with *Jeong* and *Hann* are culture-specific concepts whose general applicability is not widely proclaimed (see Rhi, 2013, for related discussions). The endeavor to grasp these concepts in a rational, objective manner will naturally fail, because of the vast differences in how they are understood by different individuals in varied settings. As described previously, *Maum* is more than the sum of different psychological concepts.

Sometimes *Maum* can refer to the heart, a person, a character, spirit, and will; even the body itself can be included. *Maum* comes and goes. It is a container, and an individual is contained within. It can be thought and it can differ from thought.[2]

Despite its wide range of definitions, *Maum* plays a central role in a person's well-being in Korea, and so it needs to be considered in therapy to address the patients' individual needs and sorrows. The *Maum* is thus a very important metaphor, one whose complexity makes it difficult, if not impossible, to fully study.

Nevertheless, the *Maum* can guide therapeutic approaches (Kabat-Zinn, 1990, 2005). Mindful, or in the Korean sense *Maumful*, meditation has, for example, become very popular in the last few years. In this context, it is said that

> if you have time to meditate, then the unclear water of the *Maum* becomes clear, and you start hearing the sound of your *Maum*: a sound of your soul that was unheard before. When this happens, health and peace come to your body and *Maum*.

In light of the importance of *Maum* for many individuals, psychologists and scholars should be willing to take a closer look. This would include an ongoing exchange with the patient or research participant, since meanings can change over time or vary in different settings. Ambivalence is part of the process, because co-construction of meaning is not static but a continuous process, one that will not lead to a clear definition, such as: This is *Maum*! An observation that is true for many psychological concepts.

NOTES

1. A student of mine wrote: "*Maum* is water." This analogy is similar to one found in Taoism, when Tao (以道而治病) is said to be something impossible to describe with words, but that naturally and smoothly flows like water. According to the philosopher Lao-tzu, Tao can heal diseases.
2. In Lee's book "From *Maum* to *Maum*" (2013), the author says that if there is some distance between him and an object, there is thought, but if there is no distance between the two, there is *Maum*.

REFERENCES

American Psychiatric Association (Ed.). (2000). *Diagnostic and statistical manual of mental disorders* (4th ed.). Washington, DC: Author.

Choi, S., & Choi, S.-H. (1991, October). An attempt to arrive at a socio-psychological conception of *Hann.* Paper presented at the annual conference of the Korean Psychological Association, Joung Ang University, Seoul, South Korea.

Jung, A. (2008, August). *A pattern of dialogue: From Maum to Maum.* Paper presented at the Fifth International Conference on Dialogical Self, Queens' College, Cambridge, England.

Kabat-Zinn, J. (1990). *Full catastrophe living: Using the wisdom of your body and mind to face stress, pain, and illness.* New York, NY: Delacorte.

Kabat-Zinn, J. (2005). *Coming to our senses: Healing ourselves and the world through mindfulness.* New York, NY: Hyperion.

Kim, U. (2005). *Landscape and mind: Essays on East Asian landscape painting.* Seoul, South Korea: Thinking Tree.

Lee, O. (2013). *From Maum to Maum.* Seoul, South Korea: Gimm Young.

Rhi, B.-Y. (2013). Human mind within and beyond the culture: Toward a better encounter between east and west. *Shim-Song Yon-Gu, 28*(2), 107–136.

Seong-Rae, P. (2005). *Science and technology in Korean history: Excursions, innovations, and issues.* Fremont, CA: Jain.

Sohn, H.-M. (2001). *The Korean language.* Cambridge, England: Cambridge University Press.

Yoon, K.-J. (2007). My experience of living in a different culture: The life of a Korean maigrant in Australia. In M. Besmeres & A. Wierzbicka (Eds.), *Translating lives: Living with two languages and cultures* (pp. 114–127). Queensland, Australia: University of Queensland Press.

CHAPTER 6

ONE OF MANY STORIES ABOUT FREUD

My Story as a Freudian Clinician[1]

Roger Bibace
Clark University

I should preface my lecture with some of my own therapeutic and clinical insight—namely, that this lecture is selective. By selective I refer to the bias of my own egocentricity and the role psychoanalysis has played in my interests, values, and intellectual growth. Since both Freud and I were psychotherapists, I believe it is fitting to begin the lecture this morning with a few quotes from the conclusion of James Davies' book, *The Making of Psychotherapists: An Anthropological Analysis.* Davies (2009) asks, "What are the distinctive aims of the psychodynamic institute? How do these influence the professional socialization of trainee practitioners?" (p. 251) His response to these questions parallels the idea of Freud's *Analysis Terminable and Interminable* (1937) and the therapeutic question of whether or not there is a natural end to an analysis. Davies writes,

Particulars and Universals in Clinical and Developmental Psychology, pages 91–99

> Furthermore, unlike training in more skill- than idea-based professions, where practical attainments can reach high levels of perfectibility, the kind of abilities garnered from psychodynamic socialization are characterized by non-completion. Like in Kabyle rituals where material exchange binds people in unending cycles of reciprocity (Bourdieu, 1972), the project of the institutes, as with the project of therapy, never reaches completion. The gift given in the project of therapy, never reaches completion. The gift given in training obliges a return—a lasting commitment. The trainee has thus entered a story whose narrative extends infinitely—personhood is never fully obtained, and the final aims of analysis are never achieved. (Davies, 2009, p. 255)

This quote brings up a few major themes of this lecture, the major theme being that of relationships. It is precisely the relationships between people, such as the therapist and the patient, and the relationship with oneself that sets the foundation for conflict and insight.

RELATIONSHIPS OF CONFLICT, INSIGHT, AND CHANGE

As long as we live there is conflict. But conflict, if properly analyzed, leads to insight, and insight leads to change. For many years the belief of insight and change guided the teaching and practice of my supervisors. But change did not always occur. As a result, my fellow students and I were taught that the "insight" revealed was only an "intellectual" insight. In order for change to occur, emotional insight was needed. This differentiation—between emotional and intellectual insight—was essential to understanding the relationship between insight and change. Decades later, I was taught a new explanation essential to understanding the relationship between insight and change. Allen Wheelis (1975) claimed that change should be amended to the following sequence: conflict—insight—will—action—change. Wheelis added "will and action" to the insight and change relationship. But will as a concept became controversial for analysts who subscribed to a deterministic interpretation of Freud rather than the alternative humanistic interpretation of Freud articulated by Robert Holt (1975).

What did I make of all this for my clinical work? I focused on the importance of activity. Especially in my later years as a psychotherapist, I remember asking my patients: What are you going to do when you get home tonight to avoid these "fights" with your wife? When I became director of the Psychological Services Center (PSC) at Clark University in 1965, I did most of the intake interviews. And in that historical era there were quite a few students who had been in therapy previously in high school or before they came to Clark. I took to asking them two questions: What did you learn from these previous experiences in therapy? Have you changed in any way since your experiences in therapy? It was disillusioning to know that almost all the students said they had not changed. And there were very few, if any, clear-cut examples of insight. Of course, the students who came to see me were a biased sample; the ones who had changed were not the ones who came to the PSC for help.

These clinical experiences underlined my focus on activity in the real world of my patients. That is, I focused on the patients relationships with their roommates, their teachers, their families, and of course their love life—the break ups or rejections with their boy or girl friends. These relationships often yielded conflict, but the patient would not change their behavior or cognition to put an end to the conflict. I remember pressing the patients for alternatives. What do you think X would do *if* you did Y? Some patients were so caught up with their conflicts they could not come up with an alternative. I would then say something like: Do you want me to tell you what some other people in fairly similar situations have done? That is, I was relying on George Herbert Mead's concept of the "generalized other" (Mead, 1934) and George Kelly's ideas of "constructive alternatives" (Kelly, 1969). I would also preface this with the statement, "I don't know if this will work for you" or "it's up to you" or "you can try something like this if it makes sense to you." And if the patient agreed, we would then talk about how to make a hypothetical alternative become a changed reality. The best alternatives, as judged by their impact in bringing about change, were behaviors that "pleasantly surprised" the other person in the relationship or even behaviors that "pleasantly surprised" themselves.

Note that I had come a long way, a very long way, from my training doing psychoanalytic sector therapy with patients. Sector therapy was an approach that relied on Felix Deutsch's ideas that any word introduced by the therapist "contaminated" the patient's own flow of associations (see Hohendorf, 2004). My supervisors repeatedly relied on a surgical analogy: a patient's associations were sacrosanct, any changes from the "outside" by the therapist would only distract the patient; would reveal the biases of what the therapist thought was important; or would change the cathexis, the priorities in the patient's psychic activities. So even in the history-taking phase prior to the therapy itself, the clinician minimized their verbal activities. At that time, Deutsch was teaching history taking in the Department of Internal Medicine at Harvard Medical School. He published an article titled "Associative Anamnesis." I relied and still use Jacob Finesinger's three levels of verbal activity (see Finesinger, 1948). The minimal level limits the interviewer to nonverbal behaviors, e.g., raising one's eyebrows or single words like "Uhum." Moderate levels of activity include underlining what the patient said with one's tone or mild directives such as, "Can you say more about X?" It is only at the third level of "marked activity" that a direct instruction is given to the patient, e.g., "I want you to tell me how you feel about X."

AN ANALOGY BETWEEN A THERAPEUTIC INTERPRETATION AND WEAVING

As we can see, as a therapist I have developed. But my roots still lie in psychoanalysis. Psychoanalytic Interpretations of Behavior was a course I taught here at Clark for approximately 25 years—from 1965 until 1990. It relied heavily on my clinical training in psychoanalysis, psychoanalytic theory, and my own person experience interpreting behavior from my psychoanalytic foundations. In a footnote to the *Interpretation of Dreams,* Freud (1900) commented on interpretation writing.

> Formerly I found it extraordinarily difficult to accustom my readers to the distinction between the manifest dream-content and the latent dream-thoughts. Over and over again, arguments and objections were adduced from the uninterrupted dream as it was retained in the memory, and the necessity of interpreting the dream was ignored. But now, when the analysts have at least become reconciled to substituting for the manifest dream its meaning as found by interpretations, many of them are guilty of another mistake, to which they adhere just as stubbornly. They look for the essence of the dream in this latent content, and thereby overlook the distinction between latent dream-thoughts and the dream-work. The dream is fundamentally nothing more than a special form of thinking, which is made possible by the conditions of the sleeping state. It is the dream-work which produces this form, and it alone is the essences of dreaming—the only explanation of its singularity. (Freud, 1900, Footnote 114)

To help you understand how such an interpretation in therapy would occur, I will give you an analogy. As a student of Heinz Werner, I had learned that any symbol could be construed in diverse ways, beyond verbal definitions. Further, words are often opaque in communicating a concept. In my encounter with this trainee, I asked him to create an "image" that would represent his understanding of what was meant by an "interpretation" in psychoanalysis. The following week he came back to tell me the image he had created, and he also related the image to his behaviors as therapist. The image was that of splitting an uncut diamond. The diamond cutter had to be very careful, to examine the stone from all angles before attempting to cut the diamond. This careful examination coincided, he reminded me, with the well-known role regarding silence. Or the rule, prevalent in that historical era: "Shut up and listen." Following this assessment, the diamond cutter would use the chisel to target the one specific spot that would split the stone into the valuable parts that were desirable. The analogical relationship in therapy to the precise cutting of the stone was the therapist's "interpretation." This trainee accompanied his explanation by an assertive, forward jerking of his forearm stating, "That's when I give him an interpretation."

I now had a much clearer understanding of the basis for this therapist's behavior during therapy. The following week we discussed an alternative image. The image I proposed was that of weaving. Weaving required the therapist to collaborate with the patient in transforming the raw wool by spinning all that was said into threads. The threads were the theme or themes for a particular hour. The themes themselves were made up of different colors; some were smooth, others coarse, and so on. That is, the themes were generalizations within an hour and across time, for different contexts, issues, and people. The analogical relationship between weaving and therapy then required both the weaver and the therapist to create a pattern that would constitute the whole in its formation as a product or an outcome. I emphasized that, of course, at every step both persons were constructing the materials, the threads, or the themes that were integral to the pattern. The patterns would most clearly be different as a result of the relationships between diverse therapists with the same patient. Even in the unlikely event that the final product or outcomes were the "same," the sequences in the construction of the patterns between therapist and patient would be different. Relationships determine what will emerge publicly as exchanges between people, including and especially in psychoanalysis.

RELATIONSHIPS OF TIME IN CLINICAL PSYCHOANALYSIS

For this analogy I relied heavily on many things, one being James Strachey's "mutative interpretation" (1934) based on clinical psychoanalysis, namely an analysis over a period of time. There are four strands to such an interpretation: the patient's historical past and present, and the transference past and present. When I use historical past, I mean the version, or narrative, that has mutually come to be accepted as the "past" by both the psychoanalyst and the patient. Each successively new session between the patient and therapist yields a historical present—the patient's "initial" version of the past has been retold and reinterpreted in the present session. This present retelling of the past has usually changed as a result of distorted and layered disguises and defenses that the patient has acquired since his last session. As Swift reminds us, "We don't know our own minds." This initial version will eventually—and as a principle usually—change in the retelling of the story, differentiating the historical past and present. There is a parallel development in the thoughts and feelings of the patient towards the analyst, categorized loosely as "transference." The transference past and present is similar in its emergence and analysis.

I need to point out that the previously statement is liable to be misinterpreted for at least two reasons. Many people rely on a linear idea of time. Time is believed to be the duration of an event. All events have a past, present, and future. In this approach to time, the past, present, and future are connected through "sequence." In psychoanalysis, this is only way in which time is organized. Standard sequential time of the past to present to future is a form of organization in the "conscious" level of the mind and the secondary forms of thinking and feeling. In sharpest contrast, the primary psychological processes involved in "preconscious" and "unconscious" levels of the mind include the organization of thoughts and feelings that rely on the "co-existence" of past, present, and future at every moment of a person's life. The present coexists with the past in a person's experiences through their memories; similarly, the future may also be contained in that person's momentary experiences through their imagination. The interpretations that constitute the generalizations between the analyst and the analysand are based on both primary and secondary forms of intrapsychic psychological processes. These intrapsychic psychological processes manifest themselves in the "reports or free associations" by the patient regarding their life. Most importantly, these intrapsychic psychological processes are manifested and experienced by the both persons in the course of analysis. This occurs when patients "transfer" the irrational beliefs and behaviors of their own lives onto the analyst at various times in the course of an analysis. Irrational, unconscious convictions about "others" in the life history of the patient in general become focused on the analyst in particular. These particular experiences *in the here and now* parallel a patient's general expectations of others—past, present, and future.

THE RELATIONSHIP BETWEEN ANALYST AND ANALYSAND: TRANSFERENCE AND COUNTER-TRANSFERENCE

There is another oversimplification against which to be guarded, namely that the intrapsychic processes of the patient are the sole focus of analysis. The distinction between intrapsychic and interpersonal schools of psychoanalysis, from my perspective, is too sharp a boundary. The transference interpretations in Freudian analyses are very clearly directed to the interpersonal interactions between analyst and analysand. Further, the analyst's source of data or information includes their own thoughts and feelings as the patient "free associates" and speaks about themselves. The thoughts and feelings of the analyst include the entire range of the products of primary and secondary psychological processes that result in rational and irrational conclusions within one's self and that may or may not become manifest as "behavior." The analyst listens with "free floating attention" to both what the patient is saying and the "resonance or reverberations" within one's selves as one listens in silence. All such thoughts and feelings within the analyst, when they are made conscious, are grouped under the label of "counter-transference." Both the transference and countertransference for the analyst may parallel the experiences of the patient and the analyst's own life, such as how both persons experienced authority figures at one time in their own lives as aspects of their historical past. Another example would be parallels based on the form, such as rebellion against an authority figure, but not the content of such experiences. The analogical relationship that is constructed as a formal parallel is sharply differentiated from the contents or actual experiences in these two person's lives. Again, I want to emphasize that these analogical relationships do not refer to identical or even similar experiences. In this example, the analogy establishes a functional similarity for these two people regarding their relationship to an authority figure.

People in their everyday life recognize such parallels and analogies when speaking and interacting with others. A person may or may not acknowledge publicly what they are experiencing privately. A psychoanalysis differs, in this respect, from everyday life in two very important ways. The patient does not have eye contact with the analyst. That is, the nonverbal behaviors of the analyst are not available to the patient, whereas the nonverbal behaviors of the analysand lying on the couch can be observed by the analyst and constitute what Deutsch referred to as "psychoanalytic posturology." This asymmetrical relationship constrains the patient to auditory or olfactory perception (e.g., Freud's smoking of cigars). The analyst, however, can also rely on visual perception and observations. Further, there is a direct contradiction between ordinary everyday expectations and the patient's experiences in analysis. When a person asks another individual a question, ordinarily that person gets a response. The response may not be an answer to the question asked but usually they get a response of some kind. One of the very distinctive aspects of psychoanalysis, for a patient, is the disconfirmation of this expectation. A major tool for creating transference reactions by the analyst is silence; that is, a question by the patient to the analyst results in silence. The atmosphere of the analysis is to quote Freud *gefühlskalt.* This is quite different from the "warm, accepting, empathic" atmosphere that some other approaches to psychotherapy attempt to create. How that silence is experienced and responded to by the patient is a major source of information in psychoanalysis. The stories the patients tell themselves regarding the reasons for the analyst's silence constitute the "projections" and the bases for the transference reactions by the patient.

CONCLUSION (ADDED)

There are many factors that contribute to the very broad range of *relationships* between two people, in this case, a patient and a psychoanalyst. There are expectations on both sides: values, hopes, fears. In the foregoing, we have shown that certain therapeutic schools come with certain expectations in regards to the patient-therapist relationship. In the following chapter, we will examine the ongoing processes between therapist and patient as they try to "metaphorically sit next to each other" further. Rosenbaum (in this volume) will try "to more fully explicate how these field dynamics function within psychoanalysis" including the psychoanalytic defense mechanisms. The following section will then demonstrate the dynamics between researcher and participant—outside the clinical context.

NOTE

1. Lecture given at the Vienna-Clark Symposium, "Freud in the Mirror of History," October 2009.

REFERENCES

Bourdieu, P. (1972). *Esquisse d'une théorie de la pratique, précédé de trois études d'ethnologie kabyle* [Outline of a theory of practice]. Genève-Paris, France: Droz.

Davies, J. (2009). *The making of psychotherapists: An anthropological analysis.* London, England: Karnac.

Finesinger, J. (1948). Psychiatric interviewing. Some principles and procedures in insight therapy. *American Journal of Psychiatry, 105,* 187–195.

Freud, S. (1937). Analysis terminable and interminable. *International Journal of Psychoanalysis, 18,* 373–405.

Freud, S. (1900). *Interpretation of dreams.* Retrieved May 2015 from http://psychclassics.yorku.ca/Freud/Dreams/dreams6d.htm

Hohendorf, G. (2004). *Die psychosomatische theoriebildung bei Felix Deutsch (1884–1964). Ein beitrag zur geschichte der psychoanalyse des körpers (1884–1964)* [The psychosomatic theory construction by Felix Deutsch (1884–1964)]. Husum, Germany: Matthiesen.

Holt, R. R. (1975). The past and future of ego psychology. *Psychoanalytic Quarterly, 44,* 568.

Kelly, G. A. (1969). Personal construct theory and the psychotherapeutic interview. In B. Maher (Ed.), *Clinical psychology and personality. The selected papers of George Kelly* (p. 226). New York, NY: Wiley.

Mead, G. H. (1934). *Mind, self, and society: From the perspective of a social behaviorist.* Chicago, IL: University of Chicago Press.

Strachey, J. (1934). The nature of the therapeutic action of psychoanalysis. *International Journal of Psychoanalysis, 15*, 127–159.
Wheelis, A. (1975). *How people change.* New York, NY: William Morrow.

CHAPTER 7

AN INTERPERSONAL THEORY OF PSYCHOLOGICAL DEFENSE MECHANISMS

Philip J. Rosenbaum
Haverford College

ROGER BIBACE: AN INTERPERSONAL THINKER

One of the fondest memories I have of Roger Bibace is of him discussing his unique approach to research in the weekly kitchen meetings held at Clark University. Roger espoused that the research setting needed to be "more egalitarian, democratic, and naturalistic." One way he thought this could be achieved is with the researcher sitting next to the participant so they were each overlooking the same object of inquiry, the same field. Not only does sitting next to one another level the traditional hierarchy found in the roles of scientist and participant (Danzinger, 1994), but it also makes it more naturalistic, bringing more validity to the study as the influence of the scientist's authority is lessened (though never nonexistent). There always seemed to be something very human in sitting alongside someone looking at something, whatever it might be, together. Sort of like saying that although we are or might be different in a number of ways (age, gender, social role, income, class, and so on), we can both share this space and

Particulars and Universals in Clinical and Developmental Psychology, pages 101–118

look at the same things. Or, in the words of the interpersonal psychiatrist Harry Stack Sullivan (1953), "Everyone is much more simply human than otherwise" (p. 32).

That Roger would select a technique emphasizing our shared humanity is not surprising to those who know him. In his teaching, clinical practice, and research he has always sought to understand and express what makes us human. Whether it was passionately talking about the dignity of schizophrenics, emphasizing their struggle to relate and make connections, or the importance of being sensitive to students' needs, Roger is a consummately empathic and caring individual. Although, I could not know it at the time, the emphasis on sitting next to one another and being with each other, sometimes referred to as joining or witnessing, stayed with me throughout my graduate school training as a clinical psychologist and postgraduate training as a psychoanalyst.

PSYCHOANALYTIC THEORIES AND DEFENSE

Of course, just because two people are sitting next to one another does not mean they are seeing the same thing. There are many possible reasons for this. Some include different possible life experiences, which may impact how we construct and make sense of what we see. For instance, someone not raised with the traditional idea of a classroom would likely consider a group of students sitting and staring as someone faces away from them while talking, differently than someone who has attended classes. Our expectations about what will occur within specific contexts or at different times may also impact what we attend to. For example, the man dressed up patriotically and singing the "Star-Spangled Banner" may make sense on the Fourth of July, but stand out on May 4th (Bruner, 1990). Similarly, perspectives and values about living will influence how individuals make sense of what they see.

Conscious or unconscious uses of defense mechanisms are other reasons for why people who sit together may see the same thing differently. Projection, denial, cognitive dissonance, paranoid-schizoid thinking (black and white), repression, selective inattention, and so forth hamper our abilities to formulate experience in its fullness and complexity or to even take note of what may be happening around us. In this respect, defenses serve multiple purposes. They keep us focused on what we need to be focused on, so that we are not overwhelmed, or so that we feel secure and comfortable in our environment and actions (McWilliams, 1994). At times, however, defenses prevent us from observing and acting in more beneficial ways. Then we may act in ways that appear to work against us, sabotaging our efforts at being in the world. For instance, someone who has learned to "avoid conflict" due to possibly getting wounded, or directing the anger of someone toward them, may have a hard time recognizing conflicts in the future and asserting themselves in situations that are not as dangerous.

Within psychoanalysis, defenses have been historically thought of as being intra-psychic. They occur within the individual preventing them from feeling something understood as threatening or scary to their psychic selves. Defenses protect our egos and selves from what could be debilitating wounds. Defenses protect our images ourselves, what we consider important to who we are, and also how other people see us, which we may be more or less aware of (McWilliams, 1994). In this respect, they operate along a range of consciousness, with some being more conscious than others. For instance, projection, when I unconsciously without awareness attribute my own feelings or motivations as belonging to someone else such that they are one way and I am not, is considered an unconscious defense to prevent me from considering aspects of myself that may be threatening (or that I just do not like). Disowning these aspects of myself, such as aggression or hostility, and locating them in someone else, may ironically (Wachtel, 2008) influence their perceptions of me in a negative fashion, which is referred to as projective identification (Ogden, 1979; Rosenbaum, 2013). Alternatively suppression, when I mostly consciously try to not feel something at a particular time, is an example of a defense that is considered more conscious.

These intrapsychic defenses are clinically very useful and at the heart of many therapeutic processes and actions. They are also very much connected with the modern theories and philosophies of their time. Specifically, they operate in what has been termed a point-to-point manner (Valsiner, 2007). A defense can be understood as protecting the self from a particular threat. In psychoanalysis this threat was often known *a priori,* as it was intrinsically connected to the dominant metatheories or overarching ideas of the time.

Metatheories are broadly articulated hypotheses and ideas intended on understanding the ongoing psychological processes occurring for individuals (within their minds as it were) that were not readily observable. For instance, Freud's conception of the Oedipus complex, or the way the baby/infant/child relates to both their mother and father, is seen as guiding and underlying normative developmental processes. Oedipal dynamics including the child's drive to possess the mother and get rid of the father are hypothesized as normatively occurring in all developmental circumstances (McWilliams, 1994; Freud, 1899/1955). These dynamics entail certain threats, known *a priori,* such as the child's fear of castration from the retaliatory father. As such they are used to understand complex psychological phenomena, such as childhood repression, and the later development of pathological symptoms.

When applied in the clinical setting, the Oedipal complex organizes the flow of the patient's associations. The analyst hears and makes sense of data and phenomena through the lens of Oedipal dynamics. Since the infant's possessive and sexual feelings toward the mother are threatening to their security, these are unconsciously repressed. Similarly, competitive feelings with the father may also be repressed out of fear of consequence. Repression while effective requires energy, which then may later lead to neurotic symptoms, and defenses. Passivity for instance, may be a way of dealing with hostile feelings (McWilliams, 1994). Interpreting these underlying dynamics frees up the energy bound up in symptoms. This connection between metatheories and phenomena ensured a circular closed relationship; the metatheory informs the threat, which generates a certain type of defense.

Since defenses are more readily observable than what presumably is going on within the individual's inner world, they are then used to support the presence of the meta-theory. In other words, the presence of certain objectively observable defenses validates metatheoretical hypotheses about what is going on subjectively. Strong metatheories help the therapist postulate what is occurring within the psyche of the patient. When the therapist becomes aware of it, he or she can then interpret it back to the metatheory. Interestingly, the patient's reaction to this can itself be interpreted and also understood within the metatheory of the therapist.

This system provided psychoanalysis with a tremendous amount of power and theoretical neatness. However, it also meant that analysis, and later therapy, ironically functioned in a reductionist way, where not only did something stand for something else, but the therapist, in possession of power and authority in many cases, already knew what *it* was. The explanatory power of these defense mechanisms and their undeniable clinical utility has contributed to them being one of the lasting legacies of Sigmund Freud and psychoanalysis.

Changes in ideas about defense have been connected to the revolutionized understandings of the goals of analysis. That is to say, as the object and aims of analysis have changed, so have the ideas about what requires defense. Following the postmodern turn in addition to focusing on their patient's intrapsychic world of fantasies, associations, and dreams, the therapist equally attends to the patient's real relationships (present and past), their interpersonal lives, and the here-and-now relationship to the patient. As a result, defensive maneuvers may also occur around the therapist's relationship to their patient. This involves the therapist's "authority and influence" on the patient, the experience of intimacy, what it is like to sit with one another, and the continual ways they are co-constructing, structuring, and negotiating their relationship (Hoffman, 1983; Mitchell, 2005).

As will be elaborated in the following section, this shift implies a changing idea of what is being defended, moving the locus from the intrapsychic toward a study of the interpersonal field (Aron, 1991; Stern, 1997) or the relational matrix (Greenberg, 1995). In other words, the focus has turned to examining the ongoing processes between therapist and patient as they try to metaphorically sit next to each other and look out over the field of the patient's life. Clearly, this idea is very much in the spirit of Roger's interpersonal thinking and it is with this in mind that we try to more fully explicate how these field dynamics function within psychoanalysis.

FIELD THEORIES AND PSYCHOANALYSIS

Kurt Lewin and Harry Stack Sullivan

The field theoretical approach in psychology and psychoanalysis has been present since the eminent German-American social psychologist Kurt Lewin (1890–1947) introduced it in the 1930s. He considered his ideas as providing a necessary counterpoint to the behaviorists who were becoming popular at the time (Lewin, 1946/1997). These highly reductionist, but also neat and seemingly applicable, theories turned the mind into a "black box" that could not be accessed, and consequently how meaning was made was not of significance (Bruner, 1990). Instead, behaviors, identified as stimulus and response, and purposefully absent of meaning, were studied. In this context, Lewin's voice arguing for a comprehensive and holistic psychology that studied meaningful and intentional conduct within a person's interpersonal context and history was a powerful alternative that influenced many, including Harry Stack Sullivan. An American psychiatrist, Sullivan was one of the founders of interpersonal psychiatry in the 1940s and 1950s. And although rarely fully explicated, field theory implicitly structured many of his central concepts, such as his theory of personality organization and participant observation, and continues to be important (Stern, 2013a; Sullivan, 1953).

Field theories argue that there are a range of factors affecting individual conduct, personality, and experience (Lewin, 1935, 1936, 1943, 1946/1997; Stern, 2013a). These include the familial, social, and cultural situations of the individual as well as more internal forces. In other words, field theories include both what is external to individuals as well as what is internal to them. It follows that field theories consider these as mutually influencing each other, such that distinctions between outer–inner, external–internal, and so forth become somewhat arbitrary, always entailing a relationship between them (Hoffman, 1998; Harris, 2005). Fields develop from the variety of contributing factors (e.g., familial, biological, cultural, and so forth), but are not reducible to these factors. In this respect, fields are considered emergent properties. Within a field the ongoing relationships between the different components of the field generate feedback loops and boundaries that both constrain and enable movement (physical and ideological) within fields (Harris, 2005; Lewin, 1935; 1936; 1943; 1946/1997; Stern, 2013a; Valsiner, 2007). The characteristics of any particular field are unique to that field.

Sullivan (1953) believed that all human conduct occurred within interpersonal fields. While he differentiated between personality and self, he considered each constituted as fields. Sullivan defined personality as the sum total of appraisals, or evaluations and observations recognized both by that individual and by others. Personality thus includes appraisals that the individual himself/herself may not recognize. In contrast, Sullivan defined the self as including only what the individual himself/herself recognized or understood (Sullivan, 1953). In other words, personality was an observable phenomenon, whereas self was a more private and subjective one (Greenberg & Mitchell, 1983). Notably, both are field phenomena, dependent upon the ongoing feedback from social relationships, which provide the key ingredients supporting the development of an individual's more stable and enduring traits.

Sullivan (1953) termed the expression "self-system" to describe how the self regulates these ongoing feedback processes of evaluations and appraisals.[1] Although it invokes more mechanical imagery, his idea was that the self-system regulates primarily the experience of anxiety, keeping it at manageable levels. This speaks to ongoing defensive processes, primarily what he called "selective inattention." Unlike Freudian repression, which keeps threatening feelings pushed down and unconscious, selective inattention works more like wearing blinders. It prevents individuals from attending to events and experiences that disrupt the security of the self (Rosenbaum, 2015). This shift has repercussions for thinking about defensive processes, moving the emphasis from being mainly intrapsychic and concerned with internal forces and drives, to being more interpsychic and concerned with how that person feels perceived, understood, and how he/she co-constructs experiences with others.

Tangentially, but interestingly, about 10 years after Sullivan's death, Madeline and Willy Baranger also utilized ideas from Kurt Lewin (among others) to develop a different strain of field theoretically informed psychoanalysis (see Stern 2013a for a discussion of similarities and differences). While this chapter focuses mainly on field theory as it is influenced by Sullivan and interpersonal/relational psychoanalysis, the development of a second strain underlines field theories' theoretical and practical flexibility and utility. While not substantiated, it is interesting to consider that the Barangers perhaps encountered Lewin's ideas in his writings for the Tavistock Institute in England, where a number of his articles on field theory were published (i.e., Neumann, 2005, 2013). The later influence of object relations thinkers who were involved with the Tavistock, such as Donald Winnicott, on the development of contemporary relational psychoanalysis in the United States, might be in part located as resulting from sharing Lewin as an intellectual father.

Not surprisingly, according to Donnel Stern (2013a), Sullivan's field theory has continued to have a central, although often unformulated, influence on the development of contemporary interpersonal/relational psychoanalysis, which he terms "IRP." In this respect, field theory is a linchpin for IRP, but one that functions outside of conscious awareness, much like procedural memory. Everyone recognizes that field theory informs a good deal of the therapeutic venture, but articulating how it does so seems to have defied description, if not totally escaped attention.

This may be because it is quite difficult to articulately and succinctly describe a field in its complexity. Thinking in field theory terms is both very intuitive, it makes sense given that we see and experience fields in our lives, but also very counter-intuitive as it means abandoning more traditional ideas of causality and mechanical physical interactions. It almost seems like trying to move from two-dimensional seeing to three-dimensional seeing. In fact, similar to complexity and chaos theory, descriptions of fields and field theory are rarely satisfying. They seem to quickly run into either theoretical abstraction or overly static and reductionist accounts of forces, vectors, and the like. This is somewhat paradoxical, as Lewin intended to provide a theoretically comprehensive, but also practical system. His famous equation of individual behavior B = F(PE) is simultaneously simplistic and complicated. Here, behavior is a function of the person within their environment at a particular point in time[2] (Lewin, 1946/1997). While this seems clear, articulating even a simplistic behavior can be complex.

An Example From Field Theory

To illuminate the complexity, it is worth considering an example from a field theory perspective to highlight some basic concepts that will be more fully articulated in the following section. Consider what a description of the seemingly simple action of a young child taking a cookie from a jar may sound like in Lewinian language. To begin with, the appraisals and feelings of the mother on taking cookies generate vectors of possible experiences. These vectors are potential fields with varying degrees of permeability. What the child is told by the mother, in addition to their own proclivities, structures their access to other fields. The child may have been told that asking for a cookie "is what good children do" and that "only bad children take a cookie without asking." At other times they were also told, "Smart children figure things out on their own" and "not to do what everyone says." Each statement establishes vectors and trajectories for possible conduct and making meaning about taking the cookie, which structures the development of potential future fields.

In this example, the potential subfields are bifurcated along the mother's desire for a "good" child who asks and the "bad" child who does not. The split field is often mistakenly reduced when, in fact, it entails a whole host of other possibilities. In other words, the opposite of good is not bad, but rather nongood, which possibly entails the idea of bad, but also a range of meanings that are not good (Valsiner, 2007). For instance, while mother's preference is the "good" child, the "smart" child may figure that while taking the cookie is "bad," it is also an indication of being independent and clever, which mother also values.

The possible openness of the field to multiple meanings and interpretations offers a contrast to the point-like systems described earlier (Valsiner, 2007). For these systems the similar motivation toward gratifying an urge or impulse may be brought into conflict with the parental authority. Solely locating the impulse within the self would be insufficient. In-between parent-child dynamics as well as other more basic drive-based processes have to be taken into account in understanding the development of conflict. The temptation to make meaning in a "lazy" fashion (Valsiner, 2007) reduces or constrains the field to a particular point, however, the possibility for ambiguity, based on the existence of unformulated (Stern, 1997) or undeveloped fields, continues to exist. In part, the ability to experience this depends on the other structures within the field. If, for instance, the mother cannot experience the child taking the cookie as an expression of independence, but rather only noncompliance, the other zones of meaning likely become more foreclosed than if she herself can see the event as having multiple meanings. Similarly, the child's internal direction may be strongly drawn (valence) toward keeping such a mother calm, which then limits the experience of taking the cookie.

Considering behaviors then requires knowing the valence and vectors of not only the actor, but also the others within their internal and external worlds (Lewin, 1940/1997). The outcomes of these tensions may result in identifications, counter-identifications, or partial identifications with others and their appraisals (good, bad, smart, etc.). These in turn continually shape the child's experience of themselves, as well as the field and the zones of movement within it. Development after all is recursive, constantly feeding back into itself and resulting from an almost incomprehensible number of micro moments. Thus, fields are self-reinforcing and cyclical (Wachtel, 2014), existing within ongoing feedback loops. For this reason, understanding the individual, their relating to others, and their environment proves to be an incredibly complicated task (Lewin, 1940/1997). In fact, coloring in the lines of the person and the people who compose their fields or worlds is one of the central tasks of psychoanalysis.

The patterned and cyclical nature of fields ensures that certain field dynamics, such as preferred modes of relating to others, can to degrees be recreated within the therapeutic situation. Each person brings in their own histories and so the patterns co-constructed between therapist and patient may be similar to past patterns, but are always idiographic. The relatively nonconscious and unconscious patterns of relating to self and other provide the basis for the therapeutic process, and in recent years therapeutic technique has emphasized exploring what is transpiring in the here and now between therapist and patient. The goal now, if it can be called such, is to create an interpersonal field where novel thoughts and experiences can occur, which Stern (2013b) has called "growth in the present" (p. 634). The interpersonal field contains the fields of therapist and patient as well as their own ontogenetic histories, but also the emergent field containing each of them. This emergent property, sometimes referred to as the analytic third (Ogden, 1994), can also be conceptualized as a metafield occupying a more abstract level of meaning (Levenson, 2013). From a field theoretical perspective, this may be seen as elaborating the field such that previously unsymbolized and perhaps ambiguous vectors can be expressed and explored. This process seems to involve articulating the factors that prevent the growth of the patient's ability to attend to the full range of their experience and also, importantly, describe it linguistically both within and outside of the therapeutic situation.

Processes Within Fields

There are at least three interrelated ideas apparent when working to explicate how field theory works within contemporary settings: *movement, boundaries,* and *force/energy*. These ideas also help articulate where we can begin to locate defensive processes within field theories. As a caveat, these ideas are complementary to each other and are only being dealt as separate in the following for the sake of clarity.

Movement

Perhaps no idea captures the therapeutic process better than that of movement. It can be literal, in the sense of the feeling when a patient starts "moving" in his or her life, such as making changes in his or her patterns of living. Movement is also ideological. Phillip Bromberg's (1998) idea about "standing in the spaces" is essentially one of greater ideological field mobility. Rather than being locked into a particular field by existing feedback cycles, patterns, boundaries, and other fields that have been dissociated (disowned), the patient can now move more freely between these fields. Returning to the previous example, the child could experience him or herself as at times being "bad," but also creative, bold, defiant, and so forth. This achievement requires a complicated series of events, including awareness of other fields that may have previously been foreclosed, and a cognitive capacity for symbolization and metaphor (Lewin, 1946/1997). The complexity necessitates an interpersonal other to track patterns and interpsychic and intrapsychic processes and provide a type of developmental scaffold for therapeutic processes. Similarly, as noted earlier, according to Stern (2013b), the shift from the resolution of certain developmental complexes or tracing symptoms to historical antecedents toward an ability to grow in awareness and formulation suggests an importance of freedom of expression and motion.

Boundaries

Implicit in the idea of moving between fields are the boundaries that structure the field as a gestalt emergent property and also its subfields. Boundaries also determine how much energy is required to move between or within fields. They also can be physical or ideological. For a student a semipermeable boundary, such as dormitory rooms or classrooms, is easier to navigate than a less permeable boundary, such as the faculty dining hall. Boundaries are structures that have acquired force and regulate movement. The acquisition may be derived as cultural artifacts, which semiotically structure physical environments, such as the way bathroom signs cause traffic at busy events, but also result from ontological experiences at more local and familial levels. In this respect, boundaries not only constrain or prevent conduct but enable it as well. We do not need to look any further than our own bodies as bounded fields to understand how both occur.

Energy

For Lewin (1936, 1946/1997), energy is closely related to the concept of forces, valences, and motivations. Objects within fields, including but not limited to boundaries, may attract or repel certain actions. These objects and their valences are derived from ongoing interaction with the individual's motivation to achieve a goal or perform a particular action. The desire to overcome a boundary with a negative or repulsive valence, such as the faculty dining hall, may stem more from internal motivation (conscious or unconscious) than it does from the boundaries repulsing valence. In this case, the internal valence overcomes the external valence. Of course it is more complicated. The student may transform the repulsive valence of the faculty dining hall into a challenge to overcome, such as a place to play a prank. This transformation may result from the student's desire to fit into a certain group of friends, express rebelliousness towards authority and challenge the social order, or so forth. It speaks to the development (movement) of the field from first being a state of repulsion to then becoming an attractor motivating action.

Fields do not naturally strive toward any particular state, such as homeostasis or change. Rather, the charge of the field results as an emergent property through ongoing interactions. In some cases, an individual's motivation to avoid anxiety may lead to the (re)creation of particular patterns within fields (Sullivan, 1953), while in other cases strong motivation toward certain goals may lead to hyperactive field construction, deconstruction, and impulsive conduct. Noting the direction of the field and where energy is flowing is important when considering the overall structure of the field.

Examples of Defensive Processes Within Fields

In drawing from field theory, defensive processes involve negotiating both inter-psychic phenomena, especially how one relates to others, in addition to intrapsychic processes, what one experiences within oneself. As stated earlier, there is also an ongoing relationship between the two making their separation somewhat arbitrary. Dispositions, urges, impulses (what Freud termed *trieb*) exist within mediated space, necessarily entailing at least some relationship to something else. The shift for thinking about defensive processes is profound.

Negotiating Boundaries

Defensive processes within field theory operate in various ways on the interrelated workings of movement, boundaries, and energy. For instance, during a session, a young woman sits on the edge of her seat clutching her purse tightly toward her body. She talks about anxiety that threatens to choke her and a need she feels to be responsible at all times. She wants very much for colleagues and friends to throw her a party, as she makes an important life transition, but is not sure they will. She is afraid of the potential disappointment that comes from experiencing the freedom to want from others and to express her desire to them. This, in fact, feels irresponsible and drawing attention to herself feels unacceptable. Thus, while we acknowledge that she could throw her own party, this is fraught with risk. In addition to the question of its appropriateness, it also would be another example of her feeling that she is putting in more work than others. She would feel off balance by wanting more than others and valuing their friendship more than they do. Having them arrange the party is in part a test of whether her colleagues and friends value her and also a way to feel validated by them.

Her constricted posture highlights the difficulty she experiences moving within not only the therapeutic field, but also the interpersonal field of her relationships. The motivation toward being responsible combined with the fear of disappointment are strong valences that not only lead to her avoiding a potentially scary situation, but seemingly direct so much energy toward herself as to choke her. The need to appear responsible constructs an ideological boundary that she cannot overcome. On the other side are her desires to be valued as an employee and a friend. The tension between wanting to be celebrated and not wanting to ask or stand out creates a choking feeling of being stuck. As a result, the ordinary interpersonal boundaries are experienced as more difficult to navigate around than usual, feeding into the sense of tightness that permeates her during the session. The drawing inward fortifies her defensive walls serving to further isolate and withdraw from others.

Here, her defenses are organized around maintaining these boundaries. She cannot for instance imagine that she could ask about the party and still be valued by her friends. This creates an either/or situation and the rather rigid boundary makes moving into a new space difficult as energy is bound up within maintaining the boundaries.

In our session, I commented:

> **Me:** It feels like there are two wishes, one wanting to have a party and be acknowledged, but at the same time it is important to not have to throw it yourself, so you can know that they really like you.
>
> **She:** Yes, they've thrown parties for the other people who left, so I think they will throw a party for me too, but it's almost the end of the week and I haven't heard anything and so I don't know if maybe they forgot, or if because there was one last week that they don't want to throw another one this week. I could ask someone, but then, what if they didn't want to and now felt that they had to do it out of obligation or what if they just didn't want to do it.
>
> **Me:** That would mean?
>
> **She:** Well, maybe that they didn't like me as other employees, or that they didn't think I did as good a job, I mean, which is silly, because I know I did a good job, but it was also, like we've talked about how hard it was for me at the beginning and how much pressure I felt to do a good job and so maybe, like maybe they like the work I did, but not me.

While talking about this throughout the session, her posture and stance not only conveys a feeling of the interpersonal distance she experiences at work, but also generates within me some desire to pull away as well. In this sense, her rigidity is also a form of concretizing and crystalizing her experience within a particular field of meaning-making. The invitations to explore and experience more of the field she is currently occupying, or even move to another field, are both attempts to reinitiate or restart the meaning-making processes. They can also be understood as trying to move from the more physical world to the symbolic one. Defensive processes try to limit this movement or keep the boundaries solidified.

Keeping Distance

For one patient, therapy was a last ditch effort to figure out her "commitment issues" to a Jekyll and Hyde boyfriend, both alluring and charming but also unpredictable and terrifying. Before beginning to understand these issues, we had to first figure out how we were going to relate to one another, if at all. We talked about how she wanted to be able to trust a man to help her, but she also needed to be on guard against what she felt was an inevitable betrayal where that person's needs would come before hers. This conflict was most acutely felt around the frame of the field when having to pay the therapy's fee and having to attend regularly. In her case, she experienced paying the fee and attending regularly as a threat to her independence, which was hard-fought and not tolerated as negotiated space, compromised between us.

The psychological frame structures the treatment within practical boundaries that establish how long sessions are, how much there is to pay, what to do in case of cancellations, missed sessions, and so forth. These boundaries, which also include how some therapist's respond to particular questions about themselves, and I think how they understand the purpose of treatment, serve a multitude of purposes but create a distinction between the therapeutic space and the space outside of it. This space is unique, similar to the space outside of the consulting room, but different, and for many this is what enables therapy to safely proceed. By delineating certain areas as being within the purview of analysis and certain areas as being outside of treatment, boundaries serve a gatekeeping (regulatory) function keeping out and enabling within (Lewin, 1946/1997).

As both therapist and patient are involved in establishing relationships that are asymmetrical and uneven (Aron, 1991), the frame often becomes the object of the therapeutic process. With this patient we discussed her ambivalence regarding treatment. We both acknowledged that the boundaries of the frame were a form of shameful submission to her, potentially compromising her independence. She wanted very much to engage in a relationship that would be helpful, but also that would be minimally personal. Her defensive wish was to keep her distance from me, and realizing that a relationship occurring within the frame of therapy could potentially be intimate scared her.

As we talked about these topics, we also became able to track the ways our relationship fell into a similar sado-masochistic pattern as her relationship with her boyfriend. Here, the frame serves as a sociocultural artifact of the therapeutic process combined with our roles (therapist/patient) and each of our unique histories to push our interpersonal field to assuming a particular constellation of complementary relationships (Aron, 2006). Edgar Levenson (2013) has labeled this the "isomorphic transformation" resulting from structure of language, whereby to talk about something is also to enact it. He suggests that the therapist's attempt to resist this transformation is ultimately futile, and that enacting a particular relationship with the patient is inevitable. Interestingly, awareness of these enactments does not lead to the end of enactment, but instead toward a different metalevel of enactment and so forth.

These enactments can highlight fields that have been dissociated from awareness and used to articulate the intrapsychic and interpsychic boundaries that limit movement. For instance, when we spoke about her father, an émigré from Eastern Europe, she would frequently start crying, though not knowing why or what she was feeling that led to tears. She would then describe him as being two different men. When he was out in their community, he was funny, vibrant, and engaged, the life of a party. At home, he was a very depressed man, prone to drinking and experiencing crippling paranoid anxiety. However, her descriptions lacked personal meaning and affect. It was almost like she knew a laundry list of things about him, but had not allowed herself to formulate what the list meant about him (who he was), and also for her. In time, her associations began to become more saturated with meaning, as she considered how his history impacted her, especially when she was a child. Needing to deal with his pain and distance within their interpersonal field meant that she rarely considered her needs, and if she did she experienced crippling guilt.

She was caught off guard when, as we talked about the frame, I acknowledged that it was as much to take care of my needs as her needs, and that it is what helped with this process. The idea that not only could she have needs, but also that someone would be interested in them, was new to her. Recognizing the validity of her feelings and needs was an important first step before considering a relationship where these were met. At the same time, becoming involved in a relationship where her needs were met meant articulating fields that had been dissociated. This transformed her experience of the frame and therapy as a form of submission into one where two people collaborated together.

Exploring Potential Fields

The on-going negotiation between therapist and patient ensures that the therapist acts as more than just a gatekeeper. The therapeutic setup, where the therapist positions himself or herself literally (behind, next to, across), but also metaphorically (as a cotraveler, expert guide, and observer), as well as where the patient positions himself or herself (cotraveler and tourist) all influence the field. Throughout the treatment, the therapist may be called to play different roles and respond from different perspectives (Greenberg, 1991). Being able to shift and to see these different tasks requires the therapist's nondefensive presence and own ability to move among fields.

For instance, one patient comes into a session talking about how the end of a much-anticipated event has been spoiled by people rather insensitively not keeping information to themselves. Choosing how to perceive this statement involves the opening up of a number of potential fields. In addition to the patient's disappointment and history of having things spoiled, there is also the double meaning of the term "spoiled." How was he spoiled by his parents or was he not spoiled enough? Does he want to be spoiled now? Moving to another field also means asking, "Have I done anything to spoil him, or did I spoil something for him?" Perhaps, my unexpected canceling of a session earlier that week spoiled his day, preventing him from doing something desired or needed, and he is angry with me for it.

What seems to matter in this case is working to maintain the openness of the field and facilitate the patient's stepping into it. Being a coparticipant means that the therapist, at times, may be limited in what they can see about themselves. Not only encouraging the patient to report on the analyst's own subjective experience (Aron, 1991), but maintaining an attitude of openness and curiosity that engages multiple possibilities and multiple fields can help facilitate this. The therapist explores their patient's inner and outer worlds, while maintaining an awareness and connection to their own (Ogden, 1999). Through doing so, they keep the field open to a number of possible meanings and developments.

CONCLUSION

In considering the role of psychological defenses, the move from point-to-point systems, to field theoretical ones, has heralded a shift from considering defenses as intended to keep threatening thoughts and feelings out of awareness, to also including the ways meaning is made. Locating defensive processes as occurring within interpersonal fields highlights the reciprocal process between interpsychic and intrapsychic processes. This has freed psychologists to consider and make sense of a wider variety of psychological phenomena, since working at one area will have an effect on the other and vice versa.

The focus on the holistic field of the therapeutic situation draws attention to the ways defensive processes regulate field dynamics. These include, though are of course not limited to, the experience of closeness and distance between therapist and patient, the establishment of boundaries within the therapeutic space, and also the extent to which fields of meaning can be explored and deepened. More broadly then, as the goals of psychoanalysis have shifted from resolving predetermined complexes to instead looking at what is occurring between analyst and patient, greater emphasis has been placed on the ways defenses foreclose making novel meanings of situations.

Since meaning is generated through movement either within or between fields (Hermans, 2001), there are a variety of ways of trying to generate movement and freeing up otherwise stuck psychological processes. One way is changing the valence of particular boundaries, which keep individual's pulled toward one particular narrative, opening up new possibilities. Deconstructing the historical meaning of a patient's narrative, trying to understand why the field is structured and bounded as it is, accounts for another form of meaning. Similarly moving to other fields, such as shifting perspective or exploring wishes, offers another form of meaning-making. The various ways that meaning can be made speaks to a pragmatic aspect of therapy, which considers effects more than metatheories. In other words, when field dynamics are considered understanding occurs *posteriori*, rather than *a priori*. What matters is not that defenses match up to metatheory, but rather that movement has begun to occur within a field that was previously static.

In this matter, therapy functions as an invitation for dialogue and hopefully movement for therapist and patient. Negotiating the terms of this invitation and determining how it will work is an initial obstacle to beginning treatment. While therapy is ostensibly an invitation where the patient receives help with their suffering, both parties may have different conscious and unconscious ideas and expectations about what the invitation is actually for.

The wonder of the therapeutic process is that once moved from the point-to-point theorizing of the early 20th century, all processes can be understood as potential fields waiting to be explored, deepened, occupied, and experienced. It is this potential for playing within fields and with different perspectives and meanings that helps turn the therapeutic process from one potentially dangerous and scary one to one that can also be freeing and life changing. Playing and playfulness are also important legacies of Roger's work and career. He was, and still is, a tireless explorer of humanity who balanced the seriousness required to treat people's illness with the playfulness needed to help them recover.

NOTES

1. Whereas Lewin used the expression life space to denote the field of the individual.
2. Really an elaboration of $b^t = F(S^t)$ that includes the importance of time (Lewin, 1946/1997).

REFERENCES

Aron, L. (1991). The patient's experience of the analyst's subjectivity. *Psychoanalytic Dialogues, 1,* 29–51.

Aron, L. (2006). Analytic impasse and the third: Clinical implications of intersubjectivity theory. *International Journal of Psychoanalysis, 87,* 349–368.

Bromberg, P. (1998). *Standing in the spaces: Essays on clinical process, trauma, and dissociation.* Hillsdale, NJ: Analytic Press.

Bruner, J. (1990). *Acts of meaning.* Cambridge, MA: Harvard University Press.

Danziger, K. (1994). *Constructing the subject: Historical origins of psychological research.* Cambridge, England: Cambridge University Press.

Freud, S. (1899/1955). *The interpretation of dreams.* New York, NY: Basic Books.

Greenberg, J. (1991). *Oedipus and beyond: A clinical theory.* Cambridge, MA: Harvard University Press.

Greenberg, J. (1995). Psychoanalytic technique and the interactive matrix *Psychoanalytic Quarterly, 64,* 1–22.

Greenberg, J., & Mitchell, S. (1983). *Object relations in psychoanalytic theory.* Cambridge, MA: Harvard University Press.

Harris, A. (2005). *Gender as soft assembly.* Hillsdale, NJ: Analytic Press.

Hermans, H. J. M. (2001). The dialogical self: Towards a theory of personal and cultural positioning. *Culture & Psychology, 7,* 243–281.

Hoffman, I. (1983). The patient as interpreter of the analyst's experience. *Contemporary Psychoanalysis, 19,* 389–422.

Hoffman, I. (1998). *Ritual and spontaneity in the psychoanalytic process: A dialectical-constructivist view.* Hillsdale, NJ: Analytic Press.

Levenson, E. (2013). *The fallacy of understanding and the ambiguity of change.* Hoboken, NJ: Taylor & Francis.

Lewin, K. (1935). *A dynamic theory of personality: Selected papers.* New York, NY: McGraw-Hill.

Lewin, K. (1936). *Principles of topological psychology.* New York, NY: McGraw-Hill.

Lewin, K. (1940/1997). The background of conflict in marriage. In G. W. Lewin (Ed.), *Resolving social conflicts: Selected papers on group dynamics.* Washington, DC: American Psychological Association.

Lewin, K. (1943). Defining the "field at a given time." *Psychological Review, 50*(3), 293–310.

Lewin, K. (1946/1997). Behavior and development as a function of the total situation. In In G. W. Lewin (Ed.), *Resolving social conflicts: Selected papers on group dynamics.* Washington, DC: American Psychological Association.

McWilliams, N. (1994). *Psychoanalytic diagnosis: Understanding personality structure in the clinical process.* New York, NY: Guilford Press.

Mitchell, S. A. (2005). *Influence and autonomy in psychoanalysis.* New York, NY: Routledge.

Neumann, J. (2005). Kurt Lewin at the Tavistock Institute. *Educational Action Research, 13,* 119–136.

Neumann, J. (2013). Kurt Lewin: 'Dynamic Approach Rule.' *The Tavistock Institute.* Retrieved November 24, 2014, from http://www.tavinstitute.org/projects/kurt-lewin-dynamic-approach-rule-2/

Ogden, T. H. (1979). On projective identification. *International Journal of Psychoanalysis, 60,* 357–373.

Ogden, T. H. (1994). The analytic third: Working with intersubjective clinical facts. *International Journal of Psychoanalysis, 75,* 3–19.

Ogden, T. H. (1999). *Reverie and interpretation sensing something human.* London, England: Karnac Books.

Rosenbaum, P. J. (2013). The role of projective identification in constructing the other: Why do westerners want to "liberate" Muslim women? *Culture & Psychology, 19,* 213–224.

Rosenbaum, P. J. (2015). Harry Stack Sullivan and Charles Sanders Peirce: The impact of early pragmatism on interpersonal psychoanalysis. In P. Rosenbaum (Ed.), *Making our ideas clear: Pragmatism and psychoanalysis.* Charlotte, NC: Information Age.

Stern, D. B. (1997). *Unformulated experience: From dissociation to imagination in psychoanalysis (Relational perspective book series).* New York, NY: Routledge.

Stern, D. B. (2013a). Field theory in psychoanalysis, part I: Harry Stack Sullivan and Madeleine and Willy Baranger. *Psychoanalytic Dialogues, 23,* 487–501.

Stern, D. B. (2013b). Field theory in psychoanalysis, Part 2: Bionian field theory and contemporary interpersonal/relational psychoanalysis. *Psychoanalytic Dialogues, 23,* 630–645.

Sullivan, H. (1953). *The interpersonal theory of psychiatry.* New York, NY: Norton.

Wachtel, P. (2008). *Relational theory and the practice of psychotherapy.* New York, NY: Guilford Press.

Wachtel, P. (2014). *Cyclical psychodynamics and the contextual self: The inner world, the intimate world, and the world of culture and society.* New York, NY: Routledge.

Valsiner, J. (2007). *Culture in minds and societies foundations of cultural psychology.* Thousand Oaks, CA: Sage.

SECTION III

THE PHILOSOPHER: WHAT IS THE RIGHT THING TO DO?

CHAPTER 8

ETHICAL AND LEGAL ISSUES IN FAMILY PRACTICE

Roger Bibace
Clark University

Ronald J. Comer
Princeton University

Carolyn E. Cotsonas
Cambridge Health Alliance

When patient and physician come together, they establish a special relationship. This relationship is more profound than a mere contractual agreement in regard to the patient's health. Of course, the patient chooses to entrust his or her health care and well-being to the physician, and the physician, in accepting this arrangement, agrees to perform the required services. The law also imposes on the physician a duty toward the patient to possess and employ reasonable skill and care. But in addition, the physician assumes special ethical responsibilities founded on loyalty, confidentiality, and trust. In legal terms, the physician becomes a fiduciary.

All physicians in all specialties have this special responsibility. So, too, do psychotherapists and lawyers (and others) who act on behalf of their

Particulars and Universals in Clinical and Developmental Psychology, pages 121–132

clients' critical interests. If an individual relies upon the integrity and fidelity of a professional who participates in making important decisions about that individual's life, then this special relationship is mandatory—ethically and legally.

SPECIAL PROBLEMS IN FAMILY PRACTICE

This special relationship ensures that the provider will become involved in finding solutions to the ethical dilemmas which arise in the context of a patient's life. And to the extent that the care-provider's role in serving the consumer is defined broadly rather than narrowly, the ethical dilemmas will be more acutely felt and will be surrounded by ambiguity. The family physician, in particular, is faced with a number of ethical problems that are relatively unique in the field of medicine. These ethical problems that are peculiar to the family physician are the product of the unique goal of family medicine—the goal of treating the whole family. This is a worthwhile goal, but it gives rise to certain inevitable ambiguities and conflicts, and it is from these conflicts that problems emerge.

The key point is that the family is a unit comprised of parts—that is family members. The parts of any organized whole will not always be in harmony. Indeed, in order to change and develop, the parts must frequently be in conflict. Correspondingly, the family is a dynamic whole that is constantly developing and changing, and its parts—the family members—will frequently be in conflict as a part of this developmental process. This necessarily creates a tension for the family physician who embraces the humanistic, person-centered goal of caring for entire families.

The gist of this tension can be summarized in the question that we want to explore: Whose agent are you or for whom are you working? This question comes into sharp focus for the family physician when the family members are in conflict.

Even if the family physician were to stick solely to the "medical model," which focuses on the disease rather than on the person who has a disease (Magraw, 1971), this dilemma would not always be avoidable. For example, a family physician might treat a husband for a venereal disease contracted during an extramarital affair, which is unknown to the wife. On narrow medical grounds alone, the physician and patient must now confront the issue of treatment for his wife.

But the family physician is not solely disease oriented. His (or her) definition of self as a physician takes him deeper into his patients' lives. As McWhinney (1975) writes,

> to such a physician, problems become interesting and important, not only for their own sake, but because they are Mr. Smith's or Mrs. Jones's problem. Very often in such relationships there is not even a very clear distinction between a medical problem and a nonmedical one. The patient defines the problem.

This perspective of one's doctoring role ensures that the family physician will be more readily drawn into issues outside the traditional realm of direct medical treatment. A couple's sexual difficulties, a child's fear of his parent, a husband's jealousy of his wife's attention to their children, a couple's marital discord, and a teenager's alienation from his parents: these are all legitimate foci for the family physician.

Before proceeding, it is worth asking: Why is this important, why is it worthwhile to explore a role such as that of the family physician, which gives rise to these ethical issues?

There seem to be three critical implications for this kind of inquiry. First is the issue of what is the responsibility of a training program, such as a family practice residency, to teach its trainees expectations about themselves. Educational institutions and teachers impart values wittingly or unwittingly. Stephens and Baker in a chapter entitled "The Ethical Dimensions of Behavior" speak about each physician's commitment to some value system when they write:

> The physician cannot escape playing some role in these affairs (philosophical and moral issues of life). He may play the role unwittingly, the victim of his biases, prejudices, and apparent self-interest, or he may play it in a more consciously responsible manner by subjecting his assumptions to critical evaluation, visualizing himself in a historic and social perspective. (Stephens & Baker, 1973)

It is essential that all educators, particularly those in professions that make the life experiences of other people their concern, heed this, and as McWhinney (1975) notes in describing family physicians, the "educators must have in mind a clear conception of the type of person they would like their students to become."

The second implication has to do with the professional's own sense of his or her role and what this means for one's mental and physical health and sense of well-being. Are the expectations one has for oneself vis-a-vis patients or clients realistic and attainable?

The third implication goes to the provider-consumer relationship itself. What can the consumer expect and demand of the family physician, the therapist, or the lawyer? These expectations, whether realistic or unrealistic, will determine the quality of the relationship that will in turn affect the outcome, for better or for worse.

COMPARATIVE ROLES IN FAMILY CONFLICT

The ethical dilemma that confronts the family physician (viz, "whose agent are you") when the family members are in conflict will also confront other family interventionists like lawyers and psychotherapists. The available approaches to resolving these dilemmas are likely to be quite different, however, because of the different functions and institutional settings of these various professionals. These ethical dilemmas are not answerable in terms of specific pieces of information or new "advances" for any of these family interventionists. On the contrary, in many instances advances in scientific knowledge and technology have served to heighten or confuse rather than help resolve these issues. When does life begin? When has death occurred? At what point are we as a society sufficiently endangered by aberrant behavior that we are justified in restraining an individual's liberty? In grappling with these issues, physicians, therapists, and lawyers can give some guidance to each other. They do, after all, (as members of the same society) share values, and (at times) their functions will overlap. However, because the family physician plays a special role in attempting to resolve these issues, he/she is necessarily exposed to a greater level of ambiguity and thereby subjected to greater degrees of anxiety than are the lawyer and psychotherapist when each deals with family problems.

The solutions of the psychotherapist cannot readily be applied to family medicine. This is because the working boundaries of the family physician and the family therapist are significantly different. The family therapist intervenes in the family for a delimited period of time and often during periods of family crises and/or disintegration. The family physician's intervention is ongoing. The family physician, to use McWhinney's term, "stays with" the family through illness, health, and growth (see McWhinney, 1975). This temporal feature creates a tension because the family physician has a past, present, and future with a particular family and its members. A great deal has occurred which defines the physician's role in a family through the physician's eyes and through each family member's eyes. Depending on the definition of that relationship, the dynamic that has created it, and the particular circumstances at times of intrafamily conflict, the family physician may be in an excellent position to help or he may be in a disadvantageous position. If the latter, this may be a good reason for the physician to bring in a second family interventionist, such as a therapist, to work with the family. This would not mean the family physician has failed. On the contrary, it indicates that he has been flexible enough to perceive that the crisis in this family at this particular time may necessitate the attention of both a family physician and a therapist.

This may be illustrated with an example. Assume that a family physician has been caring for various members of a certain family for a few years.

Assume also that the members the physician has most often seen have been the mother and two children. The father has been to this physician only once during a 3-year period. The couple is having marital difficulties and the wife has starred to articulate this to the family physician. Now it may be entirely possible and within the scope of his skills for the physician to counsel the couple. But it is also possible that the physician's closer relationship to the wife and children will be perceived by the husband as a source of bias, whether this is true or not. In this case, referral to a therapist may be the most appropriate help for this couple. A positive byproduct of this may be that the physician's position in the husband's eyes will remain neutral enough so that the husband can be encouraged to seek out the health care that he needs.

The law's approach to intrafamily conflict is not only delimited in time, but for the most part confined to a particular process of resolution—the adversarial process. This is not to say that the family lawyer escapes ethical dilemmas. But, again, the particular role definition of the lawyer in doing his job is tied to a legal system, which at least reduces the ambiguities. It is usually the case that if a lawyer is consulted for a particular intrafamily conflict, the law offers solutions confined to breakdown situations. Or, if the family is not this far toward disintegration and the lawyer pursues a resolution through collaboration among the conflicting members, then the lawyer cannot move back into a more traditional adversary role with that particular family. Ford, director of the Harvard Family Law Project, noted this when he observed the "persistent conflict that occurs between the adversary system—the mode within which lawyers traditionally operate—and the more collaborative model of dispute resolution which physicians and mental health personnel usually employ" (Ford, 1973). Here is a concrete example of this. Assume that an attorney has functioned as the family lawyer for the family in the last example. The lawyer over a few years has handled the family's disagreement with a landlord, has helped them start a small business, and has handled their purchase of a home. As a result, many of the details of this family's life are known to the lawyer. Assume also that the couple's marital discord leads to a decision to divorce and there is even disagreement about custody of the children. Assume further that they decide to seek the advice of their lawyer. Their lawyer may at that point insist on representing only one member of the couple. Or if the lawyer does try to help the couple resolve their dispute, he cannot ethically represent either in a custody dispute in court because in this adversarial context each side must make out the best case possible and convince the court that the opponent is wrong. If this system is to work, each side must, at least theoretically, start from a position of equal strength. In the case where the lawyer functioned as mediator, this balance would be disrupted if the lawyer then argued for one of the parties.

The adversarial system, then, defines for the lawyer a number of significant role parameters, and in doing so reduces ambiguity for the lawyer. Another fact about this system is that, particularly in the family law field, the role of law is often to resolve issues that have gotten past the point of promoting family function (e.g., divorce, child abuse, custody), or in the constitutional area to protect the family from unreasonable interference by society.

The authors do not suggest that the adversarial system is inferior to the more collaborative one of the therapist and the family physician. Indeed, in some situations, particularly where personal liberty and assertion of power are at stake, the adversarial system is one of the best safeguards available. As Judge David Bazelon (1974) has argued in an article entitled, "The Perils of Wizardry," and in a follow-up letter, the advances brought on by brain and behavior modification substantially affect and threaten human rights. In the face of this, the adversarial system forces the judgment of experts out into the open in order to "challenge their validity or to assess their weight."

The summary point then is that our legal system, based as it is on an adversarial model, works relatively well when it is called upon to protect families or individuals from unwarranted intrusions by society. This is demonstrated by the contraception and abortion cases which emphasize the constitutional right of privacy of the couple and the individual. The law is a less helpful and precise system when it moves deeper into family functioning itself. For this reason, it tries to stay out of the conduct of family life until it is forced into it in order to protect the members of the family from only the most serious forms of intrafamily conflict, such as divorce and child abuse.

Unlike the family therapist or lawyer, the family physician is involved in a more fluid and changing family dynamic over time. McWhinney (1975) suggests that "whenever the situation requires it, he can change his focus from individual to family and back again." In many respects the family physician has been left to his own resources to conceptualize and resolve how this relationship is to be carried out and how the ethical ambiguity arising from it is to be addressed. Ambiguity is an uncomfortable state of affairs for any person, but particularly for a physician. He is trained to clarify, resolve, and make decisions; and ambiguity is thought to retard this process. As a result, some physicians, irrespective of specialty, have tended to try to minimize the inherent ambiguity in these situations for themselves by employing either of two approaches. One approach may be labeled the "invalid generalization." Here, the physician (or other expert) has a rule that he applies to all relevant situations, irrespective of the specific elements involved in each situation. For example, the physician may always side with the parents' wishes in areas of abortion or he may always give exclusive consideration to the needs of the woman in periods of pregnancy and childbirth.

This approach certainly removes the discomfort and uncertainty of ethical conflicts, but it does so by ignoring the conflict, rather than by resolving it. The justification for this invalid generalization, which glosses over the specifics of the case, is this individual's past experience. That is, the physician's (expert's) past experience is codified so as to avoid the specifics of a case and its context by relying on an oversimplified rule.

The second approach may be labeled the "inadequate rule." Here, the physician tries to resolve the issue based on the specific merits of the situation at hand. This approach suffers from being too vague and unsystematic. In these instances, the expert acknowledges that one cannot make some generalizations without knowing the particulars about the people and contexts involved. So while the expert recognizes individual differences, he is unable to go beyond an *intuitive* attempt to be responsive to such differences. Such an approach appears to address itself to the situation at hand by applying the rule that all elements will be weighed; but because it defines no avenues or boundaries for this process of evaluation, it in fact provides no systematic tool for guidance at all.

THE FAMILY PHYSICIAN'S APPROACH

How, then, should the physician approach these difficult issues? The authors do not wish to develop specific solutions to specific dilemmas here, but rather to try to outline an organizational framework in which to examine these dilemmas and to consider their implications. The framework the authors have in mind centers around the family life cycle.

As noted previously, the family may be looked at as a developing organism. Theorists who rely on a developmental conception of life have argued that an organism develops by continuously undergoing changes in its structure and processes throughout its life, changes that occur when the organism is confronted by new problems, which it cannot handle with its present structure. The new problems place the organism in a state of disequilibrium, and it is forced to change its structure and tools of operation in order to restore equilibrium to its system. By this view, conflict and change are not only an inevitable, but also an essential pan of development.

Similarly, the family's development will be marked by changes in its structure. These changes are most visible when they take the form of major discontinuities or transitions in the life cycle of the family. It is at such points of discontinuity or transition that familial conflict is most likely to emerge. Therefore, it is not fruitful to deal with this or that ethical dilemma on a piecemeal basis. Rather, a parallelism is assumed between ethical issues on the one hand and the different phases of the life cycle on the other. Therefore, it is at these points of discontinuity in the family life cycle that major ethical issues will confront the family physician when he is asked—explicitly or implicitly—to take a side. This idea that transitions in the life cycle of the family will lead to the involvement of the family physician, is supported by numerous studies that have suggested that relatively major changes or stresses do indeed lead to illness onset (Rahe, 1968; Wyler, Masuda, & Holmes, 1971). Even if such transitions do not lead to some form of illness, the family physician may be drawn into these discontinuities because the family directly solicits the physician's help in dealing with its problem. Either way, it is at such points that the goal of treating all of the family members will be most taxing for the family physician.

It may be useful to think of the discontinuities that a family faces in the course of its life cycle as being of two types. First, there are those discontinuities that are common to the development of most families, discontinuities that are "normative" for a culture. For example, pregnancy and childbirth comprise a nonnative transition that may give rise to family tension and conflict. Another example is the parent-child conflicts that may surface when the child first enters school.

The second type of discontinuity in the life cycle of the family involves discontinuities that are relatively "idiosyncratic" to a family. These represent transitions that need not necessarily occur in the family's development, but which play critical roles when they do occur. They include such events as major illness of a family member, marital discord or divorce, and teenage pregnancy.

The events of teenage pregnancy and abortion exemplify the ethical dilemmas that confront the family physician at times of idiosyncratic discontinuity. When a teenage daughter becomes pregnant, the concerns and needs of each of the family members may vary significantly. The dilemma for the family physician is a difficult one. Whose need does the physician address when the family approaches him? Who is his patient? The following vignette, which was presented to family practice residents, illustrates the potential confusion:

> Doctor Jones has been the Smith's family physician for 7 years. All members of the family—wife, husband, and two daughters—have seen Doctor Jones during the 7 years for a variety of reasons. The family has seemed to be a fairly stable and happy one, although the oldest daughter, Janet, mentioned recently that she and her parents, especially her father, were talking less with each other. This daughter recently came to Doctor Jones on her own, believing she was pregnant. Doctor Jones confirmed this. Janet told her parents about her condition and said she planned to have and raise the baby. She also said she did not want to involve the baby's father in her decision. At the same time, she hinted that she would do what Doctor Jones advised her to do. During a subsequent appointment, Mrs. Smith asked that Doctor Jones talk Janet into having an abortion and said that, if necessary, she would get a court order

requiring Janet to have the abortion. In the meantime, Mr. Smith indicated that he no longer wanted Janet to live at home and refused to speak with her after learning of her pregnancy.

Some of the ethical questions that confront the physician in this situation are: (a) Whose agent is the physician: the mother's, the father's, the daughter's, the fetus's, the family's? (b) What are the boundaries of the physician's goals? Is his goal limited to resolving the abortion issue, or does it extend to such things as reuniting the father and daughter? (c) How is the physician to use his power—the power exemplified in Janet's hint that she would do what the physician told her to do? (d) What role does the physician's own value system play in this intervention? and (e) How does he resolve these and similar questions?

Thus, both normative and idiosyncratic discontinuities in the life cycle of the family will likely generate conflicts among family members, and may in turn generate ethical conflicts for the family physician. He/she will be drawn into such conflicts when the discontinuities lead to somatic difficulties or when the patient decides that the physician can be helpful in solving the problem itself.

What role or roles, then, might the physician play in dealing with the problems that emerge from family transitions? One role that the physician may be called upon to assume, particularly in normative discontinuities, is the role of the standard-bearer, the personal conduit by which societal norms are conveyed. Precisely because of his position as an observer of a wide variety of human behavior, the family physician is able to speak authoritatively on the norms or trends of our culture. He may, for example, be viewed as an expert on the appropriateness of a newborn baby's sleeping in the parents' bedroom. The role of the standard-bearer is one of offering information that others may not have access to, and the role is a legitimate one, if indeed it is the role that the patient is asking of the physician.

Another role that the family physician may be called upon to assume is the role of catalyst. This role may emerge especially in idiosyncratic discontinuities where there are, by definition, few normative elements to guide the physician, and thus the family physician's role centers not around his informational expertise, but rather around his expertise in the "process" of solving problems and making decisions. The question that confronts the physician is, "How can I best solve this family's problem in which there are not clear guidelines and in which there are conflicting interests among the family members?" The authors suggest that the best answer may be that the problem is not the physician's to resolve, but rather his to "help" resolve.

Thus, because there are no clear normative guidelines and because the needs of the patients conflict in this situation, the family physician's most appropriate role will be to help the family resolve its own problems and arrive at its own decisions. In this role, the physician's job is to teach the family members (a) how to use their own resources, (b) how to resolve their conflicting needs, and (c) how to arrive at their own decisions.

The idea that the physician can best solve his ethical dilemma and most appropriately resolve the family's problems by being a catalyst to the family's utilization of their own skills and by being a teacher in the development of such skills is likely to be an uncomfortable notion both for him and for the family members. The physician has been traditionally trained to weigh the elements which confront him, to reach a decision, and to impart this judgment with an air of certainty and authority. Ambiguity or indecision is viewed by many physicians as weakness on their part. Similarly, this role of catalyst may be resisted by patients because of their view of the physician as an expert sage, a person who should know the answer. It is also possible that some patients may not want to assume responsibility for their decisions. Some argue that these complementary roles (expert/layman) are the sole basis of the physician-patient relationship.

Though the focus here is on the physician, it should be noted that this is a description of the societal interactions prescribed for a layman interacting with an expert. These patterns have commonly been accepted until the recent rise of consumerism and the attendant revisions as to what relationship should hold between expert and layman. It is clear that these days there are many movements that are striving for greater mutuality, for a more egalitarian relationship between any expert and the layman.

In contrast to accepting this complementarity of traditional patient-physician roles, it is obvious that the very pressures that are being brought upon the physician to make a decision to resolve a conflict can themselves serve as a useful starting point in facilitating the physician's role as catalyst or teacher. That is, the physician may make the family members aware of the difficult position he is in, of the conflicting pressures that are being put on him, and of the incompatibilities inherent in the situation. Through this awareness the physician may then play a facilitative role in teaching the family how to make a decision. That is, the physician may share with the family the technique of decision making in which he has been trained so extensively. Indeed, in this approach, the family physician is helping the family develop skills that it can employ beyond their immediate situation.

This idea represents a key shift in the role of the physician. The physician moves from the status of expert and sage to teacher and catalyst; from *the* authority to *a* family resource. It probably also represents a shift in the kind of relationship that is fostered, away from the more traditional authority-centered relationship to one of greater mutuality. For as the focus of medicine is broadened, as the questions become more ambiguous and more difficult, and as the answers become less obvious and more dependent on perspective, it is important that all resources be employed. And the most important resource from both the ethical and practical viewpoint, is the patient. McWhinney (1975) points out that the physician may best let the patient "define the problem." It might be added that in this important realm, it may very well be best to allow the patient to "define the solution." These points about the ways in which the family physician can best deal with the ambiguity that emerges during discontinuities in the family life cycle raise a more general point, namely, the question of medicine's attitude toward ambiguity.

As mentioned earlier, ambiguity is a particularly uncomfortable state of affairs for a physician. However, ambiguity need not solely be construed as a limiting force. Indeed, it may push the physician to deal more effectively with various problems that confront him by challenging him to broaden his range of resources. Specifically, it may lead the physician to employ a key resource that has so often been overlooked: the patient himself or herself.

The point is that ambiguity can be viewed as a positive ally. Nowhere is this more apparent than in the cases in which ethical ambiguity leads the physician to actively incorporate the patient into the decision-making process. As Hart points out,

> It is essential that students should learn not only that each individual doctor has limitations which he should know, but that this is true also of the whole body of medical knowledge, with huge areas of imprecision and thinly formed guesswork. (Hart, 1973)

Professional roles have been imposed, wittingly or unwittingly, on patients and clients; as Balint (1957) puts it, the patient himself organizes his problems into an illness comprehensible in medical terms, although not necessarily comprehensible in terms that will lead to a useful solution.

Professional care providers must learn to reorganize their approach in order to be able to help sort out complex problems with their patients, recognizing that sometimes a presenting "legal" problem might more adaptively be construed as a behavioral problem, or that a "medical" problem might more adaptively be construed as a legal one, and so forth. In this task, the providers must look across disciplinary lines for their mutual education. And the ambiguity of human problems must not be looked upon as a threat to competence, but rather as an avenue for rethinking approaches with the most important ally in this process the patient himself or herself.

ACKNOWLEDGMENT

Originally published as: Bibace, R., Comer, R., & Cotsonas, C. E. (1978). Ethical and legal issues in family practice. *Journal of Family Practice, 7*(5),

The authors wish to acknowledge the encouragement and intellectual stimulation of John J. Frey, MD, and Richard F. Walton, MD. In addition, the authors wish to acknowledge Steven Nisenbaum, lawyer and currently a doctoral student in clinical psychology, who critically reviewed the paper and made a number of helpful suggestions.

REFERENCES

Balint, M. (1957). *The doctor, his patient and the illness.* New York, NY: International Universities Press.

Bazelon, D. L. (1974). The perils of wizardry. *American Journal of Psychiatry, 131,* 1317–1322.

Ford, M. de G. (1973). New directions in neighborhood law practice. *Harvard Medical Alumni Bulletin, 47*(5), 38.

Hart, J. T. (1973). Relation of primary care to undergraduate education. *Lancet, 302*(7832) 778–781.

Magraw, R. (1971). Medical education and health services: Implications for family medicine. *New England Journal of Medicine, 285,* 1407–1413.

McWhinney, I. R. (1975). Family medicine in perspective. *New England Journal of Medicine, 293,* 176–179.

Rahe, R. H. (1968). Life-change measurement as a predictor of illness. *Proceedings of the Royal Society of Medicine, 61*(11, Part 1), 1124–1126.

Stephens, G. G., & Baker, S. (1973). The ethical dimensions of behavior. In H. Conn, R. Rakel, & T. Johnson (Eds.), *Family Practice* (p. 220). Philadelphia, PA: Saunders.

Wyler, A. R., Masuda, M., & Holmes, T. H. (1971). Magnitude of life events and seriousness of illness. *Psychosomatic Medicine, 33,* 115–122.

CHAPTER 9

UNIVERSAL PRINCIPLES? WHAT IS THE RIGHT THING TO DO AND WHY?

The Influence of Culturally Imprinted Moral Values on Medical Students' and Physicians' Decision-Making

Alina Kriebel
Osnabrück University

Saskia Celina Stöckigt
University of Hamburg

Jehovah's Witnesses form a denomination of Christianity. While most non-believers welcome blood transfusions in life-threatening situations, Witnesses strictly refuse to receive blood transfusions, as they consider this a sin. Under extreme circumstances, withholding blood from a patient can even lead to their death. Thus if a clinician obeys their wish, they might controvert medicine's goals to preserve and promote a patient's life and health.

Particulars and Universals in Clinical and Developmental Psychology, pages 133–166

The dilemma the physician finds himself in dangles between according the patient the right to make decisions for himself or herself and, on the other hand, knowing that further surgery would prolong their life, maintaining their health. Two obligations clash: respect for the patient's right of self-determination and the duty to promote his well-being from an objective medical point of view. We call such an ethically critical situation with two conflicting moral values a "medical dilemma." This is, of course, only one example out of the endless pool of all possible medical dilemmas.

How can people view what is right and what is wrong in such strikingly different ways? One possible explanation is that they differ in values, beliefs, practices, and customs that influence their ways of meaning-making and, most of the time, those of the specific group they belong to (Heine, 2012). With this, we arrive at one of the many possible definitions of culture (For a critical discussion of "culture" and possible definitions see, e.g., Jahoda, 2012, or Valsiner, 2012). In cultural psychology, we study how the person, i.e., inside-the-head cognitions and emotions as well as behavior, is shaped by cultural content, such as social opportunities and public representations (Morling & Lamoreaux, 2008). Thus, cultural differences reside where person and environment intersect; they constitute each other. The other concept that will help us answer the question posed in the beginning of this paragraph is morality. Morality denotes interpersonal actions in which differing points of view, interests, and needs have to be taken into consideration. Justice is its core principle, but taking responsibility for others and benevolence are also key features. What we try to show is that individuals' moral values and their culture are closely connected.

This chapter explores how moral reasoning and perceptions of what ought to be right can both differ between countries (that offer a particular cultural framework for people to develop in) and also be quite similar in, yet, another way. Whereas some decisions a clinician makes seem to be universally recognized as the right course of action, the reasoning behind such choices can vary considerably from culture to culture. The aim of the study that will be described in this chapter was to see whether there are differences between the moral orientations of American and German medical students and physicians. Jensen (2008) points out that "culture is not synonymous with country or ethnicity, but rather describes communities whose members share key beliefs and behaviors" (p. 290). Indeed, there can be numerous variations within the two geographically differing nations (e.g., religion or ethnic background). People in one country do not only hold one uniform view. While it should be noted that culture is not synonymous with country, it must be recognized that the specific national circumstances, i.e., the cultural messages people are exposed to, such as the prevailing legal or educational systems, certain cultural products embodied in the media, and the specific norms and customs that are common where individuals reside, do preposition different contexts for people to develop in and definitely give rise to differing moral developments, as will be shown below.

In today's world, national borders are easily crossed. With facilitation of traveling comes an amplification of crossing cultural boundaries and the chance to experience and live in different cultures. Physicians who cross cultural boundaries bring with them their culture-specific decision-making characteristics and have to be aware of their new practice environment with its own customs. "[Y]ou can't just plop the practices of one culture into another and expect them to take root" (Markus & Conner, 2013, p. 13). Even if health professionals do not choose to cross borders, the physician-patient encounter often brings together individuals with differing cultural backgrounds, who might also have a culture-specific understanding of morally appropriate practices (see example given above). In order to avoid conflict, it is important to understand differing culture-dependent perspectives.

There is one problem that arises when entering such cross-cultural encounters or conducting culturally comparative research: *ethnocentrism*, meaning that one judges another culture solely by the values and standards of one's own culture. Given the fact that it is easy to be ethnocentric, it is challenging and maybe impossible to see different value orientations and not judge them (Zaharna, 2000). We tend to assume that practices consistent with our own moral standards, which have been acquired through socialization, are somewhat better than those of others (Heine, 2012). We are apt to view ourselves as the standard human, practicing the proper way of life; all others are just doing it wrong. Not judging moral orientations that differ from our own is a difficult barrier to overcome; becoming aware of the existence of diversity, however, and being able to reflect upon such variation, is not impossible. Overcoming "culture-blindness" (Markus & Conner, 2013), this chapter tries to examine the cultural differences from a neutral perspective, as much as this is possible; we do not rank groups along the dimension of what is considered to be right or good. How could we even agree on a leveling board? What variable would we choose in measuring a morally adequate decision? In the ethical area, there are no valid absolutes or universals; from an objective point of view, there is no evidence that one solution to a medical dilemma should be judged as superior or inferior to another solution (Gbadegesin, 2009). The focus of this chapter is simply to expand theoretical understandings of morality in medicine. We hope that we will offer valuable clues to the challenges that might occur in a world of globalized medicine and encourage research in the cross-cultural field of bioethics.

MORALITY IN MEDICINE: DOES IT MATTER?

> Like most construction projects, the science of medicine quickly rose from its base. (Noller & Bibace, 2005, pp. 101)

> The clinician practicing in the early twenty-first century is able to care for the dozens of patients that appear every day, better than at any time in the past. More is known about more diseases, and more and better treatments are available. There are multiple sources of new information. There are better laboratories, less invasive surgical instruments, and more effective drugs. Never have physicians had it so good. (Noller & Bibace, 2005, p. 108)

And yet, never have physicians had it so hard! In recent years, numerous revolutionary medical inventions, such as dialysis machines, artificial pacemakers, and in vitro fertilization, have evoked various discussions about ethics in medical professions and have led to an increased interest in ethical issues in medicine (Kuhse & Singer, 2009). Diverse fields of application have developed within the area of medical ethics, which take different approaches to ethical issues in medical situations. Already in the 1970s, the critical and reflective discipline of bioethics emerged, which main concerns include the doctor-patient-relationship.

> Clinicians must constantly deal with the uniqueness of each particular patient. No person is exactly like any other, and each must be cared for as an individual. (Noller & Bibace, 2005, p. 99)

> [T]here is a real limit to the usefulness on a particular (patient) level to the information in even the very best quality paper.... The universal truth ... does not apply to each particular patient. (Noller & Bibace, 2005, p. 103)

Noller and Bibace (2005) point out that delivering health care is more than just treating a condition; the practice of medicine is also highly influenced by ethical and moral considerations. Physicians need to grapple with ethical dilemmas on an almost daily basis. Their role does not only center on their informational expertise in treating a patient's disease, but they also need to be capable of dealing with a wide range of moral problems. Issues such as abortion, euthanasia, artificial maintenance of life, etc., arise regularly in the contemporary physician's career (Goldman & Arbuthnot, 1979).

> The interpersonal exchanges between the patient and the physician are key to the success or failure of the encounter.... The clinician is the focal point for the interaction between the universal (medical science) and the particular (the individual patient) in medicine. It is only through a mutually trusting doctor-patient relationship that the best practice of medicine occurs. (Noller & Bibace, 2005, p. 107)

The physician–patient relationship is one of a bidirectional interexchange (Self & Baldwin, 1994). On the one side, the patient trusts his or her practitioner and is involved in decisions. The physician, on the other side, agrees to perform to the best of his or her abilities. In a patient's life, events may occur that lead the practitioner to find him or herself in a moral dilemma outside the scope of regular medical treatment, where clear guidelines may be simply nonexistent (Bibace, Comer, & Cotsonas, 1978). As there are no clear-cut answers as to what is expected by the physician in these conflicting situations, what is regarded as the morally right or wrong decision is determined by the doctor's values, which Hofstede (1989) defines as "a tendency to prefer certain states of affairs over others" (p. 19). Smith (2012) argues that doing the right thing in such situations is a judgment made by each individual.

The interest in the ethical aspects of medicine is also reflected by the recent effort to include bioethics as part of the curricula in medical schools (Self & Davenport, 1996).

> Most individuals apply to medical school because they have a genuine desire to help others. They are surprised to find that there is almost no mention of an actual living, breathing human during the first two years.... They eat and sleep the formulas for bizarre biochemical reactions; they puzzle the meaning of infinitesimally small changes in the respiratory gases of rabbits; they learn the names of organs and parts of organs and parts of the parts of organs. (Noller & Bibace, 2005, p. 100)

> "F]ar too much time in medical school is spent on curing and far too little on caring" (Noller & Bibace, 2005, p. 104).

In the past, students were expected to gain ethical background through implicit learning such as observation. Nowadays, they take ethics courses to gain knowledge explicitly. By taking ethics courses, medical students supposedly benefit from beginning to learn how to deal with the difficult moral questions that will arise in their occupation as a physician. As opposed to earlier practices, in which students were dependent on the role models they were exposed to, modern formal teaching encourages critical thinking and independent reflection on certain moral topics such as patient autonomy, informed consent, confidentiality, and end-of-life decisions. Already complicated, these issues take on added complexity when the clinician and their patient have a different cultural background.

CROSS-CULTURAL DIFFERENCES: ARE MORAL VALUES UNIVERSAL?

Values and moral concerns are accorded different priorities in different cultures (Snarey, 1985). Consequently, moral reasoning in medical contexts is not culture-free. Even if people completely agree on the facts in a given situation, they can still differ in their attitudes towards these facts

(Frenkel-Brunswik, 1974). Cultural variation leads to differing values one gives to a moral consideration, relative to competing concerns (Miller, 2006): "Culture frames moral development" (Wainryb, 2006, p. 211).

Psychology has long ignored culture as an influence on behavior as it relates to health care and just recently started taking it into account. Alluding to the individualism–collectivism dichotomy (Hofstede, 2001), a myriad of research has been done on cross-cultural differences in moral orientations between Western and Eastern societies (e.g., Dien, 1982; Ge & Thomas, 2008; Jhala & Jhala, 2012; Ma & Cheung, 1996; Ruhnke et al., 2000). Researchers often point out that individualistic Western societies value rights of self-determination, personal values, and individual freedom; whereas collectivistic Eastern societies put emphasis on interdependence, care, and harmony, and ultimately focus more on the social framework of decision-making. Grol-Prokopcyzk (2013), for example, analyzed differences and similarities between American and Thai doctors by looking at their writings on medical ethics. The study shows that physicians across both cultures overlap in vocabulary, points of reference, and topics of interest, but differ greatly in their styles of moral reasoning. Reflecting Hofstede's (2001) individualism-collectivism dimension, American doctors were said to focus on the individual's rights, interest, and well-being in their rationale; whereas Thai doctors included role-based duties and values like national identity and interest, family, and religious beliefs—virtues aimed at collectivity.

"East and West. Independence and interdependence. These are, of course, messy categories" (Markus & Conner, 2013, p. 12). Undoubtedly, Western and Eastern societies differ significantly. However, there is also considerable cultural pluralism within Western and Eastern societies (Gbadegesin, 2009). A male, middle-class American of European descent sure is different from a female, working-class American of Asian descent. Nevertheless, nations are often used as rough indicators for different cultures. In this chapter, we present a study illuminating differences within the "wide Western world" by comparing two Western countries: Germany and the United States. The comparative research that will be illustrated in this paper has its legitimacy due to the specific circumstances of the two countries, like the prevailing legal or educational systems.

A POSSIBLE FRAMEWORK: KOHLBERG'S ORIENTATIONS

Moral judgment has been examined in a great number of studies throughout the last few decades (e.g., Piaget, 1932; Kohlberg, 1969, 1976; Self & Baldwin, 1994; Grol-Prokopcyzk, 2013). The best-known and probably most influential study on development of moral judgment is Kohlberg's work on moral stages, often referred to as the cognitive-developmental approach

(1969). He assumed that gains in cognitive competence as well as an increase in role-taking opportunities in social experiences contribute to going through three levels of moral development. Each of these levels contains two stages, of which the second stage comprises a more socially-oriented perspective than the first (Kohlberg, 1976). Table 9.1 gives a brief overview of Kohlberg's levels and stages of morality and what factors account for moral behavior (for more information see Kohlberg, 1969).

Kohlberg (1976) postulated that within each stage of moral development, four moral orientations, namely the normative, the utilitarian, the justice, and the perfectionistic orientation, can be differentiated. Each of them represents a decisional strategy, which emphasizes one of four universal elements that appear in each social situation, i.e., every social encounter contains normative, utilitarian, justice, and perfectionistic factors. They may be more or less prominent and influential, but they all determine each social situation. The normative orientation focuses on social and moral order, rules, and roles. A person arguing on this orientation will justify their moral decision based on what they are allowed to do, what duty or right they possess. The utilitarian orientation emphasizes consequences of action and decision-making for oneself or others. The justice orientation accentuates equality, liberty, reciprocity, relations, and contracts between people as most important aspects for making and explaining one's decision; one takes into account the fairness of an outcome for all parties affected by the decision. The perfectionistic or ideal self-orientation focuses on the individual's conscience and an image of the good self, no matter if others approve or disapprove of it. A perfectionistic reasoning individual tries to uphold their

TABLE 9.1 Levels and Stages of Kohlberg's Moral Development (Rest, 1994)

Level	Stage	Why Do We Behave Morally?
Preconventional	1	Influencing factors: obedience and punishment Do what you're told!
	2	Influencing factors: individualism and instrumental purpose Let's make a deal!
Conventional	3	Influencing factors: interpersonal relationships Be considerate, nice and kind: you'll make friends!
	4	Influencing factors: authority and society Everyone in society is obligated to and protected by the law!
Postconventional	5	Influencing factors: social contracts You are obligated by the arrangements that are agreed to by due process procedures!
	6	Influencing factors: universal principles Morality is defined by how rational and impartial people would ideally organize cooperation!

TABLE 9.2 Kohlberg's Moral Orientations and Their Focus of Reasoning

	Normative	Utilitarian	Justice	Perfectionistic
Focus of Moral Reasoning	law, order, social rules, and roles	individual and group consequences	equity, liberty, relations, and contracts	individual's conscience, self-respect, and ideal character

self-respect, serving their ideal character (Jancovic, 1979). All moral orientations represent structured wholes, i.e., underlying thought forms, which are applied consistently in the course of development through Kohlberg's stages of moral judgment (Kohlberg, 1976). A person may use one or all of the above moral orientations. This makes them hierarchically equal; no moral orientation is superior to another. For an overview see Table 9.2.

KOHLBERG'S MORAL ORIENTATIONS IN MEDICINE

Partly, Kohlberg's moral orientations are also represented in Beauchamp and Childress's four principles of medicine: autonomy, beneficence, nonmaleficence, and justice (Beauchamp & Childress, 1979/2009). The first two, beneficence and nonmaleficence, are consequentialist principles, i.e., whether an action is right or wrong is determined by its consequences. Whereas nonmaleficence points at not harming a patient, beneficence means benefiting the patient in terms of the best outcome of a treatment. Glannon (2005) notes that, "Utilitarianism is the most well-known form of consequentialism" (p. 9), which can be classified as either act- or rule-consequentialism, or act- or rule-utilitarianism. Rule-consequentialism focuses on general rules that are applicable to specific situations and is therefore comparable to the normative moral orientation suggested by Kohlberg (1976). Act-consequentialism defines an action as "morally right" when its consequences are better than the ones of alternatives. Hence, its definition is similar to the one of the utilitarian moral orientation, which also focuses on an action's consequences. Thus, beneficence and nonmaleficence as consequentialist principles are both represented in Kohlberg's normative and utilitarian orientation. Both autonomy and justice can be attributed to the justice moral orientation as they emphasize human values, duties, and rights. The perfectionist moral orientation does not appear in Beauchamp and Childress's (1979/2009) principles of medical ethics. Nonetheless, it has proven to be a valuable category of moral development and might be useful to classify moral judgment and argumentation in medical ethics.

KOHLBERG AND CULTURE

In terms of morality in different cultures, Kohlberg strongly advanced a view of cultural universality in the sequence of his six postulated developmental stages that increase complexity. He validated this position based on his assumption that the same dilemmas have to be faced in all societies and that therefore, all cultural groups had to develop similar value systems. Kohlberg also believed that more traditional cultural groups would not attain higher moral stages due to their lack of certain social experiences (Edwards, 1982). He interpreted cultural differences as evidence that certain environments are more stimulating and, thus, promote cognitive growth better than others. Consequently, he thought of his findings as fully compatible with his theory. Despite Kohlberg's attention to cultural issues, he still rejected the idea of significant cross-cultural variation in moral outlooks (Miller, 2007).

In fact, Kohlberg's hierarchy has been substantiated cross-culturally to a certain point. From a review of 45 studies in 27 countries, Snarey (1985) inferred that the moral Stages 1 to 4 can be regarded as universal. Research has shown that, whereas stage progression at the lower levels seems to be universal, there are certain national differences in the rate and terminus of moral development. Reasoning on stages higher than Stage 4 is limited mostly to individualistic middle- and upper-class individuals residing in urban and industrialized areas. They develop through lower stages at a faster pace and are more likely to achieve higher stages than individuals from traditional folk societies (Dien, 1982).

However, people from varying cultural backgrounds find themselves in different environments, and hence adapt in a different way. As opposed to Kohlberg's belief, social systems do differ and therefore require differing problem-solving modes. One cannot say that one stage is better than another; it is all dependent on the group and their particular contexts (Edwards, 1982). Edwards (1982) summarizes that, "[f]or any society, there may be a stage of moral judgment that best corresponds to the principles of social organization, forms of social interaction, and processes of conflict resolution that underlie it" (pp. 276–277).

What had been disregarded to this point were the qualitative differences in individuals' responses that have been classified as being on the same stage (Dien, 1982). The opinions and feelings of people on the same moral stage can differ dramatically. Not only can reasoning on the same moral stage support either side of the action course, two people may arrive at the same decision in ethical problems, but for differing reasons, which reflect different values (Cotsonas, Bibace, & Lang 1979). On the other hand, they might also use similar strategies of reasoning about their choices but end up deciding differently. A stage represents a way of thinking rather than a specific attitude (Jancovic, 1979). Snarey (1985) argued that even though stage progression can be viewed as somehow universal, there are culturally defined patterns in the choice between and the deliberation about the two competing issues presented in a dilemma. He believed that there was cultural variation in the stress placed on a particular value. Using Kohlberg's moral orientations can serve as a tool to assess such values as they can be applied to all stages of moral development. Jancovic (1979) argues that the particular moral orientation one uses as a basis for one's mode of reasoning is not only determined by one's cognitive maturation, but also by the specific situation to which the person is responding, and individual variables. But how can we measure what orientations a person utilizes? And what environmental circumstances might call for a specific orientation? Our study attempts to identify similarities and differences in moral reasoning between German and American medical students as well as physicians.

CONFRONTING MEDICAL STUDENTS AND PHYSICIANS WITH DILEMMAS

In order to fully understand the moral judgment component of moral behavior, it is necessary to closely look at one's responses to ethical medical dilemmas. Moral judgment is an important component in the process of decision-making (Rest, 1994). Moral action, however, is not only dependent on one's reasoning skills, but also people's motivation, how much weight they give to morality in comparison to other interests and values, their overall moral character (Rest, 1994), and other different contextual conditions (Jancovic, 1979). The present research looks at students' and physicians' responses to medical dilemmas and their decision making. This paragraph provides a detailed description of the research samples and illustrates the measurement instruments. The collected data was statistically analyzed with the statistics program IBM SPSS Statistics 20.

SAMPLES

Participants in the first sample were medical students from German universities as well as American medical schools. Twenty-one American medical students provided valid data. Two participants were eliminated as they did not provide complete responses. Since the original German sample of 93 students was significantly larger than the American one, it got parallelized with the American sample. Sex and age were aligned. In each sample there were 8 male subjects, accounting for 38% of the overall sample, and 13 females, accounting for 62%. The age in the American sample ranged from 21 to 35 years, with a mean of 26 years ($M = 25.71$, $SD = 3.84$). The average age of the German sample was also 26 years ($M = 25.52$, $SD = 3.6$), including participants from 21 to 36 years of age. The execution of a paired samples t-test confirmed the correct selection of German participants with no significant differences between the German and the American group [$t(20) = 1.16$, $p = .26$, $d = 0.25$]. Even though ages were aligned, over 85% ($N = 18$) of the German medical students were already in their third year of studies ($M = 4$, $SD = 1.64$), whereas with a percentage of 57% ($N = 12$), most American medical students were still in their first year at the time of data collection ($M = 1.72$, $SD = 1.18$). This is due to the differing school systems in the United States and in Germany. In the United States, a college degree is a prerequisite to entering medical school in all but the most unique of situations. This explains why so many of the participants were still in their first school year and also accounts for the 18 of 21 medical students who already had a diploma. Since American students have very strong backgrounds in science upon entering their training, as some medical classes have to be attended beforehand, they are academically comparable to German students, who have progressed further with the actual medical school curriculum. In contrast, only 14% ($N = 3$) of the German sample had a degree. Fifty-two percent ($N = 11$) of the German students have had formal ethical education that illuminated ethical questions in medicine. It seems as though the educational concept in the United States differs, as 15 students, equaling 71% of the whole sample, have encountered ethical issues in medicine, despite having only recently begun their training. All of the 21 selected German subjects studied at a university in Lower Saxony. The American sample was more diverse; 43% ($N = 9$) of the medical students studied in the state of New York, but students from California, Massachusetts, Colorado, Nebraska, and Texas were also included in the sampling.

The examined subjects in the second sample were a total of 47 physicians, of which 37 worked in Germany and 10 in the United States. The mean age of both samples was 52.53 years with a standard deviation (SD) of 11.39 years. In the United States, the mean age was 47.9 years ($SD = 19.78$) and in Germany 53.78 years ($SD = 7.76$). Thirty male physicians (63.8%) and 16 female physicians (34.0%) took part in the study, one subject did not specify their gender. In the American survey sample, there was also one German, one Indian, and one Iraqi physician who were all educated in their country of origin, but had a working base in the United States. They remained in the American sample, as their working environment and also their legal restriction concerning their occupation are dictated by American law.

In the German survey sample, all subjects were of German nationality, except for one physician who was Belgian-German and one who was American-German. In total, 21 physicians worked in private practice, 17 in group practice, six in a hospital, one in research and teaching, one part time in teaching and part time in private practice, and one that was retired. Most physicians, accounting for 44.7%, worked in urban areas, 21.3% in suburban, and 31.9% in rural areas. One participant did not specify. The participant's marital and family status was also ascertained because of its possible effect on personal views on both dilemmas. A majority, 87.2%, of the subjects were married, 8.6% were either single or divorced, and 4.2% were either widowed or in a not-further-specified marital status, with 87.2% of the participants having no children.

RESEARCH DESIGN

The research design was based on the method plan from Cotsonas et al. (1979), which had never been carried out. Research in the field of cross-cultural explorations is still sparse, the body of literature in this particular field is slim, and we tried to fill part of this major gap using this specific study design. In a three-part online questionnaire that was available in both German and English, German and American physicians as well as students were confronted with two medical dilemmas in order to identify, compare, and analyze their moral orientations.

Part 1: Which Moral Orientation Do You Apply to Medical Dilemmas?

In the first part of the study, subjects were confronted with two medical dilemmas that were almost identical to those of Cotsonas et al. (1979). Few changes from the original study have been made in order to suit the focus of this study and fit contemporary research. These changes will be explained in the following.

PREGNANCY VIGNETTE

Jane M. is a 17-year-old student at Central High School in Alpha, Massachusetts. Jane, a younger brother, and both of her parents have been patients of Dr. Smith, a family physician, for the past 10 years. In fact, Dr. Smith and his family know the M.s quite well; the two families often interact socially.

Last year, Jane was successfully treated by Dr. Smith for venereal disease. Jane said she had kept her sexual activities secret from her parents, and she requested that Dr. Smith not inform them about her treatment. Dr. Smith discussed alternative methods of birth control, and at Jane's request he prescribed birth control pills without consulting either parent.

This week, Jane made an appointment at an out-of-town clinic for lab test and was informed that she is pregnant. Several days later, in Dr. Smith's office:

> "Dr. Smith, I'm here because I have found out that I'm pregnant and I need your help. I think I'm about 8 weeks pregnant."
>
> "Well Jane, I will help you in whatever way I can. What are your plans?"
>
> "I'm very upset. I don't know what to do. I don't want to have a baby now. I love my boyfriend and he wants a child. We want to get married. But I can't have a child right now. I just can't! I want an abortion. Please don't tell my parents. I don't want Bill to know about the arrangements because he's trying to stop me from doing it. Please help me."

(Cotsonas et al., 1979)

In comparison to the study of Cotsonas et al. (1979), the age of the girl was changed from 17 to 16 years, as between the ages of 14 and 18, the physician can decide whether to keep confidentiality or not, but a 17-year-old is more likely to be as mature as an 18-year-old.

In both examined countries, the prevailing legal situation does not give clear guidance on whether or not to keep confidentiality.

The prominence of biomedical ethics has led to an escalation of concern about legal liability (Mappes & DeGrazia, 2006). In Germany, patient confidentiality is regulated in Section 203 in the penal code, the *Strafgesetzbuch* (StGB), and in Section 9 in the professional regulations, the *Musterberufsordnung* (MBO). According to these paragraphs, physicians ought to maintain confidentiality about any confirmation given in their professional context. Between the ages of 14 to 18 years, however, the physician has to decide if the patient is independent and emotionally and cognitively mature enough to understand the consequences of his or her decision. In the United States, patient confidentiality is enshrined in the Health Insurance Portability and Accountability Act Privacy Rule. Like in Germany, physicians in the United States have to preserve any information about their patients that they receive in a medical context. This rule applies to legal adults, aged 18 years or older, and emancipated minors. If the physician does not class a minor as "emancipated," their parents function as personal representatives and decide on further treatment. In both countries, having ensured that the patient's choice is rational and well-informed, the doctor can relate to the principle of patient's autonomy and keep confidentiality. To summarize German and American legal regulations, one can say that both German and American physicians have the right but not the duty to tell the minor patient's parents about her pregnancy. Therefore, as the girl in the vignette is 16 years old, and neither German nor American penal codes offer distinct rules on confidentiality in this case, the physician's values and moral orientations influence his decision.

The second vignette was about a 48-year-old man called Tom, who has been struggling with cancer for the last 4 years.

CANCER VIGNETTE

Tom P. is a 48-year-old insurance salesman who, along with his wife and two teenage daughters, has been a patient of Dr. Smith for many years. For the last 4 years, Mr. P. has been treated with conventional therapies for cancer of the colon, including one operation. Despite initially encouraging evidence that the malignancy is again progressing rapidly. Further surgery is indicated, and Dr. Smith is confident that it could substantially extend Mr. P.'s life.

However, Dr. Smith is undecided what should be said to whom. Even before the latest tests, Dr. Smith discussed possible surgical procedures and risks, and each time Mr. P. steadfastly refused to consider such recommendations. Indeed, when Dr. Smith last brought up surgery, Mr. P. firmly replied he'd "never let'em operate on me."

Moreover, Tom seems to increasingly resigned to succumbing to his cancer instead of his former optimism about "licking it." In fact, such resignation prompted Tom to assert at his last exam that he no longer really cared to hear about progress of the malignancy or prognosis or treatment recommendations. He said he was "as ready as I'll ever be to go when the Good Lord calls," so there was no point in dragging it out. In fact, he was so weary of it all the he pleaded that Dr. Smith not even tell him the outcome and significance of new tests and not bother about alternative approaches. It was just so upsetting, so worrisome, and so depressing that he really preferred not to know.

As if to emphasize his resolve to let nature take its course, Mr. P. drew up a "living will" which specified that no heroic measure be taken to sustain his life artificially if his condition deteriorated so that he could not be consulted. At the most recent appointment Dr. Smith and Mrs. P. have the following exchange while Tom is in another room getting dressed:

"Dr. Smith, how is Tom doing?"

"Mrs. P., as I explained last week, Tom's cancer is active again and it is my opinion that we must seriously consider surgery."

"Tom doesn't want that. He's resigned."

(Cotsonas et al., 1979)

The original statement of the patient, that he was ready to die when God wanted him to, was replaced by a less religious statement which says that the patient was ready to die when his time had come, in order to avoid religious influence on the subject's responses.

The dilemma the doctor finds himself in is whether to press for further treatment or to simply accept the patient's wish. In accordance with the original version of the Hippocratic Oath, medicine's goals are to preserve and promote a patient's life and health. Correspondingly, decisions are based on the doctor's expertise. To this day, physicians have the duty to advance their patient's health and maintain life. What guides medical practice nowadays, though, is promoting the patient's well-being *and* respecting his or her self-determination (Brock, 2009). Patient autonomy stands for the patient's freedom of choosing which of the available options for dealing with his or her medical problem will suit his or her values, concerns, and goals best—including the option of no treatment (Young, 2009). Brock (2009) alludes that it is widely accepted to respect a patient's wish to die. This has been institutionalized by the "right of self-determination" as mandated by law. In Germany, the patient's autonomy is anchored in Section 7, Article 1 in the *Musterberufsordnung für* Ärzte (MBO). The advance directive the man has set up is legally manifested in Section 1901a in the German civil code (*Bürgerliches Gesetzbuch*). In the United States, laws on advance directives slightly vary from state to state, but the Patient Self-Determination Act (PSDA) from 1990 is valid for the entire United States. The PSDA gives patients the right to participate and direct their healthcare decisions, to refuse or accept medical treatment, and to prepare an advance directive. Besides, the PSDA requires health institutions to inform their patients about these rights. The American Medical Association (AMA) Code of Medical Ethics (2006), which represents not laws but standards of conduct, provides ethical guidance and principles for the physician's occupation and way of dealing with certain situations and medical cases. It contains the principle of autonomy, which allows patients to make self-reliant decisions on a variety of suggested treatments. Furthermore, the AMA's Code of Medical Ethics demands physicians to maintain their patient's life. Oath taking is an important part of the inauguration of medical students in the United States, and universities' oaths include the physician's duty to do their best in order to maintain their patients' health (Kao & Parsi, 2004).

Overall, in both examined countries legal regulations do not resolve the conflict between the patient's right for autonomous decisions on healthcare, his advance directive, and the doctor's duty to maintain life and health. Therefore, the doctor has to decide based upon personal preference, opinion, and moral.

After reading each vignette subjects were asked to answer three—respectively four for the cancer vignette—open-ended questions in order to elicit their moral orientation toward the dilemma. At the end of each vignette, subjects were requested to decide whether to keep discretion or not, respectively press for further treatment or not.

OPEN-ENDED QUESTIONS FOR EACH VIGNETTE

1. As Dr. Smith, how would you reply? (In your own words; for example, "Mrs. P., . . . ")
2. What is the conventional way a physician would deal with this type of situation?
3. What factors, if any, would lead you to treat this case in a way other than a conventional manner?

(Cotsonas et al., 1979)

4. If you were Mr. P. in this situation, how would you like to be treated by your physician?

As the main focus of this study was on Kohlberg's moral orientations applied to the medical context, it was of great relevance to firstly explicitly define the four categories. Then, the answers given by participants in part 1 of the questionnaire were deductively coded as reflecting none, one, or more than one of the proposed orientations. By applying Kohlberg's moral orientations as a continuation of the work from Cotsonas et al. (1979), this procedure is a deductive and qualitative content analysis.

According to the definitions by Kohlberg (1976), the emphasis of a normative argument is on legal rules or professional guidelines, patient's rights or the physician's duties. In the pregnancy vignette a physician could argue to keep confidentiality as it is his or her duty to keep information, or they could decide to tell the girl's parents as she is still a minor. Likewise, a doctor could accept the patient's wish due to the notion of his right of "self-determination," or try to press for further treatment as it is the doctor's duty to preserve life in the cancer vignette. The utilitarian orientation is indicated when the participant's concern centers on the outcome and consequences of a decision. Talking about the pregnant girl's options, her family and boyfriend being able to support her in a difficult time of her life, or not wanting to jeopardize her trust are all signs of the utilitarian orientation in the pregnancy vignette. If a subject mentioned the consequences of respecting Tom's wish or prolonging his life, respectively, this style of reasoning should also be coded "utilitarian orientation." If interests of the involved individuals are raised and weighed against each other, and the participant makes "fairness" their prime concern, such as Jane as the most affected person by the dilemma or Bill having the right to know about her pregnancy as he is the father of the child, it is a matter of the justice orientation. In the cancer vignette one could point out Tom as the most affected person by the problem, and therefore he should have ultimate authority to decide or focus on the impact his choice also has on his family. In the perfectionist orientation, the participant's focus is on the doctor's concept of self, highlighting their conscience and perception of their role as a physician, reflected by mentioning how they see themselves, like someone who a patient should be able to trust or emphasizing their view, like stressing what they commit themselves to. Based on the work of Cotsonas et al. (1979), a coding manual (Table 9.3) for moral orientations was developed and used to code the collected data in order to explore moral orientations of German and American physicians and medical students.

Part 2: Which Moral Orientation Do You Prefer?

In the second part of the questionnaire, subjects were asked to rank four prepared statements for each vignette according to their personal degree of agreement. The statement that most represented the participant's stance was asked to be ranked first, the second most congruent second, and so on. Each statement represented one of the four moral orientations. The statements were presented dependent on the decisions made by the subject in the first part of the questionnaire, either maintaining confidentiality or not, respectively pushing for further treatment or not. The four listed answers all agreed on the same course of action that had previously been chosen by the respondent, but gave different reasons in accordance with one moral orientation. The statements were taken from Cotsonas et al. (1979) and have been slightly changed in order to emphasize the elements of the responses that represent the moral orientation.

Demographic Data

The third part of the questionnaire gathered demographic data of the subjects, such as age, gender, marital status and family, place of study, residence, medical specialization, ethnical and religious background, and ethical education. In this part, the German and English version of the questionnaire differ in terms of the offered options of residence and place of study, according to the different states in Germany and the United States.

WHAT DO STUDENTS SAY?

As consequences of a doctor's choice can be dramatic, students have a particular need to develop adequate moral reasoning strategies. Since the number of doctors who practice medicine transculturally increases, this section aims at raising the awareness of cross-cultural differences in what is considered justifiable moral reasoning. Moreover, it provides indications on

TABLE 9.3 Coding Rules and Prime Examples for Kohlberg's Moral Orientations as Categories

Category	Meaning	Coding Rules	Prime Examples	
			Pregnancy	Cancer
Normative Orientation	The participant's argumentation is based on legal rules or professional guidelines	Determinants of one's moral choice are law-abiding aspects, such as the patient's right to autonomy or professional guidelines for physicians and their duties, such as the principle of confidentiality Indicative of this orientation is when the participant justifies their moral decision based on what they are allowed to do, what duty or right they possess; use of words like "must," "must not," "have to" or "are not allowed" point to the normative orientation	As a minor, you must understand that I have to notify your parents.	I respect his right to make decisions about his body, but I want to make sure he is making a fully informed decision (. . .).
Utilitarian Orientation	The participant's concern centers around the outcome and consequences of a decision	Determinants of one's moral choice are direct consequences for the individual or the group, for the patient or the physician Indicative of this orientation is when different courses of action that can be taken into consideration are mentioned, alternatives are weighed against each other	I would stress the benefits of having family members to depend upon during difficult periods in one's life.	I will continue to urge him to get the treatment that I know can save his life–death may seem like the easiest option but death is permanent.

(continued)

TABLE 9.3 Coding Rules and Prime Examples for Kohlberg's Moral Orientations as Categories (continued)

Category	Meaning	Coding Rules	Prime Examples	
			Pregnancy	Cancer
Justice Orientation	The participant makes 'fairness' their prime concern	Determinant of one's moral choice is its fairness; interests of the involved individuals are raised and weighed against each other; the focus of this orientation is on equity, contract, and reciprocity in relationships Indicative of this orientation is when the participant mentions the impact one's choice has on others or emphasizing how the patient is the most affected person by the situation	I respect your dominion over your own body but I must counsel you to discuss your decision with your boyfriend. Honesty is a fundamental part of any relationship and this is a very dark secret.	After all, he should not be this egoistic and think about your daughters and you as well.
Perfectionistic Orientation	The participant's focus is on the doctor's concept of self	Determinant of one's moral choice is the participant's conscience and perception of their role as a physician; by emphasizing their personal view, they try to uphold their self-respect, serving their ideal character Indicative of this orientation is when the participant stresses what they commit themselves to and how they see themselves	I am prepared to help you with all means available to me within the scope of my medical competences, and everything "humanly possible", for you to make an acceptable decision	Accepting this is not easy for me as a doctor either. I want to help whenever I can, save lives and lengthen them; but sometimes a shorter and therefore, a more fulfilling life, is the better choice.

how to include ethical issues in the medical school's framework. The more aware students become of differing moral orientations, the more flexible they can respond to patients' orientations with underlying values that might differ from their own.

To examine the impact of American and German culture, in the sense that the countries' macrosystems provide a different work and study environment as well as a different national legal system, on the individual's reasoning style, it was foremost investigated if students give different priorities to different values in the same moral dilemma drawn from the ranking task. A complete description of frequencies in the ranking task would go beyond the scope of this chapter. Hence, only significant results shall be discussed in the following.

The resulting picture is not one of drastic disparities. Nonetheless, several differences could be revealed between the medical students who study in the United States and those who study in Germany. However, the reader should be aware of the fact that participants might hold more than one orientation. As pointed out above, moral orientations are not hierarchically ordered. Thus, it is somewhat artificial to evoke a ranking of statements, each of which represents one stance. Although one should be cautious and interpret results with care, findings offer interesting insights into cross-cultural differences and valuable allusions to how individuals with differing cultural backgrounds prioritize differing values.

Pregnancy Vignette

Ninety-five percent ($N = 20$) of the American medical students would keep confidentiality in the case of the 16-year-old pregnant girl. Only one participant would tell Jane's parents. In the German population, 86% ($N = 18$) would also not disclose any information about the case; three subjects would. However, most participants from both countries would still advise Jane to involve her parents in the decision-making process.

From the 20 participants of the American sample, who would all keep confidentiality, only 19 ranked the statements. Frequencies can be seen in Figure 9.1.

In order to assess whether or not the two populations differed in terms of their orientation preferences, Fisher's exact test was run over the data. The ranking of the statement representing the utilitarian orientation shows a significant discrepancy, in terms that the American sample thought of it as more important and more congruent with their own stance [Fisher's exact test: χ^2 (3, $N = 37$) = 8.9, $p = .045$, Cramer's $V = .49$]. The rankings of the justice orientation, in which the doctor weighs involved people's interests against each other, display even more significant differences between the

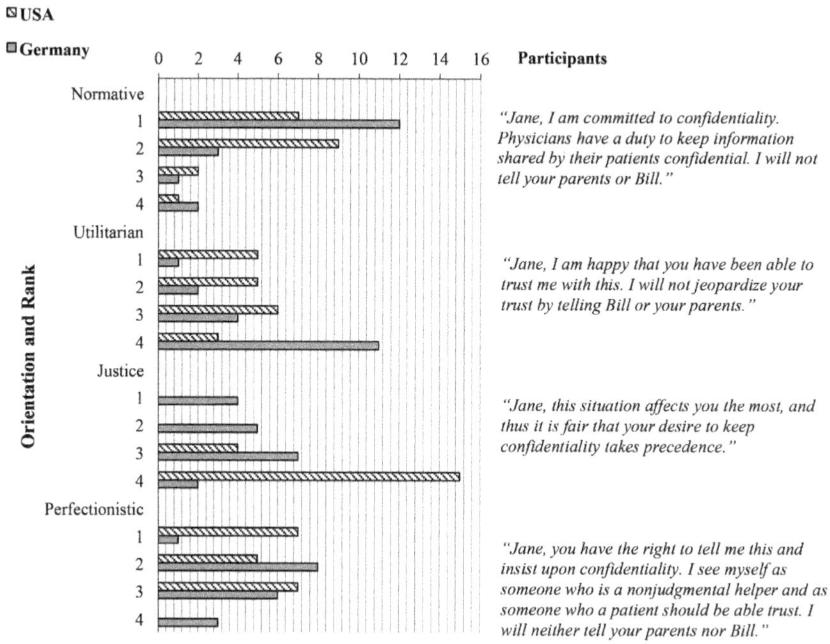

Figure 9.1 Rankings when confidentiality is kept in the pregnancy vignette.

American sample and the German group. In opposition to the American population, German medical students favor the justice orientation, agreeing to Jane's wish for confidentiality as she is the most affected individual by the situation, [Fisher's exact test: χ^2 (3, N = 37) = 19.8, p < .001, Cramer's V = .731]. The ranking of the perfectionistic orientation, which puts the ideal self of the doctor into focus, also differed considerably between German and American participants who give more weight to it [Fisher's exact test: χ^2 (3, N = 37) = 7.77, p = .041, Cramer's V = .472].

Cancer Vignette

Eight from the 21 American participants, accounting for 38%, would try and press for further treatment in the cancer vignette. Accordingly, the other 62% (N = 13) would accept the patient's wish. Interestingly, the exact same numbers apply to the German population.

For the bigger group of people, who would not push for medical treatment, cross-cultural differences arise once again. Figure 9.2 shows how participants from both countries ranked the statements.

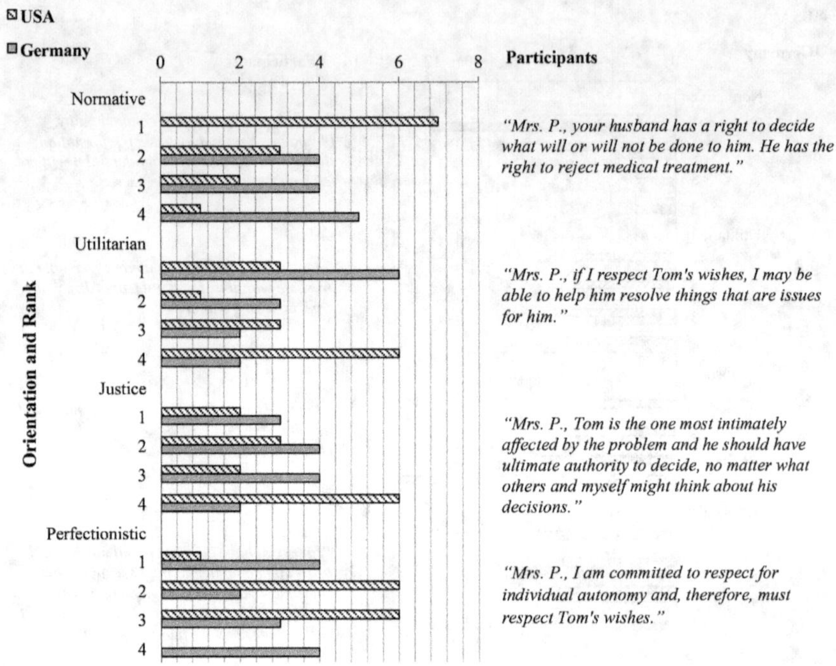

Figure 9.2 Rankings when the patient's wish is accepted in the cancer vignette.

In the American sample, the patient's right to reject treatment, resembling the normative orientation, had been given a higher rank than in the German sample. Fisher's exact test reveals a significant difference, [Fisher's exact test: χ^2 (3, N = 26) = 10.63, p = .012, Cramer's V = .635]. Again, the American sample ranked the statement reflecting the perfectionistic orientation significantly higher than the German medical students, [Fisher's exact test: χ^2 (3, N = 26) = 8.2, p = .04, Cramer's V = .582].

A Possible Explanation?

The majority of participants from both countries decided to keep confidentiality in the pregnancy vignette, and the same amounts of people in both countries would press for further treatment, the same amount would simply accept the patient's wish in the cancer case. Also, in both countries, the physician tried to involve the patient's parents in the pregnancy vignette. This was tried to be achieved withouht having to break confidentiality. In the given case this could be tried by discussing how beneficial it would be for Jane to include her parents in the decision. All in all, there does not seem to be a difference in the moral choice between the two countries.

However, even if students agreed on the same course of action, reasons for why they did differed cross nationally. When information was chosen not to be disclosed in the pregnancy vignette, German participants ranked the statement standing for the utilitarian orientation significantly lower than Americans. What could be the reason for this? Overall, Americans are said to place great emphasis on ethical decisions that are based on individual autonomy (Ruhnke et al., 2000). "Ethic of autonomy" has achieved dominance in the United States, defining the moral agent as an "autonomous individual who is free to make choices" (Jensen, 1997, p. 332). According to Hofstede (2001), the United States is the most individualistic country. The results pointed out previously could allude to the large occurrence of individualistic objectives within the American sample. At first glance, this may not be the case as the utilitarian orientation is meant to put the consequences of a moral choice into focus. In fact, the statement that has been chosen for the ranking task of the questionnaire, however, emphasizes the consequences for the doctor rather than concentrating on outcomes affecting the patient or other people involved. By choosing not to "jeopardize Jane's trust" by telling her parents or her boyfriend, this statement mainly points at the individualistic consequences for the doctor. In accordance to the idea of "individualism" (cp. Hofstede, 2001), interests of the individual are thought to achieve precedence. As a contrast to that, the justice orientation got ranked significantly lower by American participants compared to the German sample. Individuals exercising this orientation take into account the fairness of an outcome for all parties affected by the decision. The main focus of the justice orientation is rights, such as equality, reciprocity, and fairness of a decision. The statement stresses Jane as the most affected person by this situation and thus highlights that her desire for the doctor to keep confidentiality should take precedence. Rather than setting priorities to individualistic aspects, German medical students try to balance reasons, deliberating about what course of action is the fairest.

A different approach to individualistic reasoning about what course of action to take is also reflected in the significant difference in the use of the ideal-self orientation. Fisher's exact test indicated that Americans ranked the perfectionistic orientation significantly higher than German students in both vignettes. Supporting the presumption that Americans tend to be more individualistic than Germans, they also apply the perfectionistic orientation more often in the pregnancy vignette, when confidentiality is kept, and also in the "Cancer Dilemma," when the patient's wish for no further treatment is accepted. Living in the United States, a highly individualistic country, has the effect that values of personal beliefs get cultivated, and unique ideals get emphasized. Independent selves view themselves as individuals free from constraints (Markus & Conner, 2013). In the self-oriented perfectionistic orientation, one's personal role is pointed out, making the individual self the focus.

WHAT DO PHYSICIANS SAY?

Two main hypotheses concerning moral orientations among physicians in the United States and Germany were tested using the collected data. Furthermore, it was tested whether or not Kohlberg's claim for hierarchical equality among his moral orientations is warranted.

Hypothesis 1: American Physicians Argue More Normatively Than German Physicians

Differences in the number of lawsuits filed against physicians and their resulting fear of comparatively high penalty charges lead to more defensive medical practice in the United States (Summerton, 2000). In 2011, the National Practitioner Data Bank registered 11,424 malpractice reports in the United States and more than 10,000 indemnity payments because of medical mistreatments in the United States (National Practitioner Data Bank, 2013). In contrast, only 11,107 arbitration processes were requested at the German Medical Council, the *Bundesärztekammer* (2013), in the year 2011. All patient accusations due to medical malpractice had to be reviewed by the *Gutachterkomissionen und Schlichtungsstellen*, and only 1,901 approvals of such claims were granted that did not even necessarily have to lead to a lawsuit. One should carefully regard, though, that the *Bundesärztekammer* is not involved in *all* trials against physicians and that their assessment of the examined cases is not precedent to liability. Adding to the above given statistics, the United States is considered to be a "common law" country and, therefore, has a more restrictive attitude toward statutes and legal rules than Germany, which is a typical "civil law" country with strong constitutional laws (Van der Burg, 2009). Due to the common practice of defensive medicine, the high number of lawsuits, and the restrictive views on laws in the United States, this hypothesis states that physicians in the United States argue more normatively than their German colleagues, always keeping an eye on their liability.

Pregnancy Vignette

Overall, 89.2% of the German and 80% of the American physicians decided to maintain confidentiality in this case and to not tell their minor patient's parents about her pregnancy, which is a total majority of 87.2% of all responding physicians. Table 9.4 shows relative, expected, and absolute frequencies of normative moral orientations within the open responses of German and American physicians towards the pregnancy vignette.

TABLE 9.4 Frequencies of Normative Moral Orientations in Pregnancy Vignette in the United States and Germany

			Pregnancy Vignette Normative Orientation		
			Non-Existent	Existent	Total
Place of Practice	USA	Quantity	8	2	10
		expected frequency	5.7	4.3	10
		% within USA	80.0%	20.0%	100.0%
	GER	Quantity	19	18	37
		expected frequency	21.3	15.7	37.0
		% within Germany	51.4%	48.6%	100.0%
Total		Quantity	27	20	47
		% within place of practice	57.4%	42.6%	100.0%

Eighty percent of the American physicians did not argue normatively, whereas 51.4% of the German physicians did not show normative forms of reasoning in their responses. Thus, counter-intuitively, 20% of the answers given by American physicians and 48.6% of the answers given by German physicians were normatively oriented.

This shows that American physicians do not argue more normatively than their German colleagues. In total, a majority of 57.4% of the physicians did not argue on a normative basis. The statistical analysis did not show any significant differences between the two places of practice in regards to the normative orientation in the pregnancy vignette, [Fishers' Exact Test: χ^2 (1, $N = 47$) = 2.643, $p = .154$].

Cancer Vignette

A total of 80.9% of all physicians, accounting for 81.1% of the German and 80% of the American physicians, would accept their patient's wish for no further intervention. In contrast to the pregnancy vignette, it is evident that Americans argue more normatively in the cancer vignette than the German population. Table 9.5 displays the frequencies of normative orientations in the physicians' responses towards the cancer vignette. Ninety percent of the American physicians used a normative style of reasoning, i.e., they refer to laws, rules, and guidelines. Only one American physician did not argue normatively in this case.

Only 48.6% of the German physicians showed normative styles of reasoning in their responses towards the cancer vignette. A total of 57.4% of the physicians argued normatively. A slight but significant difference between

TABLE 9.5 Frequencies of Normative Moral Orientations in Cancer Vignette in the United States and Germany

			Cancer Vignette Normative Orientation		
			Non-Existent	Existent	Total
Place of Practice	USA	quantity	1	9	10
		expected frequency	4.3	5.7	10
		% within USA	10.0%	90.0%	100.0%
	GER	quantity	19	18	37
		expected frequency	15.7	21.3	37.0
		% within Germany	51.4%	48.6%	100.0%
Total		quantity		27	47
		% within place of practice	42.6%	57.4%	100.0%

the two nations in regards to the use of the normative orientation towards the cancer vignette was found, [Fisher's Exact Test: χ^2 (1, N = 47) = 5.507, p = .029, Cramer's V = 0.34]. Cramer's V indicates a moderate association between the variables.

A Possible Explanation?

In the cancer vignette, Americans justified their decision more often using a normative moral orientation than German physicians. This might be due to the Americans' restrictive view on legal regulations, documents, and professional guidelines. The patient's advanced decision in the cancer vignette against further treatment represents a legally valid document that might influence the American physician's style of reasoning and virtually pulls for the normative orientation. In contrast, a recent study by Wandrowski, Schuster, Strube, & Steger (2012) showed that physicians in Germany do not base their medical decision on patients' advance decisions and, therefore, might not include them in their reasoning. Contrary, no differences were found between the frequencies of American and German physicians' decisions whether or not to press for further treatment in the cancer vignette. This shows that different styles of reasoning do not necessarily lead to different decisions, but that even with different arguments and different priorities of values, physicians may come to the same conclusion and suggestion of treatment. In contrast, no significant differences were found between German and American physicians in the pregnancy vignette. This might have been an effect of the design of the vignettes, which emphasized different aspects of medical decision-making and, hence, may have evoked differing answers in the two groups.

Hypothesis 2: American Physicians Argue More Perfectionistic—Or Ideal Self-Oriented—Than German Physicians

As already pointed out above, the United States is a highly individualistic country, which strongly emphasizes personal beliefs and ideals (Hofstede, 2001). Thus, the second hypothesis states that American physicians point out their own role as practitioners more clearly than German physicians, i.e., they use the perfectionistic moral orientation more often than their German colleagues.

In total, only five perfectionistic-oriented answers were given, one in the pregnancy vignette by an American physician and four in the cancer vignette by two American and two German physicians. As the total frequencies are very low, a chi-square test of independency between a perfectionistic moral orientation in the pregnancy vignette and a perfectionistic moral orientation in the cancer vignette is not indicated. Likewise, no chi-square tests could be calculated to test the independency of a perfectionistic moral orientation in both vignettes and the physician's place of practice.

In total, 42 physicians, equaling 89.36% of the sample, did not use perfectionistic-oriented styles of reasoning to respond to the presented dilemmas. As no physician used the perfectionistic orientation in both dilemmas, no continuity or dependence of answers given to the pregnancy vignette or answers given to the cancer vignette can be assumed.

Are Kohlberg's Moral Orientations Hierarchically Equal?

Another aim of this study was to investigate Kohlberg's notion that all four moral orientations are hierarchically equal, i.e., no moral orientation is superior or inferior to others. A comparison of American and German physician's preferences for certain statements was relinquished in order to have a bigger sample to review Kohlberg's assumption. In accordance with Kohlberg's assumption of hierarchical equality, all statements should have been ranked first with equal frequencies. Table 9.6 shows the frequencies of how often a statement was ranked as most important and most compliant with the physician's attitude.

In order to simplify the results, the statements for each decision and vignette were summarized to normative, utilitarian, justice, and perfectionist oriented statements. Three subjects did not rank the statements for the

TABLE 9.6 Frequencies of Initial Placing of Moral Statements in Pregnancy and Cancer Vignette

	Normative Oriented Statement as Rank 1	Utilitarian Oriented Statement as Rank 1	Justice Oriented Statement as Rank 1	Perfectionist Oriented Statement as Rank 1	Total
Pregnancy Vignette	22	10	3	9	44
% within pregnancy vignette	50.0%	22.72%	6.81%	20.45%	100.0%
Cancer Vignette	11	11	16	8	46
% within cancer vignette	23.91%	23.91%	34.78%	17.39%	100.0%
Total	33	21	19	17	90
% within both vignettes	36.66%	23.33%	21.11%	18.88%	100.0%

pregnancy vignette, and one subject did not rank the cancer vignette statements, which leads to a total of $N = 44$ for the pregnancy vignette and $N = 46$ for the cancer vignette. It is apparent that 50% of the subjects ranked the normative statements of the pregnancy vignette first, whereas only 6.81% found the justice oriented statement to be most important. In contrast to that, the justice oriented statement in the cancer vignette was most often ranked as the most important one (34.78%). Assembling both vignettes, the normative oriented statements appear to be the most important ones (36.66%), whereas, as already alluded to in the section above, the least attention was given to the perfectionistic statements (18.88%).

Are Kohlberg's moral orientations hierarchically equal then? Maybe not. Kohlberg's claim for hierarchical equality among all moral orientations could not be verified and does not seem reasonable. There might be a preference for normatively oriented reasoning in medical contexts. It should be carefully noted, though, that the design of the task did not allow an equal ranking of two or more statements. Therefore, one could have rated two statements as equally important but was not able to do so in the task. To investigate this further, an additional study should be carried out with a greater sample and in more countries in order to investigate whether or not all cultures share the preference for normatively oriented reasoning.

DOES EXPERIENCE MATTER?

As pointed out previously, environmental events such as the occurrence of a higher number of lawsuits and amounts due in the United States might mediate the moral orientation of physicians in the United States. They generally treat law as "the most respected and binding type of rule" (Grol-Prokopczyk,

2013, p. 96) due to concerns about the risk of being sued or having a complaint lodged (Summerton, 1995). Through doctors' experiences with the occurrence of lawsuits in the United States, their moral reasoning is said to evolve from legislative resolutions rather than their own reflections (McQuade, 1991). This section therefore looks at influences from the occupational field and examines whether differences between practicing American physicians and soon-to-be-clinicians, who still hit the books, can be revealed. Actually facing a high number of lawsuits filed against general practitioners, combined with high compensation sums, might promote a normative mode of reasoning in their moral judgment of medical situations. In contrast, American students who have not yet been involved in medico-legal problems and have not had judicial experiences are thought to reason less normatively than experienced doctors. The distribution of this specific orientation in the open response to the pregnancy vignette (see Table 9.7) was looked at first.

No significant results can be found between the two groups, [Fisher's exact test: χ^2 (1, N = 31) = 0.034, p = 1.00, Cramer's V = .033]. In the cancer vignette, however, there is an apparent tendency, as can be seen in Table 9.8; doctors tend to argue more normatively than students, [Fisher's exact test: χ^2 (1, N = 31) = 3.77, p = .058, Cramer's V = .349].

Then, it was compared what ranking participants from the two populations assigned to the statement that stood for the normative orientation. In the pregnancy vignette, [Fisher's exact test: χ^2 (3, N = 29) = 3.71, p = .292, Cramer's V = .353], as well as in the cancer vignette, [Fisher's exact test: χ^2 (3, N = 31) = 1.58, p = .821, Cramer's V = .234] no significant differences could be revealed in the ranking of the normative orientation between American medical students and doctors.

TABLE 9.7 Frequencies and Percentages: Use of Normative Orientation in the Pregnancy Vignette

			Degree of Professionalization		
			Doctor	**Student**	**Total**
Does the participant utilize the normative orientation?	no	number	7	14	21
		expected number	6.8	14.2	
		% within country	70,0%	66,7%	67,7%
	yes	number	3	7	10
		expected number	3.2	6.8	
		% within country	30,0%	33,3%	32,3%
Total		number	10	21	31
		% within country	100,0%	100,0%	100,0%

TABLE 9.8 Frequencies and Percentages: Use of Normative Orientation in the Cancer Vignette

			Degree of Professionalization		
			Doctor	Student	Total
Does the participant utilize the normative orientation?	no	number	2	12	14
		expected number	4.5	9.5	
		% within country	20,0%	57,1%	45,2%
	yes	number	8	9	17
		expected number	5.5	11.5	
		% within country	80,0%	42,9%	54,8%
Total		number	10	21	31
		% within country	100,0%	100,0%	100,0%

A Possible Explanation?

The hypothesis that American students argue less normatively than American doctors due to their lack of experience with judicial proceedings did not find significant support. However, the tendency of physicians to argue using the normative orientation more than students in the cancer vignette suggests a slight discrepancy. Again, as already proposed previously, this might result from the differences in the vignettes. In the cancer vignette, legal rules or professional guidelines are explicitly mentioned by referring to the patient's advance directive, serving as prime for the normative orientation, activating the doctor's concern about legal issues. The apparentness of legal aspects might facilitate normative argumentation in the doctor's perception.

An alternative explanation could be that medical students get prepared adequately for what to expect in their future lives as physician. Legal aspects take up an important part of their curriculum, and they learn from the beginning how lawsuits can have major consequences for them. The practice of "defensive medicine" (McQuade, 1991) might not only be due to judicial experiences, but also evolved out of the raised awareness of legal proceedings and actions taken against physicians. This consciousness is partly attained by universities' education. Supportive of this idea is the significant finding that American medical students stress the normative orientation much more than German students in the cancer vignette in the ranking task of the questionnaire. American students are clearly much more predisposed for judicial issues of a case and also more likely to choose congruent law-abiding actions.

CONCLUSIONS

Is there one right way to treat a patient or should each patient be looked at individually? Are moral principles universal and classify as common sense, or does each person hold their own particular stance? These questions are not easy to answer.

> [T]he clinician . . . is the only person who is in a position to make decisions about the care of a specific patient, but . . . this role requires a knowledge of universal principles—those of medical science. (Noller & Bibace, 2005, p. 99)

> [R]ecommendations [on how to treat a patient] are not applicable to an individual patient. They only apply to the average patient, an individual who does not exist. (Noller & Bibace, 2005, p. 106)

> [T]here is no such thing as an "average patient." (Noller & Bibace, 2005, p. 103)

These quotes underline that universal principles should be used to care for patients, but that there is no such thing as "universal truth," and clinicians need to take particular aspects of one individual patient into consideration. The physician-patient encounter frequently brings together individuals from different cultures who hold different views of morally appropriate practices. Since our study looked at moral differences on the national group level, it is, of course, only with care that one can draw conclusions to the individual level only based on the individuals' nationality or ethnicity. Just because a medical student comes from the United States does not make him a more normatively arguing individual. What could be shown, however, is that the circumstances of a country, such as the influential American legal system, *can* have an impact on peoples' moral reasoning, at least on the group level. Under no means do we want to undermine that there are multiple ways in which an individual can be affected by culture and how this culture might be represented within themselves. Likewise, the physician has to carefully analyze each patient's stance before deciding on a course of action. They have a particular need to develop competencies of adequate moral judgment, as potential consequences of their decisions can be dramatic. Of course, not everyone would agree on one specific procedure in conflicting situations. Factors, such as cultural background, can influence peoples' values. By choosing one option of action and therefore prioritizing one value, another one gets automatically transgressed. Knowing about different value orientations does not mean we have to agree with them, but it will most certainly help our understanding of the patient's situation. Clinicians should gain knowledge of potential dilemmas that can occur in their daily job routine as well as develop decisional strategies that lead to more critically reflected and, eventually, to more secure actions. When encountering a patient with a view different from their own, health professionals should acknowledge their perspective. This is especially important if they find themselves working in a culturally different environment with its own decision-making strategies in morally conflicting situations. As has been pointed out in our study, not every individual reasons about a moral decision in the same way and broad cultural differences could be revealed.

REFERENCES

American Medical Association (Ed.). (2006). *Code of medical ethics.* Chicago, IL: American Medical Association.

Beauchamp, T. L., & Childress, J .F. (1979/2009). *Principles of biomedical ethics* (6th ed.) New York, NY: Oxford University Press.

Bibace, R., Comer, R., & Cotsonas, C. E. (1978). Ethical and legal issues in family practice. *The Journal of Family Practice,* 7(5), 1029–1035.

Brock, D. W. (2009). Medical decisions at the end of life. In H. Kuhse & P. Singer (Eds.), *A companion to bioethics* (pp. 263–273). Oxford, England: Wiley-Blackwell.

Bundesärztekammer (Ed.). (2013). *Tätigkeitsbericht 2012 der Bundesärztekammer* [Activity Report 2012 of the German Medical Council]. Cologne, Germany: Deutscher Ärzte-Verlag GmbH.

Cotsonas, C. E., Bibace, R., & Lang, E. (1979). *Family physicians' responses to medical/ethical and medicolegal dilemmas: An approach.* (Unpublished manuscript). Clark University, Worcester, MA.

Dien, S. D. (1982). A Chinese perspective on Kohlberg's theory of moral development. *Developmental Review, 2,* 331–341.

Edwards, C. P. (1982). Moral development in comparative cultural perspective. In D. A. Wagner & H. W. Stevenson (Eds.), *Cultural perspectives on child development* (pp. 248–279). San Francisco, CA: W. H. Freeman.

Frenkel-Brunswik, E. (1974). Some theoretical and empirical aspects of the problem of values. In N. Heiman & J. Grant (Eds.), *Else Frenkel-Brunswik: Selected papers* (pp. 292–313). New York, NY: International Universities Press.

Gbadegesin, S. (2009). Culture and bioethics. In H. Kuhse & P. Singer (Eds.), *A companion to bioethics* (pp. 24–35). Oxford, England: Wiley-Blackwell.

Ge, T., & Thomas, S. (2008). A cross-cultural comparison of the deliberative reasoning of Canadian and Chinese accounting students. *Journal of Business Ethics, 82,* 189–211.

Glannon, W. (2005). The patient-doctor relationship. In W. Glannon (Ed.), *Biomedical ethics* (pp. 23–46). New York, NY: Oxford University Press.

Goldman, S. A., & Arbuthnot, J. (1979). Teaching medical ethics: The cognitive-developmental approach. *Journal of Medical Ethics, 5,* 170–181.

Grol-Prokopczyk, H. (2013). Thai and American doctors on medical ethics: Religion, regulation, and moral reasoning across borders. *Social Science & Medicine, 76,* 92–100.

Heine, S. J. (2012). *Cultural psychology.* New York, NY: W. W. Norton.

Hofstede, G. (1989). *Culture's consequences: International differences in work-related values.* New York, NY: Sage.

Hofstede, G. (2001). *Culture's consequences: Comparing values, behaviors, institutions, and organizations across nations.* Thousand Oaks, CA: Sage.

Jancovic, M. P. (1979). *Structure versus content in Kohlberg's theory of moral judgment: An investigation of moral orientations within stages of moral reasoning.* (Unpublished doctoral dissertation). Clark University, Worcester, MA.

Jensen, L. A. (1997). Different worldviews, different morals: America's culture war divide. *Human Development, 40,* 325–344.

Jensen, L. A. (2008). Through two lenses: A cultural–developmental approach to moral psychology. *Developmental Review, 28,* 289–315.

Jhala, C. I., & Jhala, K. N. (2012). The Hippocratic oath: A comparative analysis of the ancient text's relevance to American and Indian modern medicine. *Indian Journal of Pathology & Microbiology, 55*(3), 279–282.

Kao, A., & Parsi, K. (2004). Content analyses of oaths administered at U.S. medical schools in 2000. *Academic Medicine,* 79(9), 882–887.

Kohlberg, L. (1969). Stage and sequence: The cognitive-developmental approach to socialization. In D. Goslin (Ed.), *Handbook of socialization, theory and research* (pp. 347–480). Chicago, IL: Rand McNally.

Kohlberg, L. (1976). Moral stages and moralization: The cognitive-developmental approach. In T. Lickona (Ed.), *Moral development and behavior: Theory, research, and social issues* (pp. 31–53). New York, NY: Holt, Rinehart and Winston.

Kuhse, H., & Singer, P. (2009). What is bioethics? A historical introduction. In H. Kuhse & P. Singer (Eds.), *A companion to bioethics* (pp. 3–11). Oxford, England: Wiley-Blackwell.

Ma, H. K., & Cheung, C. (1996). A cross-cultural study of moral stage structure in Hong Kong Chinese, English, and Americans. *Journal of Cross-Cultural Psychology, 27*(6), 700–713.

Mappes, T. A., & DeGrazia, D. (2006). *Biomedical ethics.* Boston, MA: McGraw-Hill.

Markus, H. R., & Conner, A. (2013). *Clash! 8 cultural conflicts that make us who we are.* New York, NY: Hudson Street Press.

McQuade, J. S. (1991). The medical malpractice crisis—Reflections on the alleged causes and proposed cures: Discussion paper. *Journal of the Royal Society of Medicine, 84,* 408–411.

Miller, J. G. (2006). Insights into moral development from cultural psychology. In M. Killen & J. G. Smetana (Eds.), *Handbook of moral development* (pp. 375–398). Mahwah, NJ: Erlbaum.

Miller, J. G. (2007). Cultural psychology of moral development. In S. Kitayama & D. Cohen (Eds.), *Handbook of cultural psychology* (pp. 477–499). New York, NY: Guilford Press.

Morling, B., & Lamoreaux, M. (2008). Measuring culture outside the head: A meta-analysis of individualism-collectivism in cultural products. *Personality and Social Psychology Review, 12*(3), 199–221.

National Practitioner Data Bank. (2013). *Annual report 2011.* Retrieved May 31, 2013, from http://www.npdb-hipdb.hrsa.gov/resources/reports/2011NPDBAnnualReport.pdf

Noller, K. L., & Bibace, R. (2005). The centrality of the clinician: A view of medicine from the general to the particular. In R. Bibace, J. D. Laird, K. L. Noller, & J. Valsiner (Eds.), *Science and medicine in dialogue: Thinking through particulars and universals* (pp. 99–198). Westport, CT: Praeger.

Piaget, J. (1932). *The moral judgment of the child.* London, England: Kegan Paul.

Rest, J. R. (1994). Background: Theory and research. In J. R. Rest & D. Narváez (Eds.), *Moral development in the professions: Psychology and applied ethics* (pp. 1–26). Hillsdale, NJ: Erlbaum.

Ruhnke, G. W., Wilson, S. R., Akamatsu, T., Kinoue, T., Takashima, Y., Goldstein, M. K., & Raffin, T. A. (2000). Ethical decision making and patient autonomy. A comparison of physicians and patients in Japan and the United States. *Chest, 118*(4), 1172–1182.

Self, D. J., & Baldwin, D. C. (1994). Moral reasoning in medicine. In J. R. Rest & D. Narváez (Eds.), *Moral development in the professions: Psychology and applied ethics* (pp. 147–162). Hillsdale, NJ: Erlbaum.

Self, D. J., & Davenport, E. (1996). Measurement of moral development in medicine. *Cambridge Quarterly of Healthcare Ethics, 5*(2), 269–277.

Smith, M. S. (2012). The lived experience of doing the right thing: A parse method study. *Nursing Science Quarterly, 25*(1), 82–89.

Snarey, J. R. (1985). Cross-cultural universality of social-moral development: A critical review of Kohlbergian research. *Psychological Bulletin, 97,* 202–232.

Summerton, N. (1995). Positive and negative factors in defensive medicine: A questionnaire study of general practitioners. *British Medical Journal, 310,* 27–29.

Summerton, N. (2000). Trends in negative defensive medicine within general practice. *British Journal of General Practice, 50,* 565–566.

Valsiner, J. (2012). Introduction: Culture in psychology: A renewed encounter of inquisitive minds. In J. Valsiner (Ed.), *The Oxford handbook of culture and psychology* (pp. 3–24). Oxford, England: Oxford University Press.

Van der Burg, W. (2009). Law and bioethics. In H. Kuhse & P. Singer (Eds.), *A companion to bioethics* (pp. 56–64). Oxford, England: Wiley-Blackwell.

Wainryb, C. (2006). Moral development in culture: Diversity, tolerance, and justice. In M. Killen & J. G. Smetana (Eds.), *Handbook of moral development* (pp. 211–240). Mahwah, NJ: Erlbaum.

Wandrowski, J., Schuster, T., Strube, W., & Steger, F. (2012). Medical ethical knowledge and moral attitudes among physicians in Bavaria. *Deutsches Ärzteblatt International,* 109(8), 141–147.

Young, R. (2009). Informed consent and patient autonomy. In H. Kuhse & P. Singer (Eds.), *A companion to bioethics* (pp. 530–540). Oxford, England: Wiley-Blackwell.

Zaharna, R. S. (2000). *Overview: Florence Kluckhohn value orientations.* Retrieved from http://academic2.american.edu/~zaharna/kluckhohn.htm

CHAPTER 10

INDIVIDUALISTIC AND ORGANIZATIONAL ANALYSES OF INFORMED CONSENT

Roger Bibace
Clark University

BETTY'S STORY IN THE FILM NEAR DEATH

Frederick Wiseman's (1989) film, *Near Death*, follows the lives of several patients as they, their families, and their medical caregivers confront life-threatening illnesses. The scenes were filmed at a major, urban, tertiary-care medical center. One patient's "story" was selected for analysis by the authors of the articles that follow. Each author, analyzing the same film sequences, brings a particular perspective to the task of examining the process of informed consent in the context of the conversation in the film.

The film story involves the care of "Betty" who has been intubated five times in 6 months as a result of chronic obstructive pulmonary disease (COPD) and has recently suffered a stroke. She is in the intensive care unit (ICU), presently intubated, unable to speak, and able to gesture only with great difficulty. She is conscious and apparently competent. From a medical standpoint, the choices include removing the intubation tube, the possible

Particulars and Universals in Clinical and Developmental Psychology, pages 167–180

need to reintubate or possible performance of a tracheotomy, or foregoing any of these interventions with the likely consequence of death.

The major participants (see Appendix) in the sequence disagree about how to proceed. Betty's husband, a retired physician, does not want to terminate treatment. The ICU physician ("Dr. Intensive") and head nurse ("Nurse") believe Betty would rather choose death than be reintubated, and in any case, believe her condition to be chronic, thus requiring a tracheotomy should Betty agree to continue treatment. (They believe Betty wants no treatment of any kind, however.) The family's attending physician ("Dr. Attending") agrees with Betty's husband in wanting to continue treatment and considers reintubation a viable alternative. Most importantly, Betty's wishes are unclear. The different caregivers provide divergent interpretations of Betty's attempts to communicate. It may be that she changes her mind during the course of her care. Like the participants in the film, the viewer remains uncertain about what Betty wants.

Our Research Group on Informed Consent has been meeting on a regular weekly basis for more than a year. The following study we report on was motivated by our group's assumption that the doctrine of informed consent was based on a questionable psychological premise (Bamberg, 1991). That is, we believed that the intent of the laws related to informed consent was to provide patients with information that would enable them to understand clearly the choices that they could exercise. In practice, however, our research group believed that, for a variety of reasons, providing information had somehow become the equivalent of understanding. It is this assumption that our group questioned. Several of our articles raise diverse psychological issues and assumptions about a "conduit metaphor" (Budwig, 1991), which has led some investigators to equate "information" and "understanding."

I began this investigation by assuming that the individual was *the* preferred unit of analysis. And the individual to be focused on should be the physician, since it is the physician's responsibility to insure that informed consent has been obtained. Lastly, a physician's style of doctoring could be analyzed according to a pre-established set of norms. I was also clear, in my assumptions, as to which of four doctoring styles (see later paragraphs) were appropriate for clinical activities related to informed consent.

The combination of these assumptions underlying my approach was rooted in my socialization as a psychologist. As Kimble (1984) points out, in psychology, the *epistemic differential* between experimental and clinical psychologists revolves around whether to pay attention to *part processes* within an individual manipulated experimentally, or attempt to use other methods, e.g., clinical and naturalistic methods to determine what the *whole* person is like. In both cases, however, psychologists focus on individuals as the unit of analysis. This individualistic emphasis was, in my professional life, compounded by family medicine's focus on the doctor–patient relationship. For the past 16 years, I have been concerned with doctor–patient relationships: based on my direct observation of doctors interacting with one or more patients, and leading Balint groups in which doctors present difficulties they are having with a particular patient. In *all* of these interactions, the focus is on a *dyad,* but even more specifically on the characteristics of the *person* who is talking to me, namely the physician. Lastly, this individualistic emphasis was enhanced by the opportunity to rely on an empirical-analytic approach to doctor–patient relationships. Byrne and Long's (1978) study of 100 physicians in some 2,400 doctor–patient interactions in England had generated four doctor styles—from extreme doctor-centered styles relying on specific behaviors, such as the physician attempts to "gain information," followed by "analyzing and probing," to patient-centered doctoring styles characterized by clarifications, interpretations, and reflections of the patient's feelings. To be able to rely on normative data for a reliable scoring system with face validity is, for many psychologists, a traditional and compelling virtue.

An individualistic analysis allows us to compare Dr. Intensive, Dr. Attending, and the respiratory therapist with respect to how patient-centered they are in their doctoring styles with Betty. Such individualistic analyses would enable comparisons among clinicians. I assumed that doctoring styles that emphasized interpretations based upon the *clarification* and *reflection* of the patient's feelings were most desirable. In contrast, doctoring styles that merely *provided information* were less likely to result in real understanding by the patient. The distinction between "information" and "understanding" was our group's point of departure; gauging a patient's understanding was our interdisciplinary objective. However, such individualistic analyses appeared inadequate in that they did not *specify* the "contexts" in which these doctor–patient interactions occurred. A number of factors, readily apparent to clinicians in medical settings, influenced the shift to include organizational features in which these doctor–patient interactions occurred.

HISTORICAL ISSUES

Historical issues reflect the socioeconomic changes in societal values in different historical eras generally, and these are reflected in the healthcare system. Informed consent as a legal doctrine was enacted during an era when civil rights were a dominant social issue. But the organizational principles regulating doctor–patient interactions in that historical era were taken for granted. The sharp antinomy between the 1960s and the 1980s and 1990s in medical practice in the United States is reflected in two aphorisms. In earlier times, "The more you did, as a physician, the more you earned," whereas in a contemporary managed care system, "The less you do, the more you earn."

Organizationally, there have been numerous changes in these two historical eras—all designed to restrict costs. For instance, the diagnostic related groups (DRGs) have combined with fiscal deficits in hospitals to create a "mood," which may and sometimes does pit doctors and their patients against hospital personnel administrators or professionals alike.

INCREASED AMBIGUITY: "WHOSE AGENT ARE YOU?"

There has been a major shift over the past two decades, from a private fee-for-services arrangement between physician and patient to a public, third-party reimbursement system. This change has brought about an alliance between third-party payers and hospitals. Physicians, construed as providers, are now constrained to function within the guidelines of both third-party payers and the hospitals in which medical services are offered. All these changes have made a physician's answer to a patient's question "Whose agent are you?" much more ambiguous. A physician and patient, in this historical era, may agree on a course of treatment; yet that choice may not be sanctioned by the hospital and third-party payer. The laws about informed consent should, but do not, take such organizational contexts into account. Thus, for an organizational analysis, all of the above, in addition to the factors traditionally considered in individualistic analyses, find their final expression in what transpires in a specific doctor–patient interaction with respect to issues of informed consent.

How did these professionals, as individuals, cope with the ambiguities inherent in dealing with Betty, a patient whose ability to communicate is limited to nods and ambiguous gestures? How did this group of professionals reflect our societal values, changes, and pressures on the healthcare system? Most clearly and repeatedly expressed by the hospital personnel is the need, or should we say institutional pressure, to get this patient out of the intensive care unit. Because there are limited facilities, personnel must "prioritize"—the question has now become "Whose medical needs are most urgent?" not how optimal care for this patient can be maximized.

In a different historical era, the *benevolence* (see Kuhn, 1962) of a physician could be implemented by active physician advocacy on behalf of the patient. Now, the DRGs place constraints on physician advocacy. Peer reviews can censor and punish a physician who repeatedly favors a patient's needs at institutional expense—a juxtaposition that is at the core of the DRG system, the juxtaposition between *group norms* (the universalistic orientation) and what is idiosyncratically desirable *for this patient* (the particularistic orientation).

Dr. Intensive and the respiratory therapist buttress their stance against intubation by reiterating the patient's consistently stated refusal for any interventions. The ICU professionals are against the patient being intubated for the sixth time! It is clear that there is a conflict between the "intensivists," the ICU personnel, and the patient's own doctor. The ICU physician states the philosophy of the unit, the reliance on a "Quaker consensus" that includes the "patient's wants, the nurses' wants, the doctors' wants, the family's wants; and every time you have difficulty, it's because one of those elements is out of sync." And here Dr. Intensive, the unit physician, emphatically states that the patient's doctor is out of "sync." That is, Dr. Intensive is relying on an individualistic interpretation of Dr. Attending's behavior. Conversely, Dr. Attending, arguing with the Nurse, justifies the previous five intubations: "Since her troubles are transient, intubation was an appropriate form of therapy." When the respiratory therapist states that her "concern is, being she's been re-intubated five times in 6 months." Dr. Attending replies, "Yeah! But each time with a reversible phenomenon—look how much better she is *now*." Dr. Attending can compare Betty's current medical status to *her past history*.

From an individualistic orientation, Dr. Attending could come across as presumptuous and paternalistic, a physician who makes decisions *for* Betty. However, he is also the only professional who talks about Betty as a person, reminding Betty and others that she is a "very intelligent and strong woman who has always known what you wanted to do about your own health, and that your wishes would be exactly what we would live by... would be our guidelines." He has known this patient and her husband, Henry, *over time*. He has known Betty as a *person* between the crises, and not only on a medical intensive-care unit.

In the above I am relying on assumptions made in family medicine. Dr. Attending is *not* a family physician, but his relationship to Betty is one in which he "knows the patient's name"—to use Stephens' (1975) metaphor. It is in the historical context of repeated doctor–patient interactions that trust can flourish, that negotiated truths about a patient's past are more likely to be arrived at by doctor and patient, and that consensually validated ideas and feelings about self and other can be developed by doctor and patient.

Or synonymously, in the language of experimental design, continuity of care in a doctor–patient relationship allows for repeated measures of any one event; for extensive sampling of different events; for more representative sampling of the same or different events under diverse conditions. Such experimental designs, I am arguing, lead to more valid conclusions than can a cross-sectional sample, especially when the cross-sectional sample has no controls. In contrast, the longitudinal study of an *N* of 1 allows for comparisons for both doctor and patient to their own base rates—base rates that may refer to a quantitative index (for example, blood pressure) or to subjective feelings. And quantitative and qualitative indices may vary in both doctor and patient as diagnostic clues (Bibace, n.d.; Bibace, 1982; Balint, 1968).

The reader will note that the physicians and nurses are also making assumptions regarding who or what should be the appropriate unit of analysis. For instance, Dr. Intensive, adopting an individualistic perspective, assumes that Dr. Attending is out of "sync." However, at no time do any of the participants discern the possibility that the institutional rules about a patient's stay on the ICU, or typical medical procedures for such a disease, viewed institutional roles readily subsume the impersonally, maybe out of "sync" for this reality of different relationships to the patient at this time. Physicians and nurses have been socialized to an individualistic unit of analysis.

The contrast between these two doctors is not merely a reflection of their personalities, but also mirrors important aspects of major attitudinal, conceptual, and clinical differences among diverse specialists in medicine—those who take pride in understanding the pathophysiology of a disease proper, and those who argue that it is also crucial to understand the person who has the disease. In the realm of informed consent, when a patient's choice is at stake, these differences are underscored. That is, the differences between Dr. Intensive and Dr. Attending *can be interpreted as differences in specialty attitudes, intellectual styles, and clinical orientations.*

The organizational approach would further highlight how the health-care system has changed and is changing in the United States, and that one extremely important change, for both physician and patient, is the organizational constraints (DRGs, peer review) that now intrude into the relationship between doctors and patients. Whereas formerly a physician could clearly and unequivocally be the patient's agent, now other allegiances (hospital policies, the managed care system of a practice) interfere with such commitment. Indeed, some physicians reflecting this recent *historical shift* in their role, state that they now consider themselves "employees" of their institution (Bibace, n.d.).

From an organizational perspective, a concept such as an "institutional role" might help to understand the differences among the three professionals and the alliances between Dr. Intensive and the respiratory therapist, versus Dr. Attending and Betty's husband. Institutional roles make the consistent differences among the professionals more understandable. Further, institutional roles readily subsume the reality of different relationships to the patient.

Throughout, the tentativeness of my conclusions is based on our group's shared opinion about our own stance as observers and interpreters of this documentary. This study has highlighted the desirability of conducting studies based on *the kind of data that has yet to be reported in the literature on informed consent*—that is, systematically eliciting both the physician's and patient's thoughts and feelings as they are allowed to become, like ourselves, observers and commentators of their own videotaped interactions. It is the lack of such data that should properly constrain *all* interpretations of Betty's interactions with both doctors and the respiratory therapist.

DIVERGENT CONCEPTIONS OF DOCTOR–PATIENT RELATIONSHIPS

The doctor–patient relationship remains at the center of controversies within medicine. There are, for instance, major disagreements between so-called primary-care specialties and tertiary-care specialties. Even more specifically, the intellectual basis for family medicine requires family physicians to deal with the person who has the disease and not merely the disease. This orientation sharply contrasts with many tertiary-care specialties that deal with the patient as the *host* of the disease, not as a person whose ideas and subjective feelings also need to be considered.

This controversy within medicine has been led, in large part, by the self-identification of family medicine in the late 1960s with the counterculture (Stephens, 1975). The social reform movement of the 1960s—including civil rights and the rise of feminism—also gave credence to more egalitarian forms of doctor–patient relationships. I believe that it is through such junctures that the spirit of the law and the ideals of the doctor–patient relationship can be joined. Such integrations have been concretized, in family medicine, through a national curriculum that emphasized the Four C's: One should interact with patients in a *comprehensive, caring* way, as well as a commitment to *curing* a person's diseases; the caring and curing should be maintained over time, that is, care should be *continuously* provided by the same physician.

It is still the case nationally that the distinction between curing and caring is dismissed by some specialties and given lip service by an even greater number of physicians. Thus, the universalistic orientation focuses on *curing* the pathophysiological aspects of disease. The particularistic orientation requires both *curing* and *caring* for this *person* who has a disease. Comprehensiveness is also deemed necessary in family medicine because generalists are educated to look beyond the presenting complaint or medical condition to a person's lifestyle in his or her familial context. Finally, family medicine posits that continuity of care is essential. It is through continuity of care (that is, care over long periods of time) that one can develop a sense of how individuals vary from their own base rates (Bibace, 1982). Sensitivity to variations in base rates for a particular person is a criterion for implementation of the ideal of providing personal care.

This, of course, contrasts sharply with medical interventions (either in the diagnostic or treatment phase) based on protocols. A culture that fosters homogenization should not be surprised that such "of-the-rack" rather than "tailor-made" practices are also reflected in medicine as well as other areas of life. Indeed it was one of our foremost jurists, Oliver Wendell Holmes (1891), who stated in 1860:

> The truth is that medicine, professedly founded on observation, is as sensitive to outside influence, political, religious, philosophical, imaginative, as is the barometer to the changes of atmospheric density. Theoretically, it ought to go on its own straightforward inductive path, without regard to changes in government or to fluctuations of public opinion. But... [actually there is] a closer relation between the medical sciences and the conditions of society and the general thought of the time, than would at first be suspected. (p. 177)

It is part of my argument that the universalizing tendencies in medicine have, in the last decade, regained the ascendancy. Our current historical era is obsessed with cost effectiveness, with skepticism and cynicism that is correlated with an increase in litigiousness. This is in marked contrast to the social reform era of the 1960s, of Lyndon Johnson's aspirations to the Great Society. Unfortunately, the law, in its attempt to insure a patient's rights, has dealt with medicine and physicians as if the latter were a homogeneous group. In doing so, it has obliterated a number of distinctions and controversies within medicine. The law may argue that this is as it should be. However, the legal doctrine of informed consent has not paid sufficient attention to the contexts within which consent is obtained. The law has glossed over the actualities of doctor–patient relationships.

The result has been that many physicians experience activities subsumed by informed consent as a legal imposition and not as intrinsic to doctoring. The irony is that the legal perspective is rarely self-critical when it righteously accuses physicians of "going through the motions," providing information but not understanding, and not adhering to the spirit of the law of informed consent. Conversely, from a clinician's perspective, one could ask whether the *letter* of the law should address the actualities of the doctor–patient relationship!

DISCUSSION

Initial Assumptions

I will now review my four initial assumptions underlying individualistic and organizational analyses of informed consent and indicate how they have changed in the course of our study. All clinicians and scientists, including activities implicated by informed consent, require:

1. The selection of a "unit of analysis": All clinicians and scientists are socialized by their education and training to focus on *some* rather than *other* aspects of an issue. This perennial problem has been referred to in epistemology as "levels of organization." The unit of analysis selected by a scientist or clinician is the preferred level of organization. That "level" can be analyzed from different theoretical perspectives, for example, mechanistically or systematically—irrespective of whether the level is a cell, an organ system, a linguistic segment (see Bamberg, 1991; Budwig, 1991), a person (Bibace, 1975; see also Raphaely, 1991), or, as will be argued here, an institutional role based on national and local regulatory practices (see Cotsonas, 1991).
2. The adoption of a universalistic or particularistic orientation toward that unit analysis: Universalistic analyses strive to articulate processes (be they biological, psychological, or sociological). Particularistic analyses strive to understand how this instance of the universal process is manifested. In our articles, Bamberg and Budwig most clearly adhere to the former orientations, Bibace and Raphaely to the latter. Cotsonas, as a lawyer, points to the problems emanating from the general legal requirements and the particular medical needs of a patient.
3. The kind of judgments arrived at by diverse analyses: The universalistic orientation, with the goal of knowledge, strives to be nonjudgmental for any unit of analysis. The particularistic orientation requires judgments about this patient or this physician. Judgments in law are necessarily determinations of innocence or culpability; and in clinical activities, judgments about peer professionals are often colored by blame.
4. The emphasis and breadth of context: This fourth assumption differentiates individualistic and organizational approaches. The latter approach opts for a more inclusive context, the former for a less inclusive context to understanding behavior.

In summary, all four assumptions are operative in diverse specialties within medicine and within psychology. This similarity in the assumptions applies to specialists in both medicine and psychology who value and emphasize generalizable and impersonal *processes*, that is, presumptively universal processes—be they biological processes that address pathophysiology or psychological processes that articulate principles of perception and cognition. Such specialists, in both fields, conflict with colleagues in their own discipline who value and emphasize approaches and explanations that are more particularistic and personal. Experimentalists and tertiary-care clinicians strive for universal principles. That is, they focus more exclusively and narrowly on the disease itself, while others insist that broader contexts (the person who has the disease, or the person in the familial context who is sick) should be taken into account in trying to understand problems or diseases.

Thus specialists in medicine and psychology distribute themselves according to impersonal-personal orientations, universalistic-particularistic objectives; neutral-judgmental outcomes, and more or less inclusive contexts as foci.

Grounding the Assumptions

The four assumptions are interrelated in Wiseman's (1989) documentary through Wiseman's foci (see Bamberg's article, 1991), through our group's divergent units of analysis, regarding what is to be analyzed as relevant to obtaining informed consent, through our group's divergent theoretical perspectives about universalistic or particularistic orientations, through the context selected or presumed to be relevant for analysis, through our group's changes in their judgments about the two physicians, and through changes within a member of the group, as well as different judgments among members of the group.

Regardless of the unit of analysis selected by investigators, the other three assumptions have to be addressed. That is, the interpretive framework of the investigator may target the person (or persons) involved (in this segment, Dr. Intensive or Dr. Attending) or the scene that subsumes all these people (that is, the systemic characteristic of this intensive care unit, in this institution, in this national healthcare system, in this historical era).

However, any unit of analysis can converge on particulars or on putative psychological or social processes. Further, the objectives of such analyses may be attempts to understand the biopsychosocial processes or to arrive at judgments about responsibility and culpability. Such objectives are, of course, not limited to the law. Many theoretical frameworks in behavioral science either implicitly or explicitly allocate blame. I believe that the analyses of persons lead to more explicit allocation of blame or judgments by investigators who approve or disapprove of how the informed consent activities were carried out. Approaches that rely on scientific analysis of the processes (irrespective of whether these processes are psychological or sociological) often purport to be neutral. However, as recent philosophers of science have pointed out (Fleck, 1979; Pellegrino & Thomasma, 1988), all interpretations are driven by both epistemological and value perspectives. The attempts by scientific investigators to hew to the neutrality stance often result in judgments of approval and disapproval that are implicit. The reader is often required to "unpack" the interpreter's narrative to determine *who* is being blamed or found wanting with respect to the implementation of informed consent.

According to this argument, decisions about the unit of analysis are often made without considered reflection. The preferred unit of analysis is taken as a given. This is the case because researchers, clinicians, lawyers, and ethicists have been socialized into beliefs about what should be the proper unit of analysis. For instance, readers of this journal prefer families as the unit of analysis. Ethicists, on the other hand, typically focus on individuals.

Current Assumptions

Following this initial study, I have revised my original assumptions and procedures for further study. In the light of our joint analyses, I now think that our initial assumption that information is not equivalent to understanding is still correct but not sufficiently comprehensive. *Understanding informed consent should be contextualized in and is a prerequisite for both empirical studies and clinical activities.*

The argument for contextualization in the clinical domain is based on the ideals and clinical practices of family medicine. The argument for contextualization in the research domain is based on criteria for comprehensive, longitudinal, experimental designs.

Family medicine has demonstrated the values of comprehensive, continuous treatment of patients. From this perspective, understanding between doctor and patient is fostered as a result of numerous doctor–patient interactions; it is concerned with minor and major medical conditions and life crises of patients in their familial and community contexts. That is, *the context for understanding is the history of that doctor–patient relationship.* This is in sharp contrast to specialists who limit their contacts with a patient to episodic treatments of particular diseases, or who, because they are specialists and not generalists, focus their attention solely on some diseased parts of the body and overlook the sick person in his or her familial context.

I posit that there is a concordance between the philosophical and clinical orientations of family medicine and a comprehensive experimental design for investigating informed consent. A comprehensive experimental design should allow for representative sampling of behaviors across diverse conditions. Further, such a design should be repeated over time. Such repeated measures over time and conditions represent comprehensive, longitudinal studies. Through such an experimental design, controlled comparisons are possible, and controlled comparisons are the objective of experimental design. How does the episode selected for this pilot study match up with these clinical and experimental ideals?

Clinically, we are told that there have been several intubation episodes prior to the current hospitalization. From a family medicine perspective, some crucial doctor–patient interactions are not examined. Thus, the viewer of the documentary does not know what, if any, advanced directives had been undertaken by Dr. Attending with Betty and her husband, or whether he explored Betty's thoughts and feelings after the first hospitalization and intubation. This cycle of recovery, recurrence of hospitalization, and intubation was repeated a number of times. There is a lack of information about what happened to Betty in between these previous hospitalizations. Despite these omissions, our group, including this writer, interpreted Dr. Attending's behavior as presumptuous and paternalistic. I now wonder if his presumptions were based on prior doctor–patient interactions! Is his doctoring style with Betty consistent across his patients? Or is his paternalism particular to Betty or patients like Betty? One cannot make any interpretations at this point with a comfortable degree of confidence.

Each episode can be assumed to include three components that enable comparisons of doctor–patient interactions: prehospitalization interactions, interactions during hospitalization, and posthospitalization interactions. Betty's repeated hospitalizations allow for repeated measures of three doctor–patient interactions in each episode. Such *N*-of-1 studies would allow for meaningful connections between clinical practice in medicine and an experimental analysis of informed consent.

In contrast, our current pilot study does not allow for the kinds of comparative analyses mentioned above. Indeed, the diversity of analyses does not even claim reliability in their interpretations. However, we should point out that there are few empirical studies in this area. As a result of this study, we are able to point out some meaningful connections between some forms of clinical practice (family medicine) and comprehensive experimental designs (longitudinal studies with repeated measures).

In summary, the same tensions that one can articulate within the behavioral sciences and in diverse specialties in medicine are also present in clinical, legal, and scientific studies of informed consent. This article has begun to clarify some issues (choice of units of analysis, personal/impersonal orientations, culpability versus scientific understanding, and the role of context) as bases for these tensions. This article, like the others by our research group, highlights the importance of interdisciplinary perspectives brought to bear on the same comprehensive set of data. Such studies may not only articulate these issues but also point to possibilities for integration; such interpretations would hopefully result in clinical activities, with respect to informed consent, that are both humanistic and grounded in scientific understanding.

ACKNOWLEDGEMENT

Originally published as: Bibace, R. (1991). Individualistic and organizational analyses of informed consent. *Family Systems Medicine, 9*(4), 297–306. Republished in this volume with kind permission of APA publications.

APPENDIX: DRAMATIS PERSONAE

[MsP]	Mrs. Betty Powers—the patient
[DrP]	Dr. Henry Powers—Mrs. Powers's husband
[MrP]	Mr. Powers—Dr. and Mrs. Powers' son*
[DrA]	Dr. Frank Attending—the long-time attending physician
[DrI]	Dr. Brad Intensive—the head of the ICU treatment team
[NuN]	Nurse N—the head nurse
[lnF]	Dr. F—a resident intern
[ReD]	Maureen Dillen —the respiratory therapist
[NuL]	Nurse L—a nurse involved with the case
[NuP]	Nurse P—a nurse involved with the case
[NuR]	Nurse R—a nurse involved with the case
[NuS]	Nurse S—a nurse involved with the case
[NuW]	Nurse W—a nurse involved with the case
[NuX]	Nurse X—a nurse involved with the case
[NuZ]	Nurse Z—a nurse involved with the case
[DrR]	Dr. Relief—the head of the weekend ICU team

* Never actually on-film and, in this, representative of many others.

REFERENCES

Balint, M. (1968). *The doctor, his patient and the illness* (2nd ed.). London, England: Pitman Paperbacks.

Bamberg, M. (1991). Voices of curing and caring: The role of vagueness and ambiguity in informed consent discussions. *Family Systems Medicine, 9*(4), 329–342.

Bibace, R. (n.d.). *Personal reports in "Balint-type weekly groups for faculty family physicians."* (Unpublished manuscript, available from author).

Bibace, R. (1975, September). *Interactional complexities in diverse social contexts: A structure-function analysis.* Paper presented at the annual meeting of the American Psychological Association, Chicago, IL.

Bibace, R. (1982). Longitudinal norms in family medicine research. *Journal of Family Practice, 14,* 607–608.

Budwig, N. (1991). The conduit metaphor: Language and informed consent. *Family Systems Medicine, 9*(4), 313–327.

Byrne, P. S., & Long, B. E. L. (1978). *Doctors talking to patients.* Exeter, England: Royal College of General Practitioners.

Cotsonas, C. E. (1991). The law and the limits of the law of informed consent. *Family Systems Medicine, 9*(4), 307–312.

Fleck, L. (1979). Genesis and development of a scientific fact. Chicago, IL: University of Chicago Press.

Holmes, O. W. (1891). *Medical essays, 1842–1882.* Boston, MA: Houghton-Mifflin.

Kimble, G. (1984). Psychology's two cultures. *American Psychologist, 39,* 833–839.

Kuhn, T. S. (1962). *The structure of scientific revolutions.* Chicago, IL: University of Chicago Press.

Pellegrino, E., & Thomasma, D. C. (1988). *For the patient's good: The restoration of beneficence in health care.* New York, NY; Oxford University Press.

Raphaely, D. (1991). Informed consent near death: Myth and actuality. *Family Systems Medicine, 9*(4), 343–370.

Stephens, G. (1975). The intellectual basis of family practice. *Family Practice Medicine, 2,* 423–428.

Wiseman, F. (Director) (1989). *Near death.* Cambridge MA: Exit Films (Production) & Zipporah Films (Distribution).

CHAPTER 11

THERAPEUTIC MISCONCEPTIONS

When the Voices of Caring and Research Are Miscontrued as the Voice of Curing

Michael Bamberg and Nancy Budwig
Clark University

Research on doctor-patient communication has characterized such interactions as being asymmetrical. The present article tries to shift emphasis away from the different orientations individuals bring to the communicative setting and attempts to highlight the different orientations ("voices") within a given individual. We draw on an in-depth analysis of discourse between a 21-year-old man who can be ascribed the roles of both patient and potential research subject, and an interviewer who acts in both the role of medical staff and researcher. Focusing our analysis on a limited number of linguistic forms (pronouns and demonstratives), it is argued that the use of the same form for different referents signals a conflation of two voices—the voice of health care ("caring") and the voice of "research." Furthermore, we argue that the voice of research is most likely to be interpreted by the patient/

Particulars and Universals in Clinical and Developmental Psychology, pages 181–201

research subject within the framework of curing. As such, the present article promotes a shift in emphasis from different institutional—and as such often assumed to be preexisting—orientations between the communicating parties to differing orientations within the individual that cannot help but be misconstrued in terms of the curing voice. Our conclusion focuses on the ethical and discourse analytic implications of analyzing voices in a discussion.

VOICES AS VALUE ORIENTATIONS IN COMMUNICATIVE CONTEXTS

Employing the terminology of voice or voices, we emphasize that each communicative act is governed by a value orientation. Although it is possible to describe and analyze human actions as narratives (cf. Packer, 1991), traditionally the analysis of voices has taken the language use of particular groups or individuals as displaying an underlying value orientation. For instance, investigations of the moral domain have distinguished two voices demarcating the moral orientation of justice from that of care (cf. Gilligan, 1982, 1987, 1988), and investigations of the health and medical world have differentiated between the voice of the lifeworld and the voice of medicine (Mishler, 1984; Mishler, Clark, Ingelfinger, & Simon, 1989). Taken as prototypes, these voices strive after purification and perfection, and they mutually exclude each other. In most real-life interactions, however, they are not absolutes (i.e., each voice carries residues of the contrasting voice).

In a different article (Bamberg, 1991c), we tried to differentiate between two different value orientations in physicians—the voice of "caring" and the voice of "curing." Although the voice of caring is somewhat reminiscent of Gilligan's voice of caring (Gilligan, 1982, 1987, 1988), as well as Mishler's voice of the lifeworld, its most encompassing component is a view of the individual as functioning within his or her context of personal relationships. Within this perspective, the role of the individual in his or her family and other social relationships becomes relevant in regards to the evaluation of lifestyle habits and the roles of prevention. In contrast, the voice of curing emphasizes the illness and disease aspects of the body. Within this orientation, it is more likely to decontextualize aspects of the individual's functioning, reduce them to their physical or psychological components, and along this line to deal with them rationally and scientifically As a consequence, aspects of the institutional and technical context become highlighted. Thus, the voice of curing is one that focuses on the disease and considers rationally and scientifically what steps are optimal in a rather well-defined curing process.

Rather than characterizing the voices of curing and caring as clashing in dialogue between some prototypical exemplars of physicians or nurses, and at the same time avoiding the pitfalls of denying the legitimate existence of the voice of curing, we tried to document in two separate studies how the voice of caring and the voice of curing interplay within an individual, resulting in hesitations, ambiguities, and even in straightforward self-contradictions (cf. Bamberg, 1991c; Budwig, 1991). At the center of this line of argument was the recognition that conversational sequences are not to be viewed as following a unidimensional current or an overarching communicative goal that is assumed to preexist in the mind of the speaker, only waiting to be executed in discourse. Rather, communicative actions in real-life situations are probably best understood as expressions of multivoiced individuals (cf. also Bamberg, 1991a).

The case study presented in this article is an offspring from this original point, inasmuch as we are able to document in a similar vein how different communicative orientations come to bear on the actual dialogue between a person who is a representative of a medical staff as well as a member of a research team trying to recruit a patient for a research project on the effectiveness of the medical treatment the patient experiences. The institutional context in which this dialogue is embedded is that of an informed consent negotiation (i.e., the conversation follows to some degree a ritualized format that is imposed by general expectations, the way they are laid out and codified in Constitutional amendments, specific U.S. laws, and a number of previous cases).

INSTITUTIONALIZED CONTEXT OF INFORMED CONSENT AND ITS GROUNDING IN THE CONDUIT METAPHOR

The phrase *informed consent* is used to refer to the ethical principle of respect for persons and is articulated most effectively in the often-quoted passage by Justice Benjamin Cardozo: "The root premise is the concept, fundamental in American jurisprudence, that every human being of adult years and sound mind has a right to determine what shall be done with his own body" (*Schloendorff v. Society of New York Hospital*, 1914). The Nuremberg Code (see "Permissible Medical Experiments") from the year 1949 explicitly states as its first principle:

> The voluntary consent of the human subject is absolutely essential. This means that the person involved should have legal capacity to give consent; should be so situated as to be able to exercise free power of choice, without the intervention of any element of force, fraud, deceit, duress, over-reaching, or other ulterior form of constraint or coercion; and should have sufficient knowledge and comprehension of the elements of the subject matter involved as to en-

able him to make an understanding, and enlightened decision. (Levine, 1981, Appendix 3, pp. 285–286)

Thus, informed consent as an ethical principle can be viewed as following three different subprinciples: (a) that the decision to partake in medical or experimental treatment is voluntary, (b) that the patient/subject has sufficient information in a comprehensible format, and (c) that the patient/subject has the decision-making capacity to make an informed decision (cf. also the President's Commission, 1982, Vol. 3; also see World Medical Association Declaration of Helsinki, cited in Levine, 1981).

In February 1966, Surgeon General William Stewart established in the U.S. Public Health Service's Directives on Human Experimentation that the ethical conduct of research involving human subjects was to be regulated more firmly by public agencies (see the "Basic Health and Human Services Policy for Protection of Human Research Subjects" reprinted in Levine, 1981, Appendix 1, pp. 259–268). The legal grounding for informed consent is basically a result of the outcome of litigations and disputes that arose in the context of medical practice. Over the years, courts and legislators have developed two standards to determine whether a decision is actually informed. The predominant standard is "the community of professionals standard" that requires disclosure of information that the committee of health providers would disclose under similar circumstances. The "reasonable person standard" tries to put forth a patient-centered standard, requiring the disclosure of information that reasonable patients in similar contexts would like to know in order to make a sound decision. U.S. research regulations were originally designed to be responsive to the reasonable person's standard. To assist decisions regarding the elements of disclosure, courts and legislatures have spelled out what kinds of information should be disclosed. This information includes aspects such as the content of the procedures, potential risks, possible alternatives to the procedures, and anticipated benefits of the procedures. Although the doctrine of informed consent can by no means lay out specific ways in which information is to be presented, it nevertheless stresses that the disclosure of the information in and of itself is not sufficient. In addition, the process of providing the information has to follow procedures that enable the patient or the research subject to attend to the information, to understand, to accept and remember it, and to be able to reason with it (cf. also the President's Commission, 1932, Vol. 1, p. 71).

Consent is usually given in the form of signing a consent form. However, the fact that a document bears the patient's or research subject's signature is in no way binding if the information the patient received was not sufficient for making an informed choice or if the information was not properly understood. In general, a signed consent form is different from a commercial contract. As pointed out by Levine (1981, p. 98), the consent form is more like a judiciary, which serves "as an instrument designed to guide the negotiations with the prospective subject."

Research on the complex issue of ascertaining patients' or research subjects' understanding of information has focused on a number of different problems. Silva and Sorrell (1984) analyzed the factors that influence the comprehension of information for informed consent: nature of information (amount, clarity, and complexity), method of presentation, demographic factors (e.g., age, occupation, gender, and education/vocabulary levels), and personal factors (e.g., subjects' health, patterns of recall, and attitudes toward the informed consent process). Wu and Pearlman (1988) measured information transfer according to four categories of information (rationale of the procedures, the benefits, the risks, and the possible alternatives) and compared their measurement with post hoc interviews of patients and physicians. The President's Commission report concludes:

> Research has identified a number of influences on the success of the communication process and the nature of the message received. These include the particular words used, the structure and the framing of the information, the timing of the disclosure, and the setting in which the discussion takes place. (President's Commission, 1982, Vol. 1, pp. 89–99)

In spite of the critical orientation that most of the research on informed consent communication as well as the President's Commission report adopts, there is a central shortcoming in this work regarding the function of informed consent communication. This central shortcoming lies in the reduction of communication to serve the function to convey and transfer information (cf. Budwig, 1991). Unfortunately, this view is being nourished by a number of widely shared folk models (e.g., the conduit metaphor; cf. Bamberg & Lindenberger, 1984, and Reddy, 1979, for a critique of the conduit model) as well as scientific models in linguistics and cognitive psychology. According to these models, language is the means by which thought is transported from the "sending container" to the "receiving container." To uphold this transportation process, language is viewed as a sign system that refers to items in the world the sending container has picked out to be labeled. This article challenges this basic framework within which the notion of informed consent is situated. To be more specific, we argue that the conduit notion cannot handle particular kinds of understandings or misunderstandings that are grounded in what we like to call "quantity of communication." In contrast, as long as our understanding of informed consent is guided by the conduit model, and as long as we reduce language to its referential properties only, we end up with an insufficient understanding of informed consent—an understanding that is bound to quantify the factors that lead to understanding or misunderstanding in the search for specific reasons rather than to assessments of participants' frameworks that do not mesh in communications between experts and novices.

INVESTIGATION

Data

In our analysis, we used a videotaped interaction between a 21-year-old depressed man and the research coordinator taking place within the medical facility of a large West Coast city in the United States. The research was designed to determine whether the treatment factor (i.e., the therapy program offered within this facility) has any effect on the patients' well-being. The targeted candidate (research subject) for the research project (we named him Jacques) is an outpatient undergoing the treatment program due to his symptoms of depression. Thus, the procedure to obtain the consent of the patient to participate in the study concerns his agreement to undergo additional pretreatment and posttreatment interviews and to allow for the videotaping (and analysis) of the therapy sessions (also called "role play" or "role play sessions"). To obtain the patient's consent, the research coordinator (we named him Peter) has to go over the sequence and function of the normal treatment procedure and also needs to spell out how participating in this research project will subject Jacques to additional procedures. Furthermore, it is the obligation of the researcher to inform the patient/research subject about the overarching goals of the research project (i.e., as to why it is necessary for subjects to participate in the particular research procedures and to inform him or her about aspects of privacy, confidentiality, and the right to withdraw consent at any time during or after the research has been concluded).

Method of Analysis

Although previous investigations of the expression of value orientations have paid particular attention to the lexical devices chosen, we focus solely on the use of pronouns and demonstratives, especially the use of *it, this, that, we, you,* and *I.* Obviously, these forms refer to aspects of the situational context (i.e., items that are specified elsewhere and therefore are open to interpretation and miscommunication). We picked the personal pronouns *I, you,* and *we,* because their use indicates the alliances of speaker and hearer as researcher and research subject in the one role system and as a member of the health or medical staff and the patient in the other role system. *It, this,* and *that* were originally chosen as linguistic forms that potentially refer to the consent form or the act of signing the consent form, which constituted the overarching goal of the informed consent conversation. In the course of our analyses, however, these forms turned out to be extremely useful indexes for speaker and hearer in terms of signaling devices of what is assumed to be shared between them. Even more so, these forms became very useful when a speaker wanted to set up something he or she considered to be new versus something that had been referred to in previous passages of the discourse (cf. the following for similar ways of analyzing discourse: Bamberg, 1987, 1990, 1991b; Bamberg, Budwig, & Kaplan, 1991; Bamberg & Damrad-Frye, 1991; Budwig, 1986, 1989, 1990a, 1990b). Thus, not only with regard to the distinction between new versus old information, but at the same time in terms of spelling out more clearly where one is within an ongoing conversation and where the conversation might be heading, these highly ambiguous forms function pragmatically as "shifters" (cf. Jakobson, 1957/1971; Silverstein, 1987). That is, in the broadest sense, they contribute to the process of mutual understanding as pragmatic indexes, signaling how the speaker meant to be understood.

Turning to a detailed analysis of one interaction between the researcher and the patient/subject, we emphasize the following three related points:

1. We demonstrate how the use of the shifters *I, we, you, it, this,* and *that* indexes the topical segmentation of the discourse, resulting in the final outcome of the interaction, namely, obtaining the patient/subject's consent to participate in the research procedure.
2. In using this method for the analysis of informed consent processes, we aim to contribute to a better determination of the quality of information that is provided in informed consent. (cf. Benson, Roth, Appelbaum, & Lidz, 1988)
3. We also address the phenomenon termed *therapeutic misconception,* which explains how patients/subjects in psychiatric and medical research are led to the understanding (misconception) that there are direct benefits to them from participating in research. (cf. Appelbaum, Roth, & Lidz, 1982)

Analysis

Our analysis starts with the end point (goal) of the interaction, where Peter says:

> **277:** alright—basically that's what's in the paper
> **278:** okay
> **279:** what I'd like you to do

280: is—is read this over...
284: and then when you're finished reading
285: and you think you understand
286: you can just sign on the last page

That in Line 277 of the transcript refers to the whole of the previous conversation (i.e., what Peter and Jacques talked about in the previous 276 lines or clauses). *This* in Line 280 refers (deictically) to the consent form Peter held on his lap during this conversation. *That* and *this* are related insofar as the actual word *this* (i.e., the consent form) forms the basis for the law to which the patient/subject actually consented with his or her signature; *that* (i.e., an elaboration of the actual procedures within the overarching research question with the intent to provide optimal information and supposedly an optimal understanding), although not irrelevant to the law, is basically left up to the researcher's or interviewer's subjective assessment.

It is commonly assumed that the consent form should enlighten the subject sufficiently about the goals of the research as well as of the subject's role in participating in the concrete research procedures. Signing a consent form should, under normal circumstances, imply that the subject understands his or her participation and is aware of potential risks and benefits for self and for others. However, it may be in the best interest of all participants in a research project to have some prior understanding, especially of the larger framework within which the specific procedures operate. Particularly, in that participation in research presupposes trusting the expert researcher, any conversation regarding the informed consent process is to be considered as constitutive of the trust-building framework within which researcher and research participant (i.e., the subject) are supposed to cooperate. Consequently, at least according to our Western folk belief, the acquisition of information leads to better understanding, and understanding appears to be the basis of trust (cf. Patenaude, Rappeport, & Smith, 1986).

To assess the notions of quality of information and how the information may have been understood (including the potential therapeutic misconception), let us follow Peter's course of argumentation, that is, how he got to Lines 277–286 (cf. with earlier argumentation), namely, finally asking Jacques to sign the consent form.

In Lines 17–18, Peter establishes the topic for the subsequent conversation (i.e., the therapy program):

17: well—what I wanted to talk to you about
18: was like I told you earlier today about the therapy program
19: that we have in this facility

In the subsequent lines, Peter grounds his role as research coordinator within the particular facility (including the therapy program), although he seems to try to hint at the fact that the research project, of which he is coordinator, and the therapy program are not the same. The difference between the two is indexed by the use of *they* in Line 22 and *we* in Lines 25–28 and 36–38; although, from this perspective, the use of *we* in Lines 19, 27, and 37 becomes somewhat blurred (does *we* refer to the research group or to the therapeutic staff'?):

> **21:** okay—my job is
> **22:** really I am what they call research coordinator...
> **25:** what we are trying to find out is
> **26:** we're trying to find out first
> **27:** whether or not the medical facility we have here
> **28:** is helping people...
> **36:** and the second part of what we're trying to find out
> **37:** is in particular whether or not the therapy program we have
> **38:** is helping people.

In Line 51, Peter uses the same form *we*, although this time just referring to Jacques and himself (the deictic plural: you and I). At the same time, the use of *it* in the same line refers to the previous conversation, signaling that some information (and consequently some understanding) has been established between the two of them previously. Thus, the subsequent discourse (up to a point) does no more and no less than to elaborate and, it is hoped, deepen the understanding reached thus far:

> **50:** well—let me back up
> **51:** and we'll go through it slowly
> **52:** and see what we're all about...
> **55:** what we have
> **56:** we have a—a program
> **57:** that's called the therapy program

Subsequent discourse (Lines 59–134) elaborates and explains what this therapy program, as part of this particular medical facility, is all about. In going over the different aspects of this program, the researcher points out the possible merits of the program for the participating patients. Without going into a detailed analysis of this part, Peter does not seem to speak in this stretch as the research coordinator but, rather, as someone else would who knows the program well enough. At the same time, the first guess from Line 51, namely, that *it* (in "and we'll go through it slowly") refers to the therapy program, gets further substantiated from the subsequent stretch of discourse (Lines 59–134). This interpretation is furthermore confirming that the topic of the overall conversation is really the therapy program (cf. with Lines 17–19), whereas the actual role of Peter as the research coordinator as well as Jacques's role as participant in the research project (Lines 25–28 and 36–38) become more and more backgrounded.

This discourse orientation changes drastically from Line 143 on. In his discursive orientation, however, Peter introduces this change by making use of Jacques's former agreement that, in his opinion, this particular medical facility is actually good for him (Lines 29–32, not quoted here):

135: okay
136: so—now—like you said
137: you think
138: this particular medical facility here is helping you . . .
143: another way we can find this out
144: is by looking at you
145: now that you're beginning at this facility . . .
156: and when you're finished
157: when you're ready to be discharged from this facility
158: we just want to look at you again . . .
177: okay—so—now—how do we do this

Peter begins to describe the actual research procedure (i.e., what kind of testing the patient has to undergo as a research participant). Thus, retrospectively, it becomes clear that *we* in Lines 143, 158, and 177 is not referring any longer to Peter and others in their role as staff in the therapy program. Rather, *we* refers to Peter (in his role as research coordinator) and the research team. Within this reading, the topic has shifted with Line 143 from the contents and potential merits of the therapy program to an elaboration of Lines 36–38, namely, "We're trying to find out . . . whether or not the therapy program . . . is helping people."

The gist of the information in the stretch of discourse following Line 143 is that there are two parts to the research project. The first part consists of the two interviews at the beginning and at the end of the participation of the therapy program (cf. Lines 143–145 and 156–158); the other part of the research project supposedly consists of the analysis of videotaped group sessions in which the patients engage in role play. Again, for this part of the research, Peter as the research coordinator needs Jacques's consent to videotape him and to analyze the videotaped interactions with others. Accordingly, Jacques needs to be informed that his participation is voluntary and that the information obtained will be kept confidential.

This second part of the research is introduced in Lines 202–203:

202: the other part of what we're going to do
203: is the role playing—okay

And its importance for the research team is underscored in the following excerpts:

218: it's actually the best way
219: we have
220: of finding out about your interaction skills . . .
236: and it's important
237: like I said
238: that we get that information . . .
265: we put it on videotape
266: and we erase it
267: as soon as we're finished . . .
272: and that's it
273: and I'll put your name on it
274: and no one sees the videotape except myself and my two research assistants
275: okay
276: Jacques: yeah
278: alright—basically that's what's in the paper

It in Line 218 refers to *role play*, whereas *it* in Line 236 points forward to Line 238. *It* in Line 265 refers back to *information*, *it* in Lines 266 and 273 refers back to *videotape*, whereas *it* in Line 272 may refer to either the whole research project or the conversational goal (i.e., to inform Jacques about the procedural aspects of his participation in the research project and to get his consent). In regard to the use of *we* in Lines 238, 265, 266, and 267, it becomes clear with Line 274 that the research team consists of Peter and two research assistants.

Before engaging in a more fine-grained analysis of Lines 240–263, let us pause and summarize how the flow of the conversation is segmented. Having a clearer notion of the topical segmentation, we can more clearly determine the overall orientation of the discourse and how the different parts contribute to this orientation. At the outset of the conversation (see Line 18), Peter establishes the discourse topic (i.e., the therapy program). When he presents this program in more detail (Lines 61–134), he can be understood as part of this program that is designed to help patients. Thus, by creating the discourse topic (i.e., therapy program) and presenting it using the pronoun *we*, Peter speaks the "voice of health care." In other segments of the discourse, Peter speaks of a different *we*, namely, the "voice of research." This voice briefly surfaces in Lines 26–28 and 36–38 and then, later on, becomes the dominant voice starting with Line 143, finally culminating in the research coordinator's encouragement to sign the consent form in Lines 277–288. (Lines 240–263 cannot be integrated into the voice of research, but they are discussed in more detail later.)

The only point at which the two voices are distinguished and somewhat set against each other is when Peter introduces himself: "*They* call me the *research coordinator*." However, this crucial point in the conversation, where Peter stages his identity for Jacques and the future course of the conversation, by no means clarifies his role as part of the research team. Rather, his appeal to them, meaning those who gave him the name research coordinator, may also signal that he does not feel happy in this role and that his "real" identity lies somewhere else. Again, the possibility of this interpretation further suggests that Peter would like to be understood as someone who speaks the voice of health care and helping.

In sum, Peter speaks in two different voices: that of the healthcare profession and that of the research team. Both are not differentiated enough for a clear understanding of the two different underlying perspectives. In spite of the fact that nothing really changes from Jacques's viewpoint (e.g., he may have been videotaped anyway, and he most likely will undergo repeated interviews regarding his progress in the program), the fact that a research perspective is added to the healthcare perspective makes it necessary to keep them apart, because they have different origins and they pursue different goals. Both perspectives, and thus both voices through which they are established, operate optimally within a trust-building framework. However, borrowing trust that already has been established within one framework and carrying it over to establish trust for another framework may turn out to be counterproductive, because this generates hopes and illusions the research project ultimately may not be able to meet.

We are not arguing that Peter is picking this undifferentiated perspective as a strategy to improve his chances of getting Jacques's consent to participate in the research project. Actually, we are convinced of the contrary, namely, that this is the last thing on his mind. Rather, and there is some evidence for this line of thought, it is Peter's deeper identification with the voice of the healthcare profession that makes it difficult for him in his presentation of the therapy program to differentiate between the two voices that need to be kept apart in this kind of discourse. In a fine-grained analysis of Lines 240–263, we further develop this particular argument.

In the following part of the conversation (after Peter has clarified why the research team needs the information from the role-playing sessions for assessing the effectiveness of the program but before Peter informs Jacques that the sessions will be videotaped), he slips back into the healthcare profession voice:

236: and it's important
237: like I said
238: that we get that information
239: Jacques: okay
240: because what we do with it then
241: is we use it to help you in group
242: okay—like if we find out
243: umm—you're doing something
244: like some people have nervous habits
245: when they talk to people
246: when they play with their hair
247: they bounce their knee
248: or something like that
249: Jacques: mhm
250: quite distracting
251: if you're trying to have a conversation with somebody
252: sitting there
253: going like this the whole time
254: you know
255: Jacques: right
256: if we see things like that
257: we can help you
258: learn to do something else with your hands
259: okay
260: so that you don't have that
261: Jacques: right
262: alright
263: that's the kind of stuff we do with it
264: like I said
265: We put it on videotape
266: and we erase it
267: as soon as we're finished

It in Lines 240, 241, and 263 refers back to *that information* (Line 238), which later on is specified as videotaped data (Lines 264–267). Because data from videotaped therapy sessions can be reviewed and used effectively for individual treatment, we have no quarrels with the message Peter is trying to convey in this passage. Considering the previous and subsequent co-text of this passage, however, we wonder whose voice is speaking, that of the researcher or the person conducting the therapy sessions.

Jacques has already agreed to undergo treatment in this particular medical facility. Thus, to hear "we . . . help you in group" (Line 241) must sound encouraging. However, when he hears this from Peter, the research coordinator, whose goal is to "get that information" (Line 238), to "put it on videotape" (Line 265), and to have Jacques "sign the last page" (of the consent form; Line 286), Jacques is likely to misconceive the treatment of his illness and the research project as being the same thing. One may argue that the research project ultimately will feed back into better therapy programs (or their replacement by better procedures), but Jacques himself will most likely not profit from the insights that come out of the conducted research.

Peter seems to be aware of the potential misconception, and he avoids using *you* as the addressee who potentially benefits from using the more impersonal third-person plural; "some people have nervous habits when they talk to people" (Lines 244–245). In Lines 257–260, however, Peter returns to the use of *you*, supposedly in an effort to become more personal. Again, one may argue that *you* in this passage, especially because it is used interchangeably with the third-person plural, is not addressing Jacques, but rather any patient participating in the therapy program. This is correct, although our point here is that he is the research coordinator and not the therapist. The voice he is speaking in, however, is that of the nurse or the therapist and not that of the researcher.

If *it* in the lines previous to the passage in question, and subsequent to it, were referring to the therapy program, the declared topic of the interaction, we would have no quarrel with Peter's wording. Because *it*, however, refers to the videotaped data that are of relevance for the research project, treatment and research project become totally undifferentiated, leading Jacques to misconstrue research and treatment as being one and the same. This is a typical case of what is called "therapeutic misconception" (cf. Appelbaum et al., 1982; Appelbaum, Roth, Lidz, Benson, & Winslade, 1987).

CONCLUSIONS

Analyzing Voices in Discourse: Implications for Discourse Analysis

The assumption of different voices in speech is not a new discovery that emerged from the analysis of speech data we chose to present in this article. Rather, it is a theoretical construct that explains certain phenomena. The phenomena explained in the speech sample we analyzed were of a peculiar heterogeneity and vagueness regarding the correspondences between speech forms and what these speech forms symbolize. The fact that something was wrong or at least not clear became obvious to us in our first reading of the transcript. Not knowing at that time what we were up to, we had sensed a tension between two seemingly contrasting communicative orientations. On the one hand, we realized that the researcher intended to disclose information that was pertinent to the potential research subject's voluntary decision to partake in the research project (as a research subject). In other words, the researcher wanted to enlist an informed subject, who not only gives consent but, at the same time, cooperates meaningfully in the research procedures. On the other hand, however, there were indicators in the researcher's interactions that gave us the impression that the researcher was not clear about the role of the research program; it seemed as if the researcher tried to disassociate and distance himself from the research program. On closer examination of particular linguistic forms, we tried out the construct of two communicative orientations (voices) that interact and as such create the tension that originated in our first encounter with the transcript.

However, the two interacting orientations we were able to differentiate in terms of a voice of caring and a voice of research are not a priori mutually exclusive. Research can be (or should be) a trust-building, cooperative experience between researcher and subject. Within the institutional constraints in which research takes place, however, there is a general conception of research as being a means to the end of publishing and of research subjects as providing a way to quantify and generalize across a given number of exemplars. As long as research subjects cooperate within this framework, they represent good means. The interpersonal relationship between researcher and research subject within this framework presents an interfering contextual variable that usually is not in the interest of an objective research design and therefore—within this framework—should be reduced to a minimum.

It is exactly this institutionalized framework against which young students and professionals of health care institutions often rebel, because, as we believe, this framework is diametrically opposed to the caring orientation that originally led students to choose a career in the healthcare profession. Furthermore, both orientations—the voice of curing and the voice of research—share at their bottom line the same decontextualization of the role of the individual person and as such potentially clash with the voice of caring. The curing orientation reduces the individual person to the object or carrier of illness and disease, whereas the research orientation reduces the individual person to his or her participatory role in the research project as the object.

In our discourse analysis of the use of particular linguistic forms, we have identified and exposed two contrasting orientations within the same speaker. In the interaction piece we chose for analysis, the researcher is torn between two different value orientations—the voice of caring and the voice of research. Although we do not have any independent measures to confirm how the tension between these two voices was actually understood by the potential research subject, we nevertheless speculate that they could be construed as one voice, namely, as the voice of curing. Two factors support our interpretation. First, the remarks and questions of the potential research subject stood out primarily as indexes of his patient orientation. At no time during the informed consent negotiation did Jacques seem to fully accept the role of the potential research subject and orient the communication toward this goal. Second, the specialty of the situation of doing research in a healthcare setting promotes a tendency to construe research as a component of curing, that is, as part of the institutionalized sequencing of finding out what is wrong (anamnesis) in order to cure (treatment).

Our discourse analytic point of view produced two important achievements. First, this article documents the multivoiced speaker or, in Bakhtin's (1986, p. 78) terms, exemplifies the fact that "we speak in diverse genres without suspecting that they exist." As such, we added to previous assumptions regarding the "social language" of different social groups or strata and to the assumption that individual persons have different social languages "within a given social system at a given time" (Holquist & Emerson, 1981, p. 430). It is also important to note that different cultural and institutional contexts may be expressed in the same situation by the same speaker. In other words, individual persons have more than one value orientation, which at times is difficult to integrate into an overarching system. Moreover, these different value orientations can be analyzed and exposed by discourse analytic means.

The second achievement of this article is a more general orientation away from the imposition of unidimensional goals onto human motivations in interactions and toward an analysis of different value orientations in interaction. Thus, we propose to give up the 1 Person = 1 Value equation in favor of a detailed analysis of how values emerge and change in human interactions. Discourse analysis understood along those lines would automatically be understood in terms of a critical analysis of the "ideological formulation, the communicative reproduction, the social and political decision procedures and the institutional management and representation of such issues as inequality, class differences, sexism, racism, power, and dominance" (van Dijk, 1985, p. 7; cf. also Lavandera, 1988).

Analyzing Voices in Discourse: Ethical Implications

It is the ultimate aim of the doctrine of informed consent to protect the autonomy of the citizen. Consequently, the information given should be adequate so that the subject/patient can make an informed choice. Further, the information must be comprehensible for the subject/patient. The expert not only has to avoid unnecessary jargon but, more important, has to tune his or her language use according to his or her patient's social or ethnic background and to his or her particular mental or folk models that also may affect the patient's conception of treatment options (cf. Budwig, 1991; Cicourel, 1985). Finally, the consent of the subject/patient has to be voluntary. Although it may be difficult to define in concrete situations how adequate the information really was, whether it was really understood, and whether the ultimate choice may have possibly been influenced by the information that was withheld (in contrast to information actually given) or by the way the information was broken down and sequenced, adequate information, sufficient comprehension, and voluntary decision-making are nevertheless the general ethical principles that each physician and experimenter must uphold in informed consent discussions.

If we were to take each of the principles separately and examine the discussion between Peter and Jacques according to whether or not the principles were upheld, Peter would rate very highly. The information given was sufficient, the examples came from the patient's realm of personal experiences, and as such illuminated the points very well. Thus, all in all, the information was comprehensible, and Jacques's final decision to partake in the research project seemed to be a voluntary decision—resulting in what on good grounds could be called informed consent. In light of our analyses, however, we maintain that the informed consent negotiation resulted in a miscommunication, one that is commonly called therapeutic misconception (cf. Appelbaum, Roth, & Lidz, 1982; Appelbaum, Roth, Lidz, Benson, & Winslade, 1987; Benson, Roth, Applebaum, & Lidz, 1988). In addition, we claim that what is misconceived cannot be explained in terms of the actual information that was disclosed. Rather, the misconception takes place on both ends of the negotiation—the nurse/researcher and the patient/subject. Put differently, the misconception emerges in and out of the informed consent discussion. As such, the misconception is not grounded at the level of information disclosure but, rather, at the level of prior conceptions or beliefs about the different roles of research and health care—beliefs that are more deeply seated in conceptualizations about the modern self (cf. Taylor, 1989). Consequently, it is neither Jacques, who misconstrued the message, nor Peter, who coded the message inappropriately, but their understandings of who they are and whose voices they speak with that is at issue.

Rather than stopping at this point, where miscommunications are viewed as accidentally happening and where nobody is to blame, we nevertheless want to discuss two messages that can be learned from our analysis of the interaction. Both remain rather general and, of course, do not extend to the level of actual wordings, although that was the level of our previous analysis.

First, it seems to be most expedient for both parties to become clear about (a) the different goals that are pursued by the treatment of the patient and (b) the research treatment of the research subject. Only if these different goals are separated can the two roles or personae that go along with these goals be kept apart: The researcher needs to be differentiated from the nurse/health care person, and the patient needs to be differentiated from the research subject. If the two orientations—which we identified as different value orientations—can be separated, healthcare personnel and patient can form one communicative alliance, and researcher and research subject can form another. Without being able to give specific advice about how these differentiations in both parties can be achieved, we nevertheless believe that it may be helpful to reserve a part of the discussion for the topic of both parties' general expectations regarding the different goals of research and treatment. This discussion should most likely take place near the beginning of the interaction and could also be used to initiate the patient/research subject's active involvement in the discussion, which would help in ascertaining his or her basic beliefs and concerns regarding the topic under consideration.

Second, to defuse the situation even more, it may be advisable to have personnel who have no healthcare responsibilities conduct the interview and run the research project. This is at least a possible reading of the Declaration of Helsinki, Principle 1.10, which says:

> When obtaining informed consent for the research project the doctor should be particularly cautious if the subject is in a dependent relationship to him or her or may consent under duress. In that case the informed consent should be obtained by a doctor who is not engaged in the investigation and who is completely independent of the official relationship. (Levine, 1981, p. 288)

However, the introduction of a neutral person, originally designed to play a disambiguating role "in informing subjects of their rights and of the details of protocols, assuring that there is continuing willingness to participate, determining the advisability of continued participation, receiving complaints from subjects, and bringing grievances to the attention of the IRB" (Levine, 1981, p. 92) does not speak to the core of the problem. On the contrary, it overpersonalizes the problem, as suggested by Beecher (1970) and Spiro (1975). If the core of the matter lies with the identification of two different value orientations, then it is the perspective from which the process is directed that matters and not who is directing the process. Consequently, one way of clarifying potential differences in value orientations is a joint discussion of both parties' beliefs and hopes. This discussion should include generally held beliefs about research and being a patient and should move from there to specifics of the research goals in question and the specific assessment and hopes of the patient regarding his or her illness, the research treatment, and potential connections. Having highlighted the fact that these different value orientations can be found within one person, we believe that a more basic discussion of the values of these issues not just between patient/subject and physician/researcher but for laypeople and experts in general is essential—possibly in the form of a general public education process.

ACKNOWLEDGMENTS

Originally published as: Bamberg, M., & Budwig, N. (1992). Therapeutic Misconceptions: When the Voices of Caring and Research Are Misconstrued as the Voice of Curing. *Ethics and Behavior, 2*(3), 165–184. Republished in this volume with kind permission of the Taylor & Francis Group.

Research for this article was supported in part by National Academy of Education Spencer Fellowships and a Clark University research award. We are grateful for the helpful comments of Roger Bibace, Carolyn Cotsonas, Denis Raphaely, and two anonymous reviewers.

REFERENCES

Appelbaum. P. S., Roth. L. H., & Lidz, C. W. (1982). The therapeutic misconception: Informed consent in psychiatric research. *International Journal of Law and Psychiatry, 5*, 319–329.

Appelbaum, P. S., Roth, L. H., Lidz, C. W., Benson. P. R., & Winslade, W. (1987). False hopes and best data: Consent to research and the therapeutic misconception. *Haslinger Center Report, 17*(2). 20–24.

Bakhtin, M. M. (1986). *Speech genres and other late essays.* Austin, TX: University of Texas Press.

Bamberg, M. (1987). *The acquisition of narratives.* Berlin, Germany: Mouton de Gruyter.

Bamberg, M. (1990). The German perfekt: Form and function of tense alternations. *Studies in Language. 14*, 253–290.

Bamberg, M. (1991a). Conceptualization via narrative. *Journal of Narrative and Life History, 1*, 155–167.

Bamberg, M. (199lb). Narrative as perspective taking: The role of emotionals, negations, and voice in the reconstruction of the story realm. *Journal of Cognitive Psychotherapy, 5*, 275–290.

Bamberg, M. (199lc). Voices of curing and caring: The role of vagueness and ambiguity in informed consent discussions. *Family Systems Medicine, 9*, 329–342.

Bamberg. M., Budwig, N., & Kaplan, B. (1991). A developmental approach to language acquisition: Two case studies. *First Language, 11*, 121–141.

Bamberg. M., & Damrad-Frye, R. (1991). On the ability to provide evaluative comments: Further explorations of children's narrative competencies. *Journal of Child Language, 13*, 689–710.

Bamberg, M., & Lindenberger, U. (1984). Zur Metaphorik des Sprechens. Mit der Metapher zu einer Alltagstheorie der Sprache [Metaphoricity of speaking: Using metaphors to develop an everyday theory of language]. *Sprache und Literatur in Wissenschaft und Unterricht, 53*, 18–33.

Beecher, H. K. (1970). *Research and the individual: Human studies.* Boston, MA: Little, Brown.

Benson, P. R., Roth, L. H., Appelbaum, P. S., & Lidz, C. W. (1988). Information disclosure, subject understanding, and informed consent in psychiatric research. *Law and Human Behavior, 12*, 455–475.

Budwig, N. (1986). *Agentivity and control in early child language.* (Unpublished doctoral dissertation). University of California, Berkeley, CA.

Budwig, N. (1989). The linguistic marking of agentivity and control in child language. *Journal of Child Language, 16*, 263–284.

Budwig, N. (1990a). A functional approach to the acquisition of personal pronouns. In G. Conti-Ramsden & C. Snow (Eds.), *Children's language* (Vol. 7, pp. 121–145). Hillsdale, NJ: Erlbaum.

Budwig, N. (1990b). The linguistic marking of nonprototypical agency: An exploration into children's use of passives. *Linguistics, 28*, 1221–1252.

Budwig, N. (1991). The conduit metaphor: Language and informed consent. *Family Systems Medicine, 9*, 313–327.

Cicourel, A. V. (1985). Doctor-patient discourse. In T. A. van Dijk (Ed.), *Handbook of discourse analysis: Vol. 4, Discourse analysis in society* (pp. 193–202). London, England: Academic.

Gilligan, C. (1982). *In a different voice: Psychological theory and women's development.* Cambridge, MA: Harvard University Press.

Gilligan, C. (1987). Moral orientation and moral development. In E. F. Kittay & D. T. Meyers (Eds.), *Women and moral theory* (pp. 15–51). Totowa, NJ: Rowman & Littlefield.

Gilligan, C. (1988). Two moral orientations: Gender differences and similarities. *Merrill-Palmer Quarterly, 34*, 223–237.

Holquist, M., & Emerson, C. (1981). *The dialogic imagination: Four essays by M. M. Bakhtin* (Glossary, pp. 423–434). Austin, TX: University of Texas Press.

Jakobson, R. (1971). Shifters, verbal categories, and the Russian verb. In R. Jakobson (Ed.), *Selected writings 2.* The Hague, the Netherlands: Mouton. (Original work published 1957)

Lavandera. B. R. (1988). The study of language in its socio-cultural context. In F. J. Newmeyer (ECL), *Linguistics: The Cambridge survey: Vol. 4, Language: The socio-cultural context* (pp. 1–13), Cambridge, England: Cambridge University Press.

Levine, R. J. (1981). *Ethics and regulation of clinical research.* Baltimore, MD: Urban & Schwarzenberg.

Mishler, E. G. (1984). *The discourse of medicine. Dialectics of medical interviews.* Norwood, NJ: Ablex.

Mishler, E. G., Clark, J. A., Ingelfinger, J., & Simon, M. P. (1989). The language of attentive patient care: A comparison of two medical interviews. *Journal of General Internal Medicine, 4*, 325–335.

Packer, M. J. (1991, April). *Human activity and interpretation: Action, text, and narrative.* Paper presented at the biennial meeting of the Society for Research in Child Development, Seattle, WA.

Patenaude, A. F., Rappeport, J. M., & Smith, B. R. (1986). The physician's influence on informed consent for bone marrow transplantation. *Theoretical Medicine, 7,* 165–179.

President's Commission for the Study of Ethical Problems in Medicine and Biomedical and Behavioral Research. (1982). *Making health care decisions. The ethical and legal implications of informed consent in the patient-practitioner relationship* (Vols. 1–3). Washington, DC: U.S. Government Printing Office.

Reddy, M. J. (1979). The conduit metaphor—A case of frame conflict in our language about language. In A. Ortony (Ed), *Metaphor and thought* (pp. 284–324). Cambridge, England: Cambridge University Press.

Schloendorff v. Society of New York Hospital, 211 N.Y. 125 (1914).

Silva, M. C., & Sorrell, J. M. (1984). Factors influencing comprehension of information for informed consent: Ethical implications for nursing research. *International Journal of Nursing Studies, 21,* 233–240.

Silverstein. M. (I987). The three faces of "function": Preliminaries to a psychology of language. In M. Hickmann (Ed.), *Social and functional approaches to language and thought* (pp. 17—38). Orlando, FL: Academic.

Spiro, H. M. (1975). Constraint and consent: On being a patient and a subject. *New England Journal of Medicine, 293,* 1134–1135.

Taylor, C. (1989). *Sources of the self. The making of the modern identity.* Cambridge, MA: Harvard University Press.

Van Dijk, T. A. (1985). Introduction: The role of discourse analysis in society. In T. A. van Dijk (Ed.), *Handbook of discourse analysis: Vol. 4, Discourse analysis in society* (pp. l–8). London, England: Academic.

Wu, W. C., & Pearlman, R. A. (1988). Consent in medical decision making: The role of communication. *Journal of General Internal Medicine, 3,* 9–14.

SECTION IV

THE PARTNER IN RESEARCH: A CLOSER LOOK AT THE RESEARCHER–PARTICIPANT RELATIONSHIP

CHAPTER 12

AN INTRODUCTION TO PARTNERSHIP IN RESEARCH

Changing the Researcher–Participant Relationship

Roger Bibace
Clark University

Steven Dine Young
Hanover College

Leslie Rupert Herrenkohl
University of Washington

Angela Wiley
University of Illinois

Disciplines socialize experts pervasively. Furthermore, the zeitgeist cuts across disciplines so that within a given historical era, they take on what Foucault (1971) termed the same basic "episteme." Under the broad and

Particulars and Universals in Clinical and Developmental Psychology, pages 205–216

sometimes confusing umbrella of "post-modernism," it is relatively clear that the episteme of the current historical era is in a state of transition. One of the consequences of this epistemological shift within the social sciences has been a basic reconsideration of the nature of the subject matter to be studied—human beings and human society. More concretely, we argue that the fields of study of the authors (developmental, clinical, health, and educational psychology), as well as a host of closely related disciplines (anthropology, sociology, education, and medicine), are presently experiencing currents of dissatisfaction in regards to how people called "subjects" are thought of and treated in empirical research.

The most recent *Publication Manual of the American Psychological Association* (1994) substantiates the current transition. The manual recognizes a premise we share: "Appropriate identification of research participants and clientele is critical to the science and practice of psychology" (p. 13). As a substitute for the traditional term subject, this prominent national organization now suggests that its members should "write about the people in your study in a way that acknowledges their participation. Replace the impersonal terms *subjects* with a more descriptive term when possible—*participants, individuals, college students, children, or respondents* for example." Subject is now considered to be appropriate only when discussing statistics (p. 49).

While this shift in terminology is important, it should signify more than merely the substitution of one term for another. Rather it is the assumptions being made about people, as well as the methods and procedures being espoused, that we claim are in need of reconceptualization. How individuals should be construed in psychology has been a persistent controversy. The current emphasis on participants as *actors* rather than as *acted on* would not have been acceptable to behaviorists such as Watson in the 1920s or indeed B. F. Skinner in the 1950s through the 1980s. And of course, the controversy extends beyond psychology. An entire recent issue of the *American Behavioral Scientist* (Ashmore, Wooffit, & Harding, 1994) is devoted to

> one of the most fundamental and long-running debates in and on the social and behavioral sciences. The debate concerns the question of how the very entities that social scientists investigate—humans and their interactions—are to be conceptualized in the first place. (p. 733)

This chapter contributes to the further development of this crucial debate in several ways. First it extends the issue to include what we call the "research triangle," not just the researcher-participant dyad (see Figure 12.1).

We suggest that relevant audiences, the "generalized others" to which scientific works are directed, should also be part of the concepts and values that guide research with human participants. We take the position that research should be construed as an ongoing dialogical process that has no

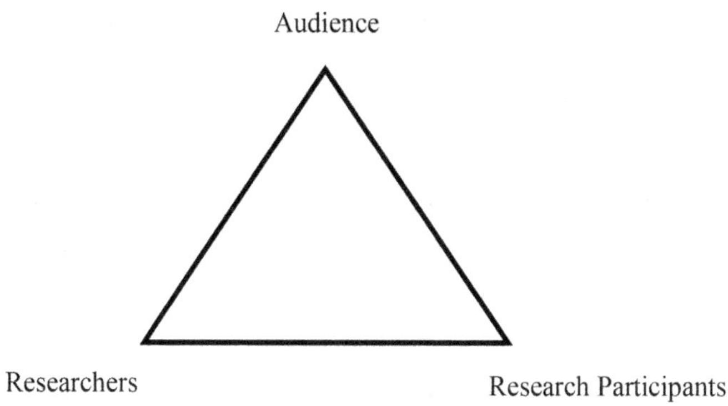

Figure 12.1 Three constituencies involved in research.

definite end point. This dialogical (or perhaps "trialogical") process minimally includes three constituencies: the researchers, the participants in the research, and the audience (other experts as well as so-called ordinary people) who read, react to, and potentially become part of *searching* and *re-searching* questions of widespread concern.

In addition to emphasizing the role of the audience in research, we also contribute by offering some suggestions for specific methodological changes that will mitigate the current dissatisfaction with the treatment of subjects. Since we conceive of research as a dialogical process, this assumption requires that a set of procedures be established in order to ensure that the collaboration of the participant and readers is "substantial." The methodological changes we suggest work to open up what has been a rather constricted and well-dammed flow of information among the three points of the research triangle. While some of these suggestions are more relevant to studies that employ qualitative or interpretive methods, others are equally relevant to quantitative studies.

Our suggestions include:

1. changing terminology from "subject" to "participant,"
2. avoiding jargon that serves to separate "experts" from "lay people" by making discussion and understanding unnecessarily difficult,
3. increasing the availability of entire sets of data to readers,
4. beginning research with participant-generated questions, and
5. instituting a feedback procedure whereby the participant has an opportunity to comment on the researcher's interpretations.

Finally, we discuss how our suggestions move toward the possibility of truly "collaborative" and more "comprehensive" research in the social sciences.

SOME METHODOLOGICAL CHANGES

Eliminating the Term "Subject"

As a first step, we support the *APA Manual's* (1994) recommendation that the term "participant" be used instead of "subject" when referring to human beings engaged in psychological research. As Danziger (1990) has aptly demonstrated, subject historically has been an unfortunate choice for psychology. On one hand, the term is inaccurate in that subjects, traditionally, often have been treated more like "objects" without subjectivity. On the other hand, even in the sense that subject is accurate (research participants are "subjected to" various procedures), it reinforces the passivity of participants. For these reasons, it would be beneficial if all social science disciplines followed this suggestion.

The strength of the term participant is that it emphasizes the active nature of an individual's involvement in the research. Clearly a child being interviewed about his experience of his parents' divorce or a woman telling her story about her psychiatric admission are both playing a crucial role in the construction of knowledge and the advancement of the social sciences. Their contribution has often been unrecognized, and the term subject calls attention only to the degree to which they were passively involved in the scientific process. A change to participant in and of itself begins to move toward their recognition as contributors. The term will become even more apt as some of the other suggestions that follow are put into practice.

It should be noted that other terms are possible, some of which might imply even more activity than participant does. For example, "collaborator" or "co-researcher" are other terms that could be used. While the ideal of participants as co-researchers is admirable, we do not believe that it accurately describes the current state of research (or even research that applies some of the suggestions in this paper). Except in the most unusual cases (see the conclusion), academic researchers will continue to take primary responsibility for developing projects and theories, seeking grants, recording findings, and preparing documents for widespread distribution. These functions place researchers in unique roles they will likely remain in, regardless of the important steps taken to give attention to the perspectives, experiences, and interpretations of the participants. A term such as co-researcher blurs this real and important distinction and thereby becomes inaccurate and disingenuous.

Mary Catherine Bateson (1989) in her book *Composing a Life* encounters the dilemma of using our current language to describe the researcher-participant relationship as she writes about the lives of five influential women, including herself:

> When I search for a word for my relationship with the women described in this book, I feel a need for a term that would assert both collegiality and the fact that the process is made possible by our differences. The thesaurus betrays me, denying me a term that affirms both symmetry and complementarity. The gap in the language parallels a gap in the culture. We are rich in words that describe symmetrical relationships, from buddy to rival to colleague. We are also rich in words that describe strongly asymmetrical relationships, many of which imply hierarchy and have curious undertones of exploitation and dominance. (p. 102)

Bateson eloquently describes the difficulty she has faced in trying to characterize her relationship to the "subjects" of her book. She raises a crucial point regarding what the English language offers to characterize relationships in general. It is not surprising, therefore, that many researchers who have reflected on these issues have been unable to transform the deeply entrenched beliefs and assumptions reached by reliance on the term subject. We hope this chapter is one attempt among many toward devising new ways of "speaking" and "thinking" regarding how we engage others who are involved in research activities. We will argue that, without denying the importance of differences in roles, a change in the way participants are thought of by researchers allows for more effective and informative investigations.

Avoiding Jargon

Technical language or jargon develops as a discipline becomes more established and specialized. Commonly understood phenomena are now referred to in ways that ordinary people cannot understand. "New" ideas surface couched in new terminology—"Old wine in new bottles."

While some specialized language is necessary in my scholarly undertaking, the overuse of jargon in speaking and writing is an obstacle in communication. Jargon keeps researchers separated not only from the participants in their study, but from much of their potential audience as well. While other researchers have called for limiting the use of jargon (e.g., Bern, 1987), few individuals who have ever read a social science journal would argue that the amount of jargon found therein is essential for the communication of ideas.

Often, the reason for the unnecessary proliferation of technical language is simply a lack of immediate awareness by researchers of the specialized nature of their language and its obtuseness to "everyday" people or even to other scholars in different disciplines. Sometimes however, there is a more conscious attempt to separate the discipline from everyday activities and create a like-minded, isolated community of specialists. While a justification for this elitism is questionable in the area of molecular chemistry, it is less defensible when the topic of study becomes depression, drug use, poverty, or other widely experienced human phenomena.

Our basic recommendation then is to eliminate jargon wherever possible and to aim toward a language that can be understood by participants and by as large an audience as possible. Often this is not exceptionally difficult as a close examination of social science writings indicates that commonly understood words can be substituted for more technical terms. When greater precision is required and specialized language is necessary, then definitions and examples are helpful. An argument could be made that repeated definitions of widely used and understood terms within a given area would be unnecessary and cumbersome. However, we point out that it is often these "understood" terms that have entered what Bruno Latour (1987) calls the "black box;" they are no longer open to question or examination. If researchers were more often forced to explicate the technical terms they use so as to communicate better, it is possible that less of this black boxing phenomenon would occur.

Increasing the Availability of Data

Increasing the availability of data is a change that would have the greatest effect on the "audience" point of the research triangle. Easier access to data challenges the univocality of the researcher's interpretation. Since it is unrealistic that any researcher would have the last word on any psychological or social phenomenon, the audience should have the opportunity to participate in actively interpreting results. Science progresses as alternative interpretations (some contradictory, some complimentary) come together in dialogue and mutually inform one another.

While this is the ideal, often in interview-based and other forms of qualitative research, the text that is being interpreted is unavailable to all but the researchers. At best, a few pages of a transcribed interview are included in papers reporting on such investigations. A situation is created in which the primary researchers have access to more data and therefore have an interpretive advantage over readers who might want to generate alternative readings. An even more lopsided presentation of data usually exists in regard to quantitative data. Whatever advantages statistical methods have for summarizing and manipulating data, they also have the disadvantage of further separating the original phenomenon of interest and interpretations of it.

To counter this tendency with both qualitative and quantitative data, we suggest that researchers make their data as readily available to as large an audience as possible. While transcripts and similar data require a great deal of written space, the widespread availability of the Internet and computer databases has made the distribution of such material much more feasible. In addition, books are a traditional publishing form that are amenable to widespread disbursement of such data. Authors could present their own interpretations of the data, which could also be available in an appendix so that readers could draw their own conclusions.

For some forms of presenting research, there are, of course, practical limitations to this suggestion. A 20-page journal article reporting on research generated from a dozen, 2-hour interviews could hardly contain much in the way of raw data. However, such data could easily be accessed. While scientific ethics have long called for researchers to be able to present their data if called upon to do so, such sharing of knowledge in the area of qualitative research is relatively uncommon. If however, the sharing of data as a means toward multiple interpretations were encouraged, efficient systems of distribution could be instituted. To begin with, having copies of data readily available that easily and quickly could be mailed or e-mailed would be helpful. Some grant monies could be dedicated to this endeavor, eliminating financial limitations as a possible discouragement toward all interested parties obtaining data.

Confidentiality is a major issue that must be addressed. As always, care should be taken to protect the identity of participants, especially in sensitive areas related to personal or clinical issues. In addition, participants need to be made aware that other individuals will have access to their stories; informed consent is essential.

Researchers should recognize that confidentiality and the desire to present as complete a data set as possible often conflict. Since transcription systems themselves are guided by researchers' theories about how oral language should be organized, coded, and presented in written form (Ochs, 1979), transcripts are, from this perspective, a step removed from videotapes or audiotapes. Researchers' transcription systems reflect their interests and the issues that they themselves are pursuing. Thus, if a reader has a slightly different interest in language data, it may not be reflected clearly in the transcript that the researcher provides.

Ideally, therefore, having audiotapes or videotapes widely available would be the best solution to this dilemma. Unfortunately, such mediums are often impossible to make confidential adequately. Although there may be certain situations in which participants might choose to waive confidentiality, those situations in which a waiver is not possible or desirable are much more common. In these instances, it is incumbent upon researchers to clarify the theories that guided their transcription system. Again, the overarching question guiding such disbursement decisions would be "How can I maintain confidentiality while simultaneously making accessible as much relevant information as possible?"

Participant-Generated Questions

Within psychology, the impetus for much of the qualitative and interpretive research has been the observation that psychology is a science that investigates how human beings construct their world with complex symbol systems such as language (Gergen, 1985; Kaplan, 1983; Mishler, 1986). Therefore, if researchers want to understand human beings, they must encounter the complexities of human language, either in spoken or written form. Thus, researchers have become interested in peoples' narrative accounts of their experience. Both open-ended and semistructured questionnaires and interviews allow participants to tell their stories. Careful thought is given to the questions that are asked so as to promote rich narratives. The same thoughtfulness is applied to many quantifiable questionnaires as well, even though the range of responses is more limited.

In an attempt to encourage participants to communicate their perspectives and opinions on a topic as clearly and fully as possible, the above scenario actually overlooks an important obstacle to that goal. While the questions are intended to allow for honest expression on the part of the participants, the fact that they are generated by the researchers prior to data gathering establishes a hierarchy of power. The researcher often stipulates both what issues are important and the sequence of questions to be investigated. Participants may be given some space to "roam," but the overall field of inquiry is dictated by the researchers.

The alternative is to allow the participants themselves to generate the relevant questions and thereby guide the research process. Focus groups are one type of procedure that have been used within the social sciences as a preliminary means of gathering information about the important questions when embarking on a new art of research (Morgan, 1988).

Other methods that focus on individuals instead of groups are also possible. In a study of substance abusers within our research group, we began our interview with the question, "What questions do you think are important to ask in order to understand substance use and abuse?" This one question allowed the participant to structure the interview around the issues they considered most important. When the participants were done responding spontaneously to this question, we present them with a list of questions that we had compiled from a review of the professional literature on substance abuse. We marked those issues that had been brought up by the participants and asked if they thought that any of the other questions were especially relevant to the experience of substance use.

This procedure was designed to remove some of the traditional authority granted to the "expert" to decide what the important questions are. Engaging participants to generate their own questions concretely communicates the researcher's attitude. This attitude empowers the participants and indicates that the researcher will be a respectful listener.

One other related procedure that can help participants gain some measure of control over the research situation is to ask them what pseudonym, if any, they preferred to use in writings that emerge from the research process. While this procedure might seem minor, it has proven to be an effective tool in bridging the expert-novice gap. Clearly, a personal name does more than neutrally denote an individual. Names have a variety of connotations—consider the difference in associations to the name "Johnny" and "Jonathan." In addition, the stories participants tell regarding the reason for the name they have chosen are often illuminating. Asking the participant to name themselves further empowers them to define themselves and to characterize their own accounts.

Participant Feedback Procedure

The most significant change to the methodological procedures of standard social science research that we will introduce is the implementation of a feedback mechanism in which participants comment on the interpretations made by researchers. Normally, the researchers' interpretations are the ending point; they would be written up and presented solely to a scholarly and professional audience.

Our suggestion is that prior to the publication of interpretations, the interpretations should be presented to the participants who generated the data in the first place. While making results available to participants has generally been a part of responsible research, we are calling for researchers to go a step further. The reactions of the participants to the researchers' interpretations should also be recorded and included as part of the final product.

This feedback loop does not preclude researchers from making interpretations that participants do not agree with. However, researchers would be compelled to include these disagreements in their work. If nothing else, this dialogical procedure is more legitimate and true to the spirit of intellectual discussion than the standard procedure in which participants are represented by the researchers and are never given an opportunity to challenge that representation.

There are some precedents in which the subtle one-sided power of the researcher to represent events has been challenged by participants. One prominent example was a response by research participants to a *New York Times Magazine* article (Prose, 1990) about Carol Gilligan's research with teenage girls (Gilligan, Lyons, & Hammer, 1990). These participants were upset by the way they had been portrayed by Gilligan and they questioned the researchers' account of their experience. Such disagreements occurred despite the fact that many feminist social scientists, including Gilligan (1982), are explicitly concerned about the role of participants in social science research.

In addition to being respectful to participants, the inclusion of their disagreements and opinions would be provocative and informative to readers. Readers would have an opportunity to observe at what points the interpretations of the participants themselves and the interpretations of experts diverge and at what points they converge. While this procedure may add some effort to the conduct of research, these added dimensions of understanding would, in many cases, justify the effort.

This suggestion may sound radical in the domain of research. However, such dialogue is commonplace and central in the helping professions. Specialists, be they teachers, physicians or clinicians, must learn to speak to two audiences: specialists like themselves and ordinary people whom they call students, patients, or clients (Bibace & Walsh, 1982; Heymann, 1995a). Furthermore, Heymann (1995b) has asserted that a similar reflexive relationship should exist in medical research. Our suggestion is to further expand the practice to include social science research participants as well.

The participant feedback procedure extends to participants what is already an established practice between researchers and their audience. Many of the most exciting areas in the social sciences are those in which public commentary, criticism, and rebuttals are present either in written or oral form. In a sense then, the feedback procedure is simply an attempt to further balance the research triangle. However, in addition to giving participants a greater voice in social science research, our highlighting of this procedure should also call attention to the public, dialogical nature of scholarly dialogue in general and lead to a reconsideration of those areas in which it is not practiced as much as it might be.

CONCLUSION: TOWARD "COLLABORATIVE" AND "COMPREHENSIVE" RESEARCH

We have been trying to envision an orientation toward research in which methods employed work to decrease the distance between researcher and participant. Inherent in this goal is a desire to disturb the unquestioned role "experts" often have in social science research.

At the same time, we have continued to maintain a distinction between researchers and participants. In our proposed research process, investigators and participants each bring equal but different domains of expertise to the research—investigators bring generalized training in theory and method, while the participants bring the lived experience of the phenomenon being studied. Knowledge is formed out of a collaboration of these distinct orientations. This movement toward differentiated egalitarianism is further elaborated in our emphasis on the active reader engaging in dialogue with the researchers and participants, thereby composing the research triangle.

There are possibilities for collaborative research beyond what we have been suggesting, however. Such an approach might feature researchers and participants starting at the same point, sitting down together and deciding on the very objective of the study. The research would proceed from there with all those involved participants similarly. In such a situation, the researcher/participant distinction changes altogether. Indeed, such research is not without precedent. For example, Freire (1988) has advocated a similar approach to education in Brazil. In the United States in the area of teacher-researcher partnerships, this form of research has been successful (Guerra & Smith, 1992; Jacobs, McCrohon, Reddy, & Rupert, 1993).

For social scientists with egalitarian tendencies who are interested in making immediate social changes, such a method might be more appropriate than the radical methods we have been suggesting. We will leave those further-reaching changes for others to discuss.

All of the suggestions that have been made are open to further refinement. They are intended to be starting points for future inquiry. Clearly, some of them are more or less appropriate for different types of research. In addition, other changes which would also work toward a restructuring of the researcher–participant relationship are certainly possible. As some of these suggestions are implemented and further thought is given to the changes, then our methods as social scientists will become more refined and better serve the goal of bringing researchers, participants, and readers closer together.

While our thinking is based, at least in part, on a desire to promote social equality, we also have a less ideological motivation as well. We believe that research in social sciences that facilitates a complex, active role for the humans being studied is "better science." It deserves this characterization because it is more "comprehensive," the standard that Pepper (1970) and others have advocated as the primary criteria for judging science. We hope that the results of such will be more developed, insightful, and in the end, useful.

ACKNOWLEDGMENT

Originally published as: Bibace, R., Young, S. D., Herrenkohl, L. R., & Wiley, A. (1999). An introduction to partnership in research: Changing the researcher–participant relationship. In R. Bibace, J. J. Dillon, & B. N. Dowds (Eds.), *Partnerships in research, clinical and educational settings* (pp. 3–14). Stamford, CT: Ablex Publishing Corporation. Republished in this volume with kind permission of Intellect Ltd.

REFERENCES

American Psychological Association. (1994). *Publication manual of the American Psychological Association* (4th ed.). Washington, DC: American Psychological Association.

Ashmore, M., Wooflit, R., & Harding, S. (Eds.). (1994). Humans and others: The concept of agency and its attributions [Special issue]. *American Behavioral Scientist, 37*(6).

Bateson, M. C. (1989). *Composing a life.* New York, NY: Atlantic Monthly Press.

Bibace, R., & Walsh, M. B. (1982). Conflict of roles: On the difficulties of being both a scientist and practitioner in one life. *Professional Psychology, 13*(3), 389–396.

Danziger, K. (1990). *Constructing the subject: Historical origins of psychological research.* Cambridge, England: Cambridge University Press.

Foucault, M. (1971). *The order of things: An archeology for the human sciences.* New York, NY: Pantheon Books.

Freire, P. (1988). *Pedagogy of the oppressed.* New York, NY: Continuum.

Gergen, K. J. (1985). The social-constructionist movement in modern psychology. *American Psychologist, 40*(3), 266–275.

Gilligan, C. (1982). *In a different voice.* Cambridge, MA: Harvard University Press.

Gilligan, C., Lyons, N. R, & Hammer, H. J. (1990). *Making connections: The relational worlds of adolescent girls at Emma Willard School.* Cambridge, MA: Harvard University Press.

Guerra, M. R., & Smith, M. (1992). *'Science is wonderful': Evolving scientific discourse in a primary resource room.* (Unpublished manuscript).

Heymann, S. J. (l995a). *Equal partners: A physician's call for a new spirit in medicine.* Boston, MA: Little Brown.

Heymann, S. J. (1995b). Patients in research: Not just subjects, but partners. *Science, 269,* 797–798.

Jacobs, R., McCrohon, C., Reddy, M., & Rupert, L. (1993, November). *Seeing with new eyes: Becoming a teacher/researcher team.* Paper presented at the annual meeting of the American Anthropological Association, Philadelphia, PA.

Kaplan, B. (1983). Genetic-dramatism: Old wine in new bottles. In S. Wapner & B. Kaplan (Eds.), *Toward a holistic developmental psychology* (pp. 53–74). Hillsdale, NJ: Erlbaum.

Latour, B. (1987). *Science in action.* Cambridge, MA: Harvard University Press.

Mishler, E. G. (1986). *Research interviewing.* Cambridge, MA: Harvard University Press.

Morgan, D. L. (1988). *Focus groups as qualitative research.* Newbury Park, CA: Sage.

Ochs, E. (1979). Transcription as theory. In B. Ochs & B. Schieffelin (Eds.), *Developmental pragmatics* (pp. 43–72). New York, NY: Academic Press.

Pepper, S. C. (1970). *World hypotheses: A study in evidence.* Berkeley, CA: University of California Press.

Prose, F. (1990, January 7). Confident at eleven, confused at sixteen. *New York Times Magazine,* pp. 22–46.

CHAPTER 13

HOW INTERESTS AND VALUES EVOLVE (SOMETIMES UNPREDICTABLY)

A Developmental Teleology of Research Encounters

Nikita A. Kharlamov
Aalborg University

Aleksandra Kaszowska
Tufts University

Roger Bibace
Clark University

What is psychological research like? What metaphor would best convey the essence of what goes on in a "typical case" of psychological research? Can we assume that psychological research works just like a photographic camera—is conducting research just like taking a snapshot of a person? Or is

Particulars and Universals in Clinical and Developmental Psychology, pages 217–234

it more like filming a person with a video camera? In research, is it one person recording the other person, or is it more like two people talking to each other? And is this still a metaphor?

Psychological research on humans, frequently referred to as *human subjects*, often involves a researcher meeting a research participant. The researcher sustains an interaction with the participant, engages in a conversation, and eventually, in the context of this interaction, performs research procedures. This simple research interaction is not that different from natural human interaction; it is just that in the course of this particular relationship the researcher invites the participant to perform specific tasks and makes measurements. Naturally, there are exceptions to this pattern. Some research only involves observation of people who are oblivious to the fact of being studied, or, with the recent explosion of online survey research, sometimes the research participants do not even have to meet the researchers in person. However, the "baseline" research encounter still presupposes humans interacting with each other. And yet, surprisingly, psychology often attempts to "bracket" this interaction, methodologically "push it out" of the research encounter (e.g., through using standardized, de-personalized measurement tools), and to work as if research indeed was more like taking a snapshot rather than talking to people. And the snapshot should be like a snapshot of a landscape and not a person, so that nothing at all changes as a result of recording the image; participants should not react to the camera, interpret the photographer's intentions, adjust their position, or even request additional pictures. Ideally, the object of study remains unchanged and unmoved by anything the researcher does.

This methodological bracketing is powerfully reinforced by the practice of ethics committees.[1] In their work of ensuring the ethical compliance of research procedures, these committees often effectively negate all possibilities for allowing or acknowledging that a developing relationship between researchers and participants exists and that this relationship involves change. And yet, change is so fundamental for all human interactions—think, for example, of how each conversation with a friend changes the friendship—if only a tiny bit so. This problematic institutional framing invites a serious reflection on the values defining the very notion of psychological research and, consequently, the basic interests that are at play when research occurs.

In this paper we discuss research with human participants from a standpoint that explicitly acknowledges that research is an interaction that involves emergence and maintenance of a relationship between the researcher and the participant. We discuss the interests that operate in research encounters in light of the assumption that the defining interest of research is epistemic, i.e., creating knowledge. However, we interpret this interest through a developmental lens, showing that it operates in context of a complex unfolding relationship between researchers and participants. We further argue that the institutional overregulation, manifest in the procedures of ethics review of social research, leads to the "myth of control"—an ideology of denying relationship and change. It leads to imposing a particular set of procedural values that are often at odds with other values necessarily present in the research encounter, particularly on part of the research participants, such as friendship or community solidarity. While our immediate context is psychological research in the United States, our basic argument is relevant beyond this discipline and beyond specific national and institutional contexts.

VALUES AND INTERESTS IN FOCUSED RESEARCH INTERACTION

In their critique of the current obsession with ethics in social research, Hammersley and Traianou (2011) identify and defend the traditional view of academic research as "a specialized activity in its own right whose only immediate goal should be to produce knowledge" (p. 381). They indicate that unless the epistemic value is treated as intrinsic to research, research activity itself is likely to lose its distinctive character and diffuse into other kinds of activities.[2]

How can we examine the values in action when researchers actually meet research participants? We suggest looking at these encounters as *focused interactions.* They occur when "people effectively agree to sustain for a time a single focus of cognitive and visual attention, as in conversation, a board game, or a joint task sustained by a close face-to-face circle of contributors" (Goffman, 1961, p. 7). This agreement is guided by interest: the practical sense of the reason for why people engage in these encounters that they rely on in their interaction. At least one interactant—a term we borrow from Glaser and Strauss's seminal paper on awareness contexts (1964)—goes about the interaction with a certain fairly specific interest[3] in mind. For example, a conversation between Roger Bibace and Nikita Kharlamov about the deadline for the draft of the present paper is an interaction of this kind. The same two people passing by each other earlier that day in the departmental mailroom and exchanging quick hellos were engaged in a much less intensively interested activity. The practical performance of *values* as present in the activities of people is manifested in particular interests defining focused interactions. Of course, some interests are not necessarily directly related to complex value systems. But others can be, and it is through examining such demonstrable interests that values can be inferred from human activities and/or the organizational and institutional contexts of those activities. To put it simply, we are concerned here with values in a pragmatic, practical sense, rather than in abstract, philosophical deliberations about values. The latter can only be relevant for our purposes if and insofar as they could be translated back to human activities.

Sustained Interest in Research Encounters

Some of Goffman's focused interactions clearly contain their interest within themselves. A conversation about weather in a departmental mailroom is likely to contain no outside interest apart from the conversation itself. But interests motivating other encounters span beyond their limits. A mailroom conversation, which is initiated by one of the interactants with the intention of setting up a meeting, is likely to begin with an exchange about weather or driving conditions. However, it will also include deliberations on dates and times, and thus it will pull in chains of other interactions preceding and following it. Harold Garfinkel (1967) has shown that humans in their everyday life and interactions routinely achieve the accountable, "organizationally demonstrable" rational status of their expressions and actions. Let us clarify this infamously nebulous formulation. Roger Bibace and Nikita Kharlamov would have little if any trouble in making their talk about weather make perfect sense as "just a conversation about weather" to anyone to observe it, as well as, of course, to each other. If a third person at any point would ask Roger and Nikita "What are you doing here?" they are likely to perplexedly answer: "We are talking about weather?" In fact, unless that third person comes from a culture in which weather is not routinely discussed in mundane conversations, they would not even need to inquire about the topic of the conversation; it would make sense in and by itself to both interactants and to any observer who is also a member of this culture. In any case, the sustained interest in setting up a meeting is there for a somewhat more prolonged period of time than the kind of interest involved in conversations about weather. Thus, Nikita Kharlamov's activities, defined by this interest, may involve also the hunt for Roger Bibace around the department, or on the failure of that hunt, a phone call.

There is a broad swath of encounters that can be expressly defined by a specific, intentional (at least on part of one of the interactants) interest sustained over time and across multiple encounters. For instance, a college lecture is defined primarily by educational interests that extend beyond the particular professor–students interaction. Nikita Kharlamov's interest in writing this paper with Aleksandra Kaszowska and Roger Bibace is a good example, as it involves multiple interactions over time, and it extends into many other interactions primarily motivated by other interests (e.g., maintaining mentor-student relationships). All these interactions have the same overarching features of accountability, i.e., they already contain in themselves (as specific indicative utterances and sequences) demonstrations, which can also serve as affirmations, that they are guided by the interest in writing a paper together. Such demonstrations are accessible to an observer (e.g., a person overhearing a conversation can record utterances referring to the purpose of a meeting as working on draft edits). Moreover, such intentional interests are often closely connected to values.

Research interactions are embedded in broad institutional systems of scientific activities (which, of course, are historically and culturally situated). If epistemic value is the primary value of research, then research encounters are those encounters that tend to be defined prospectively and retroactively (by concrete interactants in concrete organizational contexts) as encounters in which the researcher's actions are driven by the interest in obtaining knowledge. Thus, in a research setting, at least one interactant goes about the interaction with a certain, fairly specific intentional interest. And this interest is proactively, as well as retroactively, defined with respect to any particular interaction. Research interactions are thus (presumably) *teleological affairs*, which are affairs defined by their goals.

Thus far, we assumed that the primary *telos* of a research encounter, at least on the part of the researcher, is the epistemic goal of producing knowledge. In an ideal world of Max Weber's ideal types (see Burger, 2001, for a summary of this idea), the researcher who, for example, asks a participant to sign a consent form and subsequently administers a standardized questionnaire, is engaged in a focused interaction that is likely to be characterized by a sustained interest in producing knowledge. Both the interaction and the interest begin before the signing—or non-signing—of a consent form or similar research and/or legal documents, and the interest is likely to extend well beyond that particular interaction: it will motivate the initial contacting of the participant, and it will remain present even after all contact is over.

Multiple Interests and Coexisting Values

It would be far too simple to assume, however, that in a real encounter there is only one interest in action at a given time. Indeed, any given interaction at any given point is likely to be flavored by a host of different interests, i.e., rationally accountable reasons for the interactant to behave in a certain way. People talking in a mailroom can have weather in mind as well as negotiation of institutional roles and resources, and massive asymmetries between the interests of different interactants can be involved, e.g., when one person's conversation on weather is another person's gauge of the moods in this morning's department meeting.[4] Additionally, interests can change or multiply over the course of the interaction on part of both interactants.

A researcher, in addition to having an epistemic interest, is, as Hammersley and Traianou (2011) point out, both normatively and legally required to, and is likely to be oriented by, interests that can be qualified as extrinsic to the epistemic definition of research. "Minimization of harm, respect for autonomy, and the protection of privacy" (Hammersley & Traianou, 2011, p. 386) are such interests. Of importance is also the value of "politeness," i.e., the interest in maintaining a polite and civil conversation between people who are—in a standard one-off experimental research encounter—essentially strangers.

Thus, there are multiple values involved in a research encounter. On the part of the participant, the interest in maintaining an interaction with the researcher can be nonepistemic and indeed, not at all fitting with what we could, extending Mills (1940), call the "vocabulary" of epistemic interests (e.g., the indefinite "just because" motive discussed by Dyregrov et al., 2010). The same applies to the researcher.

But what is most often overlooked or neglected as banal is that these interests (and their value referents) themselves change over time. They go through developmental trajectories over the course of research encounters. Consider, for example, the possibility of a research participant being initially "excited about" participating in an experiment on short-term memory or a survey on family structure, but then losing that interest due to "boredom."

DEVELOPMENTAL TELEOLOGY OF RESEARCH ENCOUNTER

It would thus be a profound and irresponsible simplification to assert that the epistemic interest could be treated as unproblematically maintained at the same level throughout the course of the researcher's interactions with every interactant in the research process. We should also note that we have thus far almost completely left out the interests of these other interactants, among whom the foremost are the so-called "research participants." These issues are closely related, and the key concept here is *development*.

In a very broad sense, "Development of any kind and level (be it biological, psychological or sociological) is an open-systemic phenomenon in which novelty is *constantly in the process of being created*" (Valsiner, 2007, p. 35, italics in original). A research encounter belongs to the domain of systemically organized processes; moreover, in Garfinkel's (1967) terms, the organized, orderly character of this encounter itself is an ongoing practical achievement of the involved interactants. We thus need to examine what happens to the epistemic interest in the process of a research encounter, and what kinds of interests are manifest on the part of research participants. For an interest to be "manifest," it has to, at some point (prospectively, actively, or retrospectively), enter the interaction as a *method of ordering* this interaction.

The teleology we need to account for research encounters, and indeed for any other encounter, is not a static, abstract, timeless teleology, but a *developmental* teleology. We use this term in loose correspondence to Peirce (1892), but less so in relation to Hans Driesch's biology (e.g., Churchill, 1969). Considering the teleology of an encounter as developmental means acknowledging that there are multiple, possibly conflicting, goals involved in the interaction; that these goals—and consequently the interests of the interactants—can shift and change over time; and that the course of this change is open-ended. The latter is what Valsiner (2007) called the "emergence of novelty"—which, of course, corresponds to Peirce's use when he introduced the term "developmental teleology" in relation to the processual character of personality. As Valsiner (2011) underscores, development of goals, interests, and purposes, as well as creation of new ones over time, are among the most basic propensities of human psychological functioning: they essentially form the core of the majority of higher mental processes.

It follows that identifying the epistemic interest—epistemic telos—as the primary intrinsic interest characteristic of research activity does not negate the other interests operative in a research encounter. Of course, it does not imply that research cannot also be a form of, for example, political activism (as in action research). But research is only research insofar as it is characterized by this epistemic interest, and insofar as this interest is *more or less* sustained over a prolonged period of time on part of the person(s) identifying as the researcher. This argument is in line with Sandel's (2009, especially pp. 186ff) proposal for considering justice (and, correspondingly, ethics) as teleological, i.e., involving deliberations on goals (*teloi*) and virtues involved in any particular social practice. Indeed, our arguments are in a way a practical application of this notion of justice to the moral choices that every interactant routinely faces in a specific brand of encounters. Garfinkel's view of morality from this practical perspective is succinct: "the moral order consists of the rule governed activities of everyday life" (1967, p. 35).

DEVELOPMENTAL TELEOLOGY IN ACTION

Thus far we examined a research encounter in abstract terms. The questions that follow are:

What are the possible goals of researcher-participant relationships in the social sciences?
What virtues do they honor?
How does that work or not work within the institutional regulative context currently in place (or being put into place) with respect to scientific activities involving "human participants"?

To approach these questions, we now turn to some concrete examples.

Interactions in Ethnographic Encounters

There is no change without time. Change occurs in time, and can be detected "diachronically." Of all social and human sciences, ethnography is the domain in which the issues we discuss lead to most visible tensions. One of the reasons for that is that ethnography—"highly descriptive writing about particular groups of people" (Silverman, 2007, p. 12)—by definition involves some sort of "field work." That is, it involves "the researcher participating, overtly or covertly, in peoples' daily lives for an extended period of time" (Hammersley & Atkinson, 2007, p. 3). Obviously, such participation is impossible without the researcher being "out there," out of the ivory tower of the academia (or the enclosure of the laboratory), and in the "open world," be it on a sidewalk in New York's Greenwich Village (Duneier, 1999) or a Guatemalan town (Rogoff, Pérez Gonzalez, Chavajay Quiacain, & Chavajay Quiacain, 2011). Consequently, there are problems known as "access" in the literature on ethnography (Hammersley & Atkinson, 2007, Chapter 3)—how to get into the "field"—and "field relations" (Hammersley & Atkinson, 2007, Chapter 4)—how to maintain relations with various "inhabitants" of the chosen field of study. In a nutshell, the very idea of ethnography entails that the researcher is immersed in a social space populated by ordinary people who go by their daily routines (which can be anything but ordinary or self-evident for the researcher coming from elsewhere). Performing research necessitates interacting with these ordinary people and finding and maintaining a certain social position for the researcher.

Consider the case of Sudhir Venkatesh, the Indian American sociologist and ethnographer, whose doctoral dissertation dealt with the troubled community of a public housing project in a poor, mostly Black neighborhood in Chicago. His research involved several years of ethnographic observations, and his research experiences are reported in a book entitled *Gang leader for a day: A rogue sociologist crosses the line* (Venkatesh, 2008). This book would make an upsetting reading for many psychological researchers, let alone ethics committee members. What is most important in this case for us is that the field relations developed over time and included a multitude of ever changing interests and ways of ordering interactions that were far from the sanitized model of a one-off research encounter (such as the one we are familiar with as psychological researchers). For instance, Venkatesh's first attempt to conduct an "interview" with the inhabitants turned into a tense emotional experience with a group of gang members, who apparently were close to beating him up: a "university student doing research" was not a category they seemed to operate with or a member of a population they were willing to tolerate amongst them. The success of this research depended on building up relationships over multiple prolonged interactions, in which the interests and positions of the researcher vis-à-vis his interlocutors were constantly redefined and renegotiated. Everything about the project was also redefined: its goals, interests, methods, concepts, procedures, and of course, conclusions drawn. Such redefinition, however, is not exclusive to ethnographic projects.

Development of Interests in a Longitudinal Interview Project

Longitudinal interview projects involve developing a distinct relationship between the researchers and the participants. These do not always coincide with the predicted progress of the study or what was envisioned *at the outset* in terms of "benefits" to the participants as understood in, for example, the *Belmont report* (National Commission for the Protection of Human Subjects of Biomedical and Behavioral Research, 1979). In 2011–2012 Aleksandra Kaszowska, the second author of this chapter, worked on an honors project (Kaszowska, 2012) on conceptualizing the notion of home and developing a personal, comfortable environment in a completely foreign setting. This project involved five, first-year college students, who temporarily moved (migrated) to the United States in order to attend Clark University, a small urban residential college in New England. Over the span of their first semester, the participants volunteered (with no reward, monetary or otherwise) to contribute five interviews each, with intervals of several weeks between interviews. The interviews were conducted during walks on campus in a modification of the go-along method (Kusenbach, 2003). However, due to the small size of the university, the researcher-participant contacts were not limited to research encounters—the participants were asking for assistance and advice as they were familiarizing themselves with a foreign culture of the United States. During these encounters, each of them would express concerns and support for the development of the study (in the form of asking, for example, how the advisor meetings were going). Over the span of three months, each of the participants independently of each other would occasionally refer to the study as "our study" and to Aleksandra's academic advisors (whom they never met) by their first names. As the fondness of the study participation increased over time, the participants consistently reported enjoying the interviews (which they felt were just like any other conversation they had on campus, just recorded), being able to relax and "catch a breath" during the talks, looking forward to another round, and being sad about the research cycle concluding at the end of the semester. In addition to the pleasure coming from being interviewed, the participants reported never having considered quitting (despite their heavy workloads at school and shortage of free time), but claimed that they benefited from the study as well: gaining insight into psychological research (future majors), satisfying curiosity for the final results, and being able to compare their current experiences to the past experiences of the researcher (who was at the time a senior year international student). These manifested interests clearly align with the notion of "benefit to the research participant," but rather than being foreseen, defined, and structured in advance, they emerged in the process of research itself. This complex and developing constellation of interests on the part of the researcher and the participants is a good deal more complex than just the epistemic interest, and indeed, in this case the latter partly "transferred" to the participants.

Intersecting Interests in One-Off Research Encounters

Our final vignette involves one-off research encounters in Nikita Kharlamov's doctoral research project (Kharlamov, 2013) on perception of the urban environment conducted in 2010–2011. In another modification of go-along methodology (Kusenbach, 2003), the participants walked in the city of Worcester, Massachutsetts, (in a neighborhood close to the Clark University campus) together with the researcher while freely verbalizing thoughts, feelings, and associations in relation to the neighborhood, streets, buildings, etc. Most of the participants were not from Worcester, were studying at or visiting Clark University, and had very limited knowledge of the city. In an ideal version of this protocol, the researcher—who was at the time a graduate student in a psychology department—first encounters the potential participant in his study when he visits an undergraduate class, reads the recruitment statement, and leaves a sign-up sheet for interested students. He then meets an undergraduate student in a lab. Note that at this point this student is not yet a participant: her status as a "participant" will only be ascertained after what could be considered a contractual negotiation, i.e., an interaction in which the researcher presents the potential participant with a consent form and answers questions, should there be any. Once the consent form is signed, the potential participant becomes an actual participant. One possibility of manifestation of the participant's interest in continuing her interaction as such is the reward for participation in a psychological experiment. However in the case of Nikita Kharlamov's study, after the voice recorder was turned off and it was time to pay the participant their participation reward ($15), several participants, particularly those who were recruited through personal referrals, refused to take the money: all under the common premise that they felt that they enjoyed the walk, gained the opportunity to see a bit of Worcester, had fun, and did not want to get paid for that experience. As one of the participants said, "I should pay you myself for this tour of the city!" In this case there is also an emergent relationship and a constellation of interests that developed over a relatively short period of about 2 hours. "Enjoying the tour" is a clear benefit to the research participant, expressed in commonsense terms perfectly accessible to many ordinary members of many cultures (such as European and American middle-class people, who regularly travel and go on guided tours in cities, villages, and historic places)—but a benefit unforeseen in advance and not reflected, for instance, in the consent form, which only mentioned scores of risks potentially associated with walking in the city in broad daylight.[5]

THE MYTH OF CONTROL

Each of the three cases is "held together" in the final analysis by the epistemic interest, the goal of producing knowledge. But the lesson of these three cases is that real research encounters are imbued with multiple interests that are worked out developmentally as the interactions unfold over time and over multiple encounters. The epistemic interest is not a transcendent absolute that is just taken for granted, but it is continuously reassembled as the interactions and relationships develop. Change can—and indeed does—occur in the course of research interaction, just as it occurs in virtually any human interaction. To argue otherwise would essentially lead us into denial of the temporal and developmental nature of human interactions, and into subscription to a static, immovable portrayal of the world. But how does that fit with the institutional context and the values declared and enforced, for instance, through the ethics review system? In this section we unpack this issue.

Ethics and the "Standard Model" of Research Encounter

We have already alluded to the vision of research encounter that is implied in the institutional regulation of science in the United States and elsewhere. One of the facets of this regulation is ethics review by ethics committees. The ethics review process plays an ever-increasing role in defining the actual assumptions and practices that underlie the research process (Hammersley, 2009), and it thus imposes a particular vision—the "standard model"—of such research process. It originated in the United States in the context of regulating biomedical research in the wake of trials of the Nazi doctors and the public outcry at the infamous Tuskegee Syphilis Study (interestingly, there were several recent attempts to reinterpret the Tuskegee study, e.g., Shweder, 2004). The United States began incorporating ethical regulation into legislation in the mid 1970s, and now such regulation is proliferating across the world, including the European Union (e.g., in 2005, in the United Kingdom, the Economic and Social Research Council—a leading UK funding body for social research—introduced the mandatory approval of research by a Research Ethics Committee). Recently, a new scandal concerning a study done in Guatemala by U.S. scientists in the 1940s prompted calls for new—much stricter—regulations for the United States medical research (Basken, 2011). Notably, most of these egregious cases—particularly those that initially fueled the legislation—involved biomedical research, although debates continue over the ethics of psychological experiments, such as Stanley Milgram's obedience studies and Philip Zimbardo's Stanford Prison Experiment.

The tenets of the biomedical model are respect for persons, beneficence, and justice (National Commission for the Protection of Human Subjects of Biomedical and Behavioral Research, 1979). M. Brewster Smith (2000, p. 5), specifically referring to the context of psychology, gives a longer list: (a) respect for persons and their autonomy, (b) beneficence and nonmaleficence, (c) justice, (d) trust, and (e) fidelity and scientific integrity. These ethical principles receive their special tone and specific formulation when they are applied in research, and as Hammersley and Traianou (2011) point out, calling such values extrinsic by no means implies that they are somehow less important than the epistemic interest. However, there is an evident range of problems pertaining to these principles. For example, Bar-on (2006) discusses the practice of bioethics and argues that these values are oftentimes contradictory. And Hammersley (2009) underscores how the practical application of these principles in the form of ethics reviews amounts to prospective, proactive policing of whatever happens "inside" the research encounter.[6] Here we focus on one particular trait of the ethics regulation enforced by the institution of advance approval of research by an ethics committee. This trait is the literal application of the notion of informed consent.

Informed consent is crucial for the biomedical model of research. The requirement for informed consent follows out of the principle of respecting the autonomy of the person and the explicitly voluntary nature of their participation. Informed consent "is a formal process... [that] includes a clear statement of the purposes, procedures, risks, and benefits of the research project, as well as the obligations and commitments of both the participants and the researchers" (Fischman, 2000, p. 35). Obtaining informed consent in this form essentially means that the researcher and the person invited to participate in research enter a negotiated contractual relationship. The terms of this contract are stated in a signed document, and the researcher is held responsible for continually maintaining informed consent.[7]

But can a literal interpretation of an interaction as a contractual relationship—with terms clearly defined in advance—accommodate the processual, open-ended character of human interactions?

The Myth of Control in Institutional Regulation

The literal application of the principle of informed consent involves the idea that it is possible to foresee and proactively control anything and everything in the research setting. The researcher is obliged to offer the prospective participant complete information about the procedure, or, if deception (or withholding of information) is involved, to "debrief" the participant afterwards. And it is on the basis of available information that the participant has to be able to voluntarily decide to participate and to continuously maintain this decision (or to be able to withdraw from participating). The implication here is that the course of research interaction is exactly predetermined and known in advance by the researcher. Moreover, in Garfinkel's (1967) terms, the researcher organizationally accounts for it before the IRB. We call this literal application *the myth of control.*

Indeed, the legal institutional origin of this myth appears to be a specimen of what Sunstein called the "precautionary principle": the idea that "regulators should take steps to protect against potential harms, even if causal chains are unclear and even if we do not know that those harms will come to fruition" (Sunstein, 2005, p. 4). In a strong form, this principle "forbids action, inaction, and everything in between" (Sunstein, 2005, p. 4). By the same token, the strong precautionary treatment of informed consent forbids any development and any change from taking place in a research encounter governed by the contractual terms of informed consent. And the regulation, as Hammersley and Traianou (2011) note, is taken out of the hands of researchers and placed into the hands of administrators and government regulators (e.g., the Office for Human Research Protections within the U.S. Department of Health and Human Services).

A particularly revealing case of the myth of control in action is the requirement for interviews to have a predetermined research protocol in the form of a clearly written set of questions that are approved by the ethics committee in advance.[8] Such protocols essentially prohibit the researcher to come up with new questions in process of interacting with the participant. Ironically, they also forbid the participant from having a say in that relationship. As McAreavey and Muir (2011) note, the very relationship between the researcher and the participant[9] is institutionally framed in such a way that the only opportunity for the participant to take an active part in it is to reject a part of it—through refusing to answer particular questions, completing particular procedures, or having particular measurements taken—or the entirety of it—through canceling participation. The standard refrain of "Would you like to tell me anything else?" at the end of the interview, in fact, serves as a mutually accepted way of closing the relationship and ending the interview. Indeed, we seldom expect the participants to actually say anything relevant at this point in the interview.

CONCLUSION

The dire consequence of the myth of control is the explicit denial of any ongoing change and development through proactive policing of research encounters. This not only dehumanizes these encounters, it also undermines the epistemic value of research through prohibiting any development, interaction, and interest beyond mechanistically structured and procedurally defined knowledge extraction. Instead, a bureaucratic vision is created that Scott Atran (2011, p. 5) characterized as "geared to protecting American university students, or children usually living within a few miles of a university—that is, populations vastly overrepresented in research but not real world." Indeed, especially when research in question concerns higher mental processes and situated social behaviors (thinking, reasoning, decision making, moral development, cultural values, daily social practices, situated interactions in organizational contexts, etc.), the myth of control can upset and inhibit the very scientific findings that should come out of the study. Consider the cases we discussed under the notion of "developmental teleology": none of them fit a sterilized model of research encounter. In all of them, research "participants" were to various extents co-constructing knowledge. They were also doing many other things, from having fun on a city walk to living their daily lives in a low-income community. Indeed, in many (if not most) research encounters there are major mismatches between the perspectives, worldviews, and interests of researchers and their interactants. All of these unfold and change over time. Knowledge is created through the active development of these encounters and interests, and entire new domains of knowledge are opened up when researchers pay careful attention to such unpredicted developments in shared and evolving goals and researcher–participant relationships. Acceptance of such a view of knowledge requires not only an acknowledgement on the part of researchers themselves, and on the part of educators, training the next generations of researchers. It also requires concerted efforts on part of the academic and practice communities to offset or reverse the institutional movement toward overregulation and the unfettered application of Sunstein's (2005) "precautionary principle" to every aspect of research work.

Let us recall the metaphor we discussed in the beginning: (psychological) research as taking a picture of a landscape. Except for storing the picture in memory, the camera does not change after the picture is taken. There is thus another consequence of the myth of control: by focusing almost exclusively on the rights of participants and the duties of researchers to uphold those rights (or, at best, to ensure safety of the researcher in addition to participants), the overregulating institutional bodies such as IRBs effectively prevent considering change on the part of the researchers themselves. And yet, how many research encounters result in changes in the researcher! We conclude by quoting Kaya Ono, a psychologist researching the use of positive emotion terms by young Japanese people. Ono notes that in her project "the researcher's personal meanings of positive emotion terms went through changes, not only while in meeting with the participants, but also during data analysis" (2011, p. 87). Following Roger Bibace and his proposal for research as partnership (1999), she likens research to dancing: "Dancing partners create new dance together by sensing each other's movements and deciding which directions they will be taking" (2011, p. 88). But is it possible to squeeze dance into a consent form?

NOTES

1. In the U.S. they are called *Institutional Review Boards* (IRBs). Ethical compliance review is legally mandated for federally funded research, but in practice virtually all research on human participants conducted in academic settings, and in many business and applied settings, is subject to review.
2. An example of such activities would be political activism, as seems to be the case with some strands of qualitative research today. For example, Denzin, and Lincoln (2005), prominent exponents of research as political activism, do not treat activism as extrinsic to research.
3. Note the affinity between the terms *interest* and *motivation*. We focus on interest as the inferable property of situated action in interactional context, which, of course, is presumably matched by individual motivations of the interactants.
4. This issue is not lost on Goffman, whose landmark *Frame analysis* (1986) can be read as a treatise on how interactions are defined by and changed by differentiated and asymmetric interests.

5. In fact, following Loftus and Fries (2008), we could question whether or not it is ethical to administer a dense two-page consent form discussing probabilities of crime, traffic incidents and adverse weather, to people who, after all, routinely walk on campus and, at least once in a while, in the city beyond its bounds.
6. Hammersley (2009) situates ethics review within a wider movement toward increased governance of research and argues that such policing is itself unethical on a range of grounds, such as the lack of clearly agreed upon methodological and procedural standards in some fields, notably qualitative research, and lack of competence on part of the ethics committees, as well as the illegitimacy of such regulation when considered in light of the value of autonomy of academic activities.
7. In what follows we obviously side more with the "pessimistic" view of informed consent as detailed by Crow, Wiles, Heath, and Charles (2006), but for somewhat different reasons than the respondents in their study of researchers obtaining informed consent from human participants.
8. This corresponds to the typical "standardized" interview discussed by Holstein and Gubrium (2004), who propose instead to understand all interviews as "active," i.e., to conceive of both the interviewer and the interviewee as active meaning-making agents. However, they do not discuss this specifically in relation to ethics committees.
9. See Bibace, Clegg, and Valsiner (2009), on how the labeling in the US has shifted from "subjects" to "participants." Essentially, the latter are still not allowed to actually participate in knowledge creation.

REFERENCES

Atran, S. (2011). The value(s) of IRBs. *APS Observer, 24*(9), 5, 34–35.

Baron, J. (2006). *Against bioethics.* Cambridge, MA: The MIT Press.

Basken, P. (2011, December 11). Flawed 1940s study in Guatemala could mean new research rules for universities. *The Chronicle of Higher Education.* Retrieved July 1, 2014, from http://chronicle.com/article/Flawed-70-Year-Old-Study-Could/130077/

Bibace, R. (1999). A partnership ideal. In R. Bibace, J. Dillon, & B. Dowds (Eds.), *Partnerships in research, clinical, and educational settings* (pp. 175–306). Stamford, CT: Ablex.

Bibace, R., Clegg, J. W., & Valsiner, J. (2009). What is in a name? Understanding the implications of participant terminology. *Integrative Psychological and Behavioral Science, 43,* 67–77.

Brewster Smith, M. (2000). Moral foundations in research with human participants. In B. D. Sales & S. Folkman (Eds.), *Ethics in research with human participants* (pp. 3–10). Washington, DC: American Psychological Association.

Burger, T. (2001). Ideal type: Conceptions in the social sciences. In N. Smelser (Ed.), *International encyclopedia of the social and behavioral sciences* (pp. 7139–7142). New York, NY: Pergamon.

Churchill, F. B. (1969). From machine-theory to entelechy: Two studies in developmental teleology. *Journal of the History of Biology, 2,* 165–185.

Crow, G., Wiles, R., Heath, S., & Charles, V. (2006). Research ethics and data quality: The implications of informed consent. *International Journal of Social Research Methodology, 9,* 83–95.

Denzin, N. K., & Lincoln, Y. S. (2005). Introduction: The discipline and practice of qualitative research. In N. K. Denzin & Y. S. Lincoln (Eds.), *The Sage handbook of qualitative research* (3rd ed., pp. 1–41). Thousand Oaks, CA: Sage.

Duneier, M. (1999). *Sidewalk.* New York, NY: Farrar, Straus and Giroux.

Dyregrov, K., Dieserud, G., Straiton, M., Rasmussen, M. L., Hjelmeland, H., Knizek, B. L., & Leenaars, A. A. (2010). Motivation for research participation among people bereaved by suicide. *Omega, 62*(2), 149–168.

Fischman, M. W. (2000). Informed consent. In B. D. Sales & S. Folkman (Eds.), *Ethics in research with human participants* (pp. 45–48). Washington, DC: American Psychological Association.

Garfinkel, H. (1967). *Studies in ethnomethodology.* Englewood Cliffs, NJ: Prentice Hall.

Glaser, B. G., & Strauss, A. L. (1964). Awareness contexts and social interaction. *American Sociological Review, 29,* 669–679.

Goffman, E. (1961). *Encounters: Two studies in the sociology of interaction.* Harmondsworth, England: Penguin University Books.

Goffman, E. (1986). *Frame analysis: An essay on the organization of experience.* Boston, MA: Northeastern University Press.

Hammersley, M. (2009). Against the ethicists: On the evils of ethical regulation. *International Journal of Social Research Methodology, 12,* 211–225.

Hammersley, M., & Atkinson, P. (2007). *Ethnography: Principles in practice* (3rd ed.). London, England: Routledge.

Hammersley, M., & Traianou, A. (2011). Moralism and research ethics: A Machiavellian perspective. *International Journal of Social Research Methodology, 14,* 379–390.

Holstein, J. A., & Gubrium, J. F. (2004). The active interview. In D. Silverman (Ed.), *Qualitative research: Theory, method and practice* (2nd ed., pp. 140–161). London, England: Sage.

Kaszowska, A. (2012). *Temporarily living abroad: A three-level model of immersion.* (Unpublished senior honors thesis). Clark University, Worcester, MA.

Kharlamov, N. A. (2013). *Modeling sense of place: Emergence of meaningful places in encountering environments.* (Doctoral thesis). Clark University, Worcester, MA. Available from ProQuest Dissertations and Theses database. (UMI No. 3574700)

Kusenbach, M. (2003). Street phenomenology: The go-along as ethnographic research tool. *Ethnography, 4,* 455–485.

Loftus, E. F., & Fries, J. F. (2008). The potential perils of informed consent. *McGill Journal of Medicine, 11,* 217–218.

McAreavey, R., & Muir, J. (2011). Research ethic committees: Values and power in higher education. *International Journal of Social Research Methodology, 14,* 391–405.

Mills, C. W. (1940). Situated actions and vocabularies of motive. *American Sociological Review, 5,* 904–913.

National Commission for the Protection of Human Subjects of Biomedical and Behavioral Research (1979). *The Belmont report: Ethical principles and guidelines for the protection of human subjects of research.* Bethesda, MD: Office of Human Subjects Research. Retrievable from http://www.hhs.gov/ohrp/humansubjects/guidance/belmont.html

Ono, K. (2011). *What is it to feel 'ureshii,' 'tanoshii,' and 'yorokobu?': An investigation into meaning construction.* (Doctoral thesis). Clark University, Worcester, MA. Available at ProQuest Dissertations and Theses database. (UMI No. 3455142)

Peirce, C. S. (1892). The law of mind. *The Monist, 2*, 533–559.

Rogoff, B., Pérez Gonzalez, C., Chavajay Quiacain, C., & Chavajay Quiacain, J. (2011). *Developing destinies: A Mayan midwife and town.* New York, NY: Oxford University Press.

Sandel, M. J. (2009). *Justice: What's the right thing to do?* New York, NY: Farrar, Straus and Giroux.

Shweder, R. A. (2004). *Tuskegee re-examined.* Retrieved July 1, 2014, from http://www.spiked-online.com/Articles/0000000CA34A.htm

Silverman, D. (2007). *A very short, fairly interesting, and reasonably cheap book about qualitative research.* Los Angeles, CA: Sage.

Sunstein, C. R. (2005). *Laws of fear: Beyond the precautionary principle.* Cambridge, England: Cambridge University Press.

Valsiner, J. (2007). *Culture in minds and societies: Foundations of cultural psychology.* New Delhi, India: Sage.

Valsiner, J. (2011). The development of individual purposes: Creating actuality through novelty. In L. A. Jensen (Ed.), *Bridging cultural and developmental approaches to psychology: New syntheses in theory, research, and policy* (pp. 212–232). Oxford, England: Oxford University Press.

Venkatesh, S. (2008). *Gang leader for a day: A rogue sociologist crosses the line.* London, England: Penguin Books.

CHAPTER 14

COLLABORATIVE AND COMPREHENSIVE RESEARCH IN BAHIA, BRAZIL

Reframing Researcher–Participant Relationships

Ana Cecília de Sousa Bastos
Federal University of Bahia

Everything started at birth: childbirth. Roger Bibace, Kenneth Noller, and Jaan Valsiner, launching from different bases, had collaborated on a research proposal on the subject of the cultural construction of childbirth. Jaan brought that proposal to my students and me in the state of Bahia, with an invitation to collaborate on the study of meanings and circumstances of birthing in Brazil—at that time, the country with the highest frequency of Caesarian-section deliveries. Pregnancy was also considered relevant to the analysis of developmental phenomena in irreversible time,[1] taking into account its quite apparent double nature as a public and private experience.

Particulars and Universals in Clinical and Developmental Psychology, pages 235–245

My student, Ana Patricia Borges, undertook the challenge and carried out, for her master's thesis, a study on women's narratives before and after childbirth (Borges, 2005). When I came to Clark University as a visiting scholar in the fall of 2005, I had Ana Patricia's findings in my lugagge to present to Roger, Jaan, and Kenneth during our 6:30 a.m. weekly meetings. From 2006 on, many studies were developed, having been directly inspired by those meetings. The research participants were mainly Brazilian mothers (living in Brazil, the United States, and Italy). The resulting book, *Cultural Dynamics of Women's Lives* (Bastos, Uriko, & Valsiner, 2011) includes a special acknowledgement to Roger Bibace, who also composed the closing word in the book, in his chapter on partnerships in research.

Roger Bibace's partnership model was a major influence in redirecting and reframing the research in cultural psychology carried out in Bahia. Here, I will discuss some of the conceptual-methodological and practical consequences of studies that have occurred along our research trajectory over the last 10 years, entailing different sets of data. The first of these, at the level of analysis of social groups, focuses on the relationships between communities and social managers and educators; the second is related to the process of becoming parents; the third concerns the relationship between the researcher and the process of analyzing the data he or she has collected; and the fourth applies the model to autobiographical research.

First of all, it is important to make explicit that the partnership model is applied to our research trajectory, taking into account its very guidelines: not strictly as a methodological tool, but in its more general, epistemological sense, involving issues concerning validity (a theory of truth) and ethics (in considering I–other relationships). In other words, the suggestions made by Bibace, Young, Herrenkohl, and Wiley (1999) have become increasingly incorporated, totally or partially, into the work of our everyday research. Their suggestions include: (a) atitudinal shift to research participants as actors rather than as acted on—changing terminology from "subject" to "participant;" (b) avoiding jargon that serves to separate "experts" from "lay people," or the audience in general, by making discussion and understanding unnecessarily difficult; (c) increasing the availability of entire sets of data to readers; (d) beginning research with participant-generated questions; and (e) instituting a feedback procedure, whereby the participant has an opportunity to comment on the researcher's interpretations.

Collaborative and comprehensive research would be the ideal context for partnership, converging to—or departing from—a collaboration of distinct orientations: "the investigators bring generalized training in theory and method while the participants bring the lived experience of the phenomenon being studied" (Bibace, Young, Herrenkohl, & Wiley, 1999, p. 12). In Brazil, authors refer to Paulo Freire and his approach to education as developing a similar perspective.

In countries like Brazil and India, the enormous distance between everyday life, on the one hand, particularly in contexts of poverty, and psychological theories and methods on the other, almost spontaneously sets up questions about the need for developing such a dialogical approach. The researcher needs to recognize "the essential quality of the *other*," claims Chaudhary (2008, p. 35), who goes on to say that "this is the opposite of being 'ethnocentric.' A researcher must always attempt to approach a subject with the realization of what it would be like to be in the place of the *other*."

The same concern guided my own decision to adopt an ethnographical, and more recently an autoethnographical approach—implying a refusal to consider the reality of the *other* as something exotic, estranged from human reality. The *other*, in our research experience, is the family living in poverty. I came to understand that to grasp the so-called poetics of living under supposedly adverse, and many times paradoxical, circumstances, it is necessary not only to overcome the psychological blindness concerning the broad variability of modes of living, but to reassert openess toward diversity and alterity (Bastos & Rabinovich, 2009).

Roger Bibace's partnership model brings to our ongoing research a rationale that considers and enlarges the concept we were already developing in Brazil, and makes explicit its subjacent theory of truth, based more on coherence than on correspondence (Bibace, 2006; Bibace, Laird, Noller, & Valsiner, 2005). As opposed to a "top-down" approach, where the researcher decides which methods and procedures to apply based on his or her own theoretical assumptions, usually followed by statistical analysis and testing of hypotheses, a "bottom-up" approach is more open to the great range of intraindividual variability in every human being, demanding that dialogicality be embedded all along the steps foreseen in the research design; Bibace (2006) asks for patterns to be created, fitting all the parts into a whole. However, he considers that is possible to build complementarities between these two approaches, and the reasons for his belief are made explicit when he discusses the concept of partnership as an ideal (Bibace, 1999).

A partnership ideal requires that research is effectively guided by the principles of complementarity, reciprocity, symmetry, and equality. The concept refuses the traditional asymmetrical relationships marked by discrepancy in power and knowledge between the researcher (or professional) and the lay person, and by what Bibace describes as "the apostolic function of the professional who attempts to convert patients and students to his/her perspective, as an example of professional self-centeredness" (Bibace, 1999, p. 280). In addition to these ethical and organizational dimensions, a partnership ideal elaborates a comprehensive epistemological criticism to causal models based on the connection between "sequence" and "cause," which has, as a main consequence, a continuous engagement in building complementarity. Here, the process will rely on the use of analogies, and remain open to taking the best possible advantage of the tension between a nomothetic and an ideographic focus. A partnership ideal as a concept entails, therefore, ethical and epistemological dimensions, which offer ever-new possibilities of elaboration and application.

Even if not strictly following the steps systematized by Bibace, the research participant's perspective is highly valued within our process of collecting and analyzing data. In this sense, we enable each person who participates in the interview setting to ask and have answered his/her own questions, including the ones related to the way the study is being conducted. The following examples illustrate this positioning and some of its particular developments.

CONSIDERING DIFFERENT LOGIC SCHEMA

Bastos, Rabinovich, and Almeida (2010) analyzed the perspective assumed by the researcher when carrying out studies with families living in a poor Brazilian neighborhood. Bibace's partnership model was a very important tool with which to discuss the interplay of identity-alterity in this particular research context. Recognizing that research on poverty contexts and on the experience of being poor faces many epistemological and methodological challenges, the authors consider the most important challenge to be "the fact that poverty is studied by an outsider, who tries to develop measures and strategies designed to overcome the basic distancing that comes from not having the lived experience of being poor" (p. 222). Even though they are Brazilian, as insiders in the scientific community, the researchers tend to envisage and define the poor from a Eurocentric perspective: they are "the different and unknown, exotic," and this categorization reduces humans to an *us* versus *them* classification.

Partnership model guidelines help to show the *other* as a concrete person and favor an encounter, taking immersion in the reality of living in poverty and its impact on the researcher himself or herself not only as part of the methodological procedures but as part of the data. In this sense, the encounter itself is a support and a tool for understanding, and offers the researcher an opportunity for reflexivity.

An example in which the partnership model is applied more explicitly is the evaluation of social programs in a poor neighborhood of Salvador, Bahia.

Novos Alagados is a slum located in Salvador's Railroad Suburb, known for its old *palafitas*.[2] The district has gone through great physical and social restructuring, due to a multidimensional program executed by the state government and various internationally financed nongovernmental organizations. The main purpose of this program was to eradicate the palafitas, improve the district's housing, build residential structures, and develop facilities for social and recreational use, such as squares, sports courts, bicycle tracks, and roads along the seacoast, to replant the mangrove, and to prevent further construction of palafitas. Following these structural changes, specific projects were undertaken to provide services in health and education. The researchers were asked to conduct a qualitative evaluation of the project's impact from the standpoint of the community. The methodological strategies chosen throughout this process included focus groups and in-depth interviews with key participants. The discussion stressed the relevance of issues related to the subjective dynamics and agency of the residents, who mediated the transformations brought about by the social actions. Here, the use of a participatory evaluation was our main focus, together with the researchers' capacity to move along different perspectives: their own, those of the health managers, and those of the residents.

The first important conclusion to be reached was that the logic of planning is not the logic of everyday life; the administrator's logic and that of the researcher can differ from that of the research participant (logic of planning versus logic of needs). According to Bibace's partnership model, the researcher can never *assume* a particular trend concerning the answer to an item on a questionnaire or an interview; he or she must *ask* (Bibace, 1999; Dowds, Davis, & Bibace, 1999).

This point is well illustrated in this study when it comes to understanding the impact of services and actions on the reality of children and adolescents in Novos Alagados. Different groups and interviewees often mentioned children as the main beneficiaries of the program. Some statements, however, signaled important issues involving the child's relationship with the new space—for example, a possible increase in domestic violence—which went against the professionals' expectations. Although the impact of the social actions were positively evaluated, the persistent adhesion of the researchers to the "ask, don't assume" principle favored the understanding of evaluations that would not be contemplated inside the interview guide as initially elaborated. An example is the mothers' discourses when, in addition to positive considerations about how their own children were being assisted in the context of the social program, other emphases appeared, and the mothers' voices reached the status of *community voices.* They asserted that all children in the neighborhood deserved to be provided with the same quality as found in the project services. Furthermore, they said that these services should be made permanent and assigned a preventive role. The mothers' ideas were not necessarily present in what was proposed by the administrators and researchers while they were designing the study.

Assertions like these made the researchers recognize how the community voices sometimes expressed a deeper and more comprehensive understanding than their own (as researchers and social managers—who had jointly listed the items in the interview guide). The authors concluded:

> The community voices heard showed a deep understanding of the connection between actions, which are proposed as emergent, circumstantial and provisory, and everyday life, which begs for continuity. Eradicating poverty is the life work of an entire society, involving all institutions, communities and actors. However, projects such as these, while well meant, are planned to continue only for two, three, or at the most for 10 years. Everyday logic, the logic of needs, requires it to be more comprehensive and ought to consider the complexity of life. (Bastos, Rabinovich, & Almeida, 2010)

Other important understandings identified in the study concerned the paradoxical effects of social interventions and the intense way the collective memory of the community interacts with the social interventions. When participants are enabled to express their own perspectives, which entails bringing to the conversation space and time parameters different from those of the researchers, novelty is more likely to be created, making the evaluation process more comprehensive and effective. Here, for instance, the participants—using an everyday life logic as their frame of reference—contextualized the limited perspective of the researchers in the duration of their own lives and the history of the community. Some of the utterances were critical as to the nature and reach of social programs, positioning the dwellers beyond it as citizens more than users:

> So it is a process that is being installed; instead of making the family, women, community grow, there is a process of creating dependency and parasites. But there are also those people who keep their dignity, saying: "I only ask for help when I need it; if I can handle it myself I don't ask, don't like to ask." It is a different position. There used to be more sharing among the people in the community. For example, if the neighbor had flour and the other did not, she would give flour to her. But the neighbor, when she goes out on Monday she would return that cup of flour.... Thus, what we saw was always a very proud community who liked working hard for living. Everyone struggled here.

Bibace's partnership model thus contributes to the understanding of complex identity–alterity dynamics, while favoring a perspective that affirms and strengthens the research participant's agency and empowerment.

Analogous processes appeared in the research carried out with different generations of mothers, focusing mainly on narratives about childbirth. The adoption of a conversational setting for interviewing mothers from different generations offered a triangular structure inside which both mothers and the interviewer himself or herself were able to build and rebuild their narratives, making explicit explanatory systems that, otherwise, would not be considered and would be hidden by a linear narrative structure. An example is the situation in which the mother from the oldest generation developed diverse and even opposite solutions to justify her and her daughter's process of decision-making about having a normal versus a C-section delivery.

PARTNERSHIP MODEL AND DATA ANALYSIS

Another relevant situation where the partnership model has exerted an important influence is the process of analyzing data itself. The use of the model enlarges the researcher's understanding, and the opportunities created for the research participants—more waiting time for answers, the introduction of questions to better frame or to modify the answers, more attention to the diverse logics involved in their reasoning, better listening to their symbolic universe, and retroacts on the researcher himself or herself.

An interesting aspect of that process, present in the above-mentioned evaluation study, is the identification of researchers' biases related to their various roles at different moments of data analysis (Bastos, Rabinovich, & Almeida, 2010).

It can be said that the researcher applied the partnership model to their own inner dialogical conversations, being able to identify diverse perspectives linked to different roles when writing a research report for a specific "other" (the social manager, the funding agency), and when analyzing data after distancing themselves and writing an article for their peers in the scientific community.

PARTNERSHIP MODEL APPLIED TO SELF NARRATIVES

"Why not tell your own story"? This is a question often posed by Roger Bibace when discussing issues related to research on autobiographical memory. He was problematizing the general trend in developmental and clinical psychology research to take into account life stories other than the researchers' own.

The many reasons autobiographical narratives are a major concern in psychological research are not our focus here; but let us recall Freeman (1993) for a general remark contextualizing their relevance:

> [T]he stories people tell about themselves often contain revealing information about their own courses of development as well and how these have variously been enhanced or impeded by the social worlds through which they have moved. In this respect, inquiring into life histories can be of service in exploring not only the psychological realm but, in addition, the social, the cultural, and the historical. Indeed, a primary contention of this work is that there is no separating these realms from one another, except perhaps for analytic purposes: A human life, insofar as it exists in society, culture, and history, cannot help but tell us about the mode of its construction, about the complex interplay of influences responsible in significant part for its very shape. (p. 1)

The last example we have selected to illustrate how Bibace's partnership model has had a major impact on the research trajectory is our ongoing study of telling our own stories, following a collaborative autoethnographical framework (Chang, Ngunjiri, & Hernandez, 2013). Individual remembering and collective memory are articulated in a research setting in which 27 people produce and share short narratives about childhood and family, based on temporal and spatial markers (e.g., the moment when one became aware of being part of a family and of one's childhood dwelling). The research participants are encouraged to write their own stories. The group itself works as a dialogical device, continuously presenting to each participant new opportunities to generate questions, evaluate and compare answers, and rewrite personal narratives insofar as this process leads to glimpses of new layers in the process of recollecting family memories, thus improving the methodological quality of the data. It can be said that, in this case, and considering the nature of the research design, the partnership model works as a tool for validity, as the above-mentioned procedures act together to change the narratives, guaranteeing self-reflexivity.

Although we only have a preliminary analysis, these procedures appear to be in tune with the research partnership model in terms of its central features, which can be seen in combining my own report with my sister's on the house of our childhood. As she was born 6 years after me (and, of course, for other reasons concerning her own meaning-making construction around family experience), her narrative revealed a quite diverse family environment. In consequence, I added to my own narrative a temporal component, which made me consider new dimensions I had not seen before, making it work for me as a self-reflexivity tool.

FINAL COMMENTS

Bibace's partnership model entails ethical and epistemological dimensions that offer new possibilities of elaboration and application along diverse contexts, and for every stage along the process of carrying out a scientific investigation. This chapter illustrates how the use of the model in the Brazilian context expands the processes of data collection and analysis, bringing together ethical aspects and issues concerning validity.

First of all, the previous examples show how the research participant, in whatever measure he or she is sure to ask and answer his or her own questions, becomes a partner who coconstructs knowledge with the researcher. The "ask, don't assume" principle effectively modified the scope of the narratives produced, both in the case of the residents in Novos Alagados—when "community voices" could be heard—and for the mothers from different generations, who shared their experiences of pregnancy and delivery.

The perspective that the partnership model brings to research guarantees that the research participant's own logic schema is taken into account in the process of data collection and analysis. The conversational structure that was guaranteed in the examples from the previous section in this chapter sets a multidimensional structure inside which researcher and research participants were able to build and rebuild their narratives, creating a particular dynamic where explanatory systems, otherwise hidden by a linear narrative structure, are made explicit. As important as the fact that the research participants have many chances to express their thoughts, reflections, and questions is the fact that the researcher has many opportunities to listen—and to listen from diverse standpoints. For both studies—communities and mothers—it is interesting to take note of the researchers' surprise when confronted with possibilities of constructing narratives that were unexpected, at least in the beginning of the study. Unexpected narratives included the evidence for a more comprehensive concept of health among the residents of Novos Alagados than for the research team, and the use of opposite reasonings when the mother from the oldest generation justifies her and her daughter's process of decision-making as to having a normal or a C-section delivery.

From the standpoint of the researcher, the partnership model can also work as a tool for increasing validity and precision of data, inasmuch as it is a mechanism to improve self-reflexivity. The model was applied to the researcher's own inner dialogical conversations in the face of the same set of data at different moments and from diverse perspectives (the consultant I-position versus the scientist I-position). This diverse positioning sets a specific kind of triangular structure in which the researcher asks and answers his or her own questions. In the example of collaborative autoethnography, the model has a similar function: a self-reflexivity tool that brings new dimensions to analysis and understanding. To better approach and describe the qualitative structure of the phenomenon (here, autobiographical remembering), it can be said that the study increases its ability to be close to the phenomenic world, thus increasing its validity.

Finally, taking into consideration that the research activity becomes strongly based on the conversation between researcher and research participants, making more and more visible the world inhabited by those being studied it can be said that the partnership model contributes to the integration of a humanist perspective into the activity of the researchers.

NOTES

1. "It is important that irreversible time is introduced into this picture—a [...] person [exists] within a chronotope. The notion of chronotope was coined by Bakhtin for purposes of literary criticism in the 1930s [...]. Here we use

the notion of chronotope to indicate the complementary nature of time and place. Time and place are not opposite components in human lives. In philosophical thinking, we can divide the two notions in the sphere of ideas. The notion of chronotope expresses the complementary nature of time and place." (Sato, Yasuda, Kanzaki & Valsiner, 2013, p. 3).

2. Traditional housing in the Novos Alagados district consisted of *palafitas,* which are tidal dwellings, i.e., lacustrine huts built on wooden piles.

REFERENCES

Bastos, A. C. S., & Rabinovich, E. P. (2009). Realities of living. From poverty to poetry, and beyond. In A. C. S. Bastos & E. P. Rabinovich (Eds.), *Living in poverty: Developmental poetics of cultural realities* (pp. xiii–xxvi). Charlotte, NC: Information Age.

Bastos, A. C. S., Rabinovich, E. P., & Almeida, M. B. (2010). Living the world of poverty: The researcher as participant/apprentice. *Psychology and Developing Societies, 22*(2), 221–247.

Bastos, A. C. S., Uriko, K., & Valsiner, J. (2011). *Cultural dynamics of women's lives.* Charlotte, NC: Information Age.

Bibace, R. (1999). A partnership ideal. In R. Bibace, J. J. Dillon, & B. N. Dowds (Eds.), *Partnerships in research, clinical and educational settings* (pp. 275–306). Stamford, CT: Ablex.

Bibace, R. (2006). *Is and ought to be.* (Unpublished notes for a lecture). Federal University of Bahia, Brazil.

Bibace, R., Laird, J. D., Noller, K. L., & Valsiner, J. (2005). *Science and medicine in dialogue. Thinking through particulars and universals* (pp. xiii–xxiv). London, England: Praeger.

Bibace, R., Young, S. D., Herrenkohl, L. R., & Wiley, A. (1999). An introduction to partnership in research: Changing the researcher-participant relationship. In R. Bibace, J. J. Dillon, & B. N. Dowds (Eds.), *Partnerships in research, clinical and educational settings* (pp. 3–14). Stamford, CT: Ablex.

Borges, A. P. V. (2005). *Significados de gravidez e parto em mães primíparas de hospitais públicos e particulares de Salvador* [Meanings about pregnancy and delivery for primiparous mothers from public and private hospitals in Salvador, Bahia]. (Master's thesis). Institute of Psychology, Federal University of Bahia, Brazil.

Chang, H., Ngunjiri, F. W., & Hernandez, K. C. (2013). *Collaborative autoethnography.* Walnut Creek, CA: Left Coast Press.

Chaudhary, N. (2008). Methods for a cultural science. In S. Anandalakshmy, N. Chaudhary, & N. Sharma (Eds.), *Researching families and children: Culturally appropriate methods* (pp. 29–52). New Delhi, India: Sage India.

Dowds, B. N., Davis, M., & Bibace, R. (1999). Focus groups as a means for eliciting the expertise of research participants. In R. Bibace, J. J. Dillon, & B. N. Dowds (Eds.), *Partnerships in research, clinical and educational settings* (pp. 49–62). Stamford, CT: Ablex.

Freeman, M. (1993). *Finding the muse. A sociopsychological inquiry into the conditions of artistic creativity.* New York, NY: Cambridge University Press.

Sato, T., Yasuda, Y., Kanzaki, M., & Valsiner, J. (2013). *From describing to reconstructing life trajectories: How the TEA (trajectory equifinality approach) explicates context-dependent human phenomena.* Retrieved December 2014 from http://www.psy.ritsumei.ac.jp/~satot/TEA/Sato%20Yasuda%20Kanzaki%20Valsiner%20 9-26-13.pdf

CHAPTER 15

RESEARCHER–PARTICIPANT RELATIONSHIPS IN DIFFERENT SETTINGS

Theoretical and Methodological Issues Within the Framework of Semiotic-Cultural Constructivism

Lívia Mathias Simão, Danilo Silva Guimarães, Djalma Francisco Costa Lisboa de Freitas, and Suara Bastos
University of São Paulo

Hernán Sánchez Rios
Universidad del Valle

The relationship between the researcher and the research participant(s) is of essential concern in science, as shown by Bibace, Young, Herrenkehl, and Wiley (1999, Chapter 1). In this chapter, we will focus on the *process*

Particulars and Universals in Clinical and Developmental Psychology, pages 247–269

of partnership construction through verbal interactions in different settings, taking into account the dialogical tensions that are inherent within self-other-world relationships (Simão, 2012). After a brief introduction of basic ideas anchored in semiotic-cultural constructivism, we will present three recent investigations following different methodological strategies: one experimental study as well as two field studies, each of which mediated researcher-participant relationships. In one field study, the researchers interviewed members of a circus, and in the other, members of the *Nonam* indigenous community. We then discussed theoretical and methodological implications for understanding the meaning of partnership within the framework of semiotic–cultural constructivism in psychology.

SEMIOTIC-CULTURAL CONSTRUCTIVISM AND ITS IMPACT ON THEORETICAL ASSUMPTIONS: KNOWLEDGE CONSTRUCTION IN DIALOGUES[1]

In this section, research carried out by Simão (1988)—also reported in Simão (1989, 1992)—will be (re)constructively reported, aiming to highlight key aspects of the precursory conception of researcher-participant relationships, which are part and parcel of the contemporary perspective of semiotic–cultural constructivism in psychology. This research gave rise to the doctoral thesis of the first author, "Verbal Interaction and Knowledge Construction." This title later became the name of a laboratory at the Institute of Psychology, University of São Paulo, where numerous research projects in the field have been developed starting in 1991.

For 1 1/2 years, Simão (1986) met weekly with a schoolteacher and spoke with her about the teacher's relationships with her students. After having gathered a substantial body of data, Simão then tried to understand the dialogical processes of knowledge construction that occurred in the course of these meetings between the teacher and herself, as researcher. Simão's analysis showed that their verbal actions exercised mutual influence upon each other, which allowed for knowledge construction concerning the central aspect of the focused theme,[2] the so-called *phenomenon-theme*. During their interactions, what was spoken, thought, felt, expected, imagined, and desired as to the teacher–student relationship (phenomenon-theme), transformed itself,[3] a change that can be considered characteristic of the process of knowledge construction.

The researcher as well as the teacher quested for understanding certain aspects of the phenomenon-theme according to their respective interests, influencing each other in the process. It was shown that the participating teacher was the one who selected aspects of the phenomenon-theme, offering an initial frame of what was relevant for her to discuss, as she was the one experiencing it directly. The participating researcher, in turn, made inferences (also a selective process) so as to organize their discussions about the phenomenon-theme, trying to understand it with reference to her research questions and aims. By doing so, the participating researcher challenged the participating teacher's former selections of what was relevant for discussion. The teacher then had to reconstruct her version, adjusting to the suggestions made by the researcher, and vice versa. The process was, therefore, dialogical and ongoing over the course of the meetings (Simão, 1986, 1988).

Looking at these processes, it becomes evident that the knowledge which emerged was jointly constructed. This does not imply that the researcher and the research participant arrived at the same knowledge—nor that this is even possible. Therefore, arriving at the same knowledge cannot be a validity criterion, despite Engelmann's (1985) phenomenological assumption, according to which different people perceive and feel the world in a similar way. It is important to realize that "similar" does not mean "identical." Similarity both guarantees participant–researcher communication about aspects of the phenomenon-theme (perceived as shared), and requires joint negotiation of different meanings and perspectives.

Another important aspect to consider is that verbal interactions always occur in certain *contextual settings.* As such, the context of the researcher-participant interactions should be taken into account in the process of knowledge construction. This apparently obvious statement means to stress that what was talked about, thought, evaluated, etc., in this particular research situation *cannot emerge in other communicative situations*, even if the same people were involved. As pointed out by Engelmann (1985) concerning experimental situations, "verbal reports are always addressed to the experimenter as experimenter, and not to other persons"[4] (p. 3).

Consequently, the presumption that the researcher is neutral and the research subject naive in the process of scientific knowledge construction was rejected for the studies presented here. Researcher-participant dialogues are viewed as a particular kind of I-Other dialogue, in which, among other aspects, disquieting (Simão, 2003) plays a central role. Disquieting might even turn out to be a key element of semiotic–cultural constructivism in future psychological study and practice. When someone—for example, a participant—says something that challenges the other's expectations about a theme, such as the researcher's expectations, a constructive negotiation of meanings can follow. Subsequently, values and new perspectives about the theme can emerge (Marková, 2003; Simão, 2003, 2010, 2012; Valsiner, 1998, 2007).

THE EXPERIMENTAL SETTING: RESEARCHER–PARTICIPANT RELATIONSHIPS AND THE PROCESS OF CULTURAL TRANSMISSION

Djalma Freitas (2013) investigated three mechanisms of cultural transmission in an experimental setting that included four groups of subjects (see Table 15.1).

The three transmission mechanisms were:

1. Observing previous generations of participants in action.
2. Coparticipation with previous generations.
3. Contact with cultural artifacts produced by previous generations.

In Phase A of the experiment, Freitas asked all participants to draw, unaided, a boat on a sheet of paper. They were videotaped while doing so. In Phase B of the experiment, the participants were asked to draw a boat again, but this time the conditions changed as described in Table 15.1. In Phase C, the first task (Phase A, drawing the boat without help) was repeated.

Semistructured interviews were conducted in the intervals between each experimental phase in order to understand the perspective of the participants about why they had accomplished the tasks the way they did. In the course of these interviews, the individual methods of task accomplishment were examined.

The full report of this experimental work was published in the researcher's doctoral dissertation (Freitas, 2013; also Freitas & Guimarães, 2013). In this chapter, we will focus on those parts of the interviews that allow us to identify the processes of dialogical interdependence in which the efforts of the participants to construct a partnership with the researcher become apparent. Two excerpts from these interviews were selected for this purpose.

Excerpt 1 (Participant X, Phase B, 2nd Intermission and Interviews, Group 3):

> I had to observe two people drawing a boat or something like this before it was my turn. Then I noticed that they had practically drawn the same boat with the same characteristics.... I was a little bit confused and didn't know what to do when it was my time to draw. I thought that it would be appropriate not to mess with the chain, because I didn't know if what I did would influence people that were to observe me later. Then I suddenly started drawing the same shape as both people before me.... I thought that it was a chain, because those two people were doing the same thing, and when I noticed that I was systematically exposed to these two observations, I imagined that it was research related to imitation, and that it was likely that if I was having this

TABLE 15.1 Different Experimental Conditions for Drawing a Boat in Phases A, B, and C

Group	Phase A	1st Intermission & Interviews (The interviews were conducted immediately after the Phase A task.)	Phase B (Conducted immediately after Phase A.)	2nd Intermission & Interviews (The interviews were conducted immediately after the Phase B task.)	Phase C (Conducted immediately after Phase B.)	3rd Intermission & Interviews (The interviews were conducted immediately after the Phase C task.)
1. (N = 10)	Draw a boat on a sheet of paper (drawing alone). Participants did this by themselves.		1. Observe all drawings produced so far. 2. Observe the other participants twice while they are drawing a boat. 3. Draw a boat with a participant from the previous generation of participants, and then, with one from the generation to come.		Draw a boat on a sheet of paper (drawing alone). Participants did this by themselves.	
2. (N = 10)			1. Observe all drawings produced so far. 2. Draw a boat alone.			
3. (N = 7)			1. Observe the other participants (twice) while they are drawing a boat to see how they do it. 2. Draw a boat alone.			
4. (N = 10)			1. Draw a boat with a participant from the previous generation of participants, and then, with one from the generation to come. Take advice from a more experienced participant and then share his/her experiences with a new member. 1. Draw a boat twice in co-participation.			

> experience, the others probably had had the same. I would not have wanted to break this link and, suddenly, I did it this way, just like my models.

In the excerpt above, presumptions about the researcher's aims are articulated by the participant. The participant was concerned about not breaking "the chain," something that he thought was related to the study's objective. He not only solved the task by attending to the researcher's request to draw a boat, but actively tried to contribute to the hidden agenda of the researcher, as if they were partners in the experimental process. Although he was not fully aware of the study's objectives, his assumptions influenced the results of the research, and the continuity of the next participants' drawings as well. For this particular participant, the traces left by the other subjects influenced his own drawings. Thus, the trajectory of symbolic actions unfolded into the next generation of participants.

The following excerpt will show that another participant tried to decipher the study's objective, making assumptions about the intentions of the researcher:

Excerpt 2 (Participant Y, Phase B, Group 4):

> Basically, I recreated my own drawing. With the first drawing that I had done, I tried to do it in the most similar way possible.... Well, to be sincere, we had discussed the task a little bit outside the room, and it seemed to us that the experiment was trying to assimilate something from the previous experiment, so I think that I tried not to be influenced by the others and to remain the most faithful to what I had planned before.... Ah, we thought that maybe the objective of the experiment was to capture some aspect of the person that had done the drawing with us before, so it seemed that that was it, and I didn't want to follow this way, I wanted to be faithful to what I would have done.

Although at the beginning of the experiment the researcher had emphasized that the participants were not allowed to talk to each other about the experiment, the participant reports that they did converse about it. This was possible because the researcher's assistant was not present while participants were drawing their boats in Phase B and did not constrain the participants to be quiet. This apparent thoughtlessness, however, produced interesting data, to be analyzed from the perspective of partnerships in the experimental setting.

As in Excerpt 1, the participant tried to decipher the study's objective, making assumptions about the intentions of the researcher. From the participant's report in Excerpt 2, we can infer that the participants discussed and constructed a consensus about the meaning of the experimental task. Nevertheless, by violating the rule of being quiet during the experiment, and working in a direction opposing what could be the accepted solution for the task, they distanced themselves from the researcher's aims—quite the opposite of what happened in Excerpt 1. Different demands seemed to coexist within the participants: the demand to talk with each other about what is happening, the expressed and imagined demands of the researcher, the participants' personal plans/demands, and their expectancies concerning the task. They appear to emerge as representing distinct positions of the researcher; that is, the researcher in this study aims to identify the effects of a mechanism of cultural transmission (coparticipation), while the participants were simply asked to draw a boat and to talk, in semistructured interviews, about their perspectives on why they had accomplished the tasks in the ways they did. But while the researcher's intention was not necessarily to gain knowledge about the participants, the participants tried, based on what we can grasp from one report in Excerpt 2, to make assumptions about the intentions of the researcher.

Excerpt 2 stresses the relevance of the ongoing process of knowledge coconstruction between the participants and the researcher. The participants not only attended to the task, but broke the rules, reported it, and tried to justify their behavior later on. Therefore, although breaking the researcher's rule, they addressed the construction of a partnership.

Researchers need to be aware that different processes influence the experimental setting. There are processes happening *outside* the boundaries of the experiment that mediate the processes *within* the originally constituted parameters. The dialogical approach, however, allows us to observe the recursive interdependence between these two levels while the participants attend to the task proposed by the researcher. The experimental setting is structured as an open-ended system (Valsiner, 2007), in which the affective–cognitive cooperation of researcher and participants leads to the creation of nonforeseeable ways of interaction and to the construction of surprising semiotic elaborations.

Bibace et al. (1999) emphasize that the researcher is an inclusive part of the participants' actions, and vice versa. Both researcher and participants are addressing their actions to an audience; in other words, they are producing output to be analyzed by someone. Additionally, they act within a particular cultural field. The above-presented elaborations of the participants allow us to comprehend their meaning construction involving a diverse audience in their particular cultural situation. Otherness appears in the discourses as the other participants, the researcher, the study, the expected data, and as the anticipated research reports, papers, etc. Therefore, the experimental setting is a stream of relationships (Guimarães, 2010) with particular constraints that need to be negotiated by those involved. In other words, partnership in experimental research depends on an open-ended configuration of multiple relationships that can guide the participants' actions to a convergent or divergent path in regards to the investigative aims.

Figure 15.1 represents an effort to synthesize a set of relationships identified in the dialogical analysis of our experiment, focusing on "the process in which cultural aspects from a previous generation are apprehended by new generations, with consequent modifications during the process" (Freitas & Guimarães, 2013, p. 67); that is, focusing on cultural transmission. It presupposes that the semiotic elaboration of the experimental situation depends on recursive relations between the audience and the broader cultural situation of the experiment.

Figure 15.1 shows that the participant's and the researcher's actions address different aims and are constrained by diverse guides for action and meaning construction, represented by the multidirectional arrows and the box around the circle in both sides of the model. For instance, if the researcher has the aim and the obligation of constructing a dissertation from the analysis of the experimental setting, the participant would be interested in taking part in an intriguing activity that he or she had never experienced before. In this sense, partnership and interdependence in the experimental setting, understood as a dialogical and multidirectional process (Marková, 2003; Valsiner, 2007), implies an asymmetric relationship system that is not conceived as a limited set of variables. This approach is important if we are to understand the experiment as a cultural and dynamic product, taking into account situations that are idiographic and irreversible, and accepting the process of partnership construction as an important investigative aim.

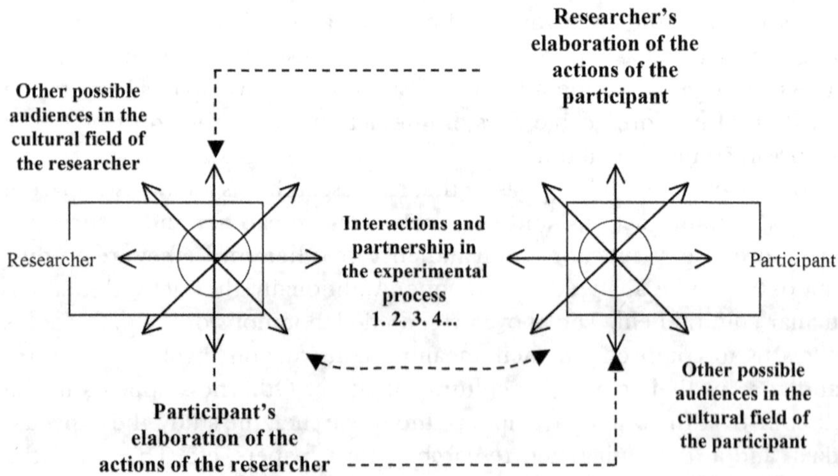

Figure 15.1 Model of the interdependent and recursive–affective exchange between researcher and participants in the reported experimental process.

THE CIRCUS: CHALLENGES AND POSSIBILITIES OF RELATIONSHIPS WITH PARTICIPANTS IN FIELD RESEARCH

The following study was conducted by Suara Bastos and aims to understand meaning-making processes in the daily lives of circus members. Bastos herself had been a circus artist years ago and had worked in three different circuses in Mexico for 4 years. Therefore, she approached a circus community near the city of São Paulo as a former insider, and profited from her knowledge of circus routines. Consequently, the time for approaching the circus in May 2012 was carefully selected in order to minimize the participants' possible resistance to the investigation. Choosing to first visit them in the morning, the researcher expected that some people would still be resting from the previous night's presentation, while others would probably be sightseeing or shopping in the city center, so that the atmosphere would be rather relaxed and calm. This strategy for approaching the circus was important because it allowed the researcher to gather important information (people in charge, show times, etc.) and, more importantly, to adapt to the environment: She would now approach the circus not as an artist, but as a researcher of psychological processes. This novel position implied the emergence of new ways of partnership construction; hence, she needed to find ways to establish a shared affective bond that would be attractive enough to make the participants wish to get involved in the research.

That this was more difficult than expected is shown by the following incident: At the end of her second visit to the circus, Bastos asked the souvenir seller (who was close to the parking lot near the circus entrance), "Do you think that the parking lot will be full, should I park my car somewhere else?" He looked at her angrily and answered, "I hope so. That's what we want, isn't it? If the circus is full, it is better for all of us." The researcher could only nod her head to demonstrate her consent. Feeling ashamed, she decided to approach another man who was close to the ticket office. She smiled at him and said, "Good night!" To her surprise, this fellow was even ruder than the first: "We here in the circus do not like giving interviews. We are all illiterate!" Both situations hit the researcher unexpectedly. Due to her previous experiences, she could not imagine that a circus member could behave aggressively toward her. These incidents made her aware of her new position within the circus and that she needed a different approach to establish research partnerships (see Bastos & Guimarães, 2014, for further details). Bastos managed to do this and although the two circus workers mentioned previously did not become participants, they later became partners of the research process, changing their initial disquieting bond with the researcher to a positive one.

Bastos (2013) eventually conducted semistructured interviews with six circus artists (two females, four males) who were between 35 and 70 years of age. After each interview, the participants were asked to take photos of anything in the circus that had an important meaning for them; for example, a miniature model of the circus. The use of photographs served as supplementary language to the interviews, and its use is justified in order to understand the meaning attributed to the items as seen through the eyes of the photographer (Neiva-Silva & Koller, 2002). Additionally, the researcher took field notes about what she observed before, during, and after the interviews. The interviews were recorded, and then the referentially semantic content as well as expressive aspects of the transcripts were analyzed (Wertsch, 1991).

Overall, Bastos observed enchantment among the participants in regards to the circus and its itinerant lifestyle. In the narratives, concerns related to the future of the circus emerged due to the difficulties it faced at the time: the removal of animals from the arena caused a significant drop in ticket sales, a fact that indicates the influence of cultural changes, since the presentation of animals had been an inherent part of the performances thus far. The new rules showed the permeability of the circus in relation to an evolving society and the necessity of adaptation to new sociocultural configurations. Some participants reported experiences of shunning by others regarding their activities and way of life. Nevertheless, the circus doors were always open to the public, since the circus depended on attracting people to come in, so that it could survive. The circus community was thus faced with a subtle and complex situation involving distancing and approximation between the public and private life, which involved constantly renegotiating boundaries.

Having given this overview, we will now discuss the identified dialogical positions and tensions that emerged in the process of partnership construction within individual interview settings. One of the circus clowns, a 40-year-old Chilean man, demonstrated a strong availability for partnership from the beginning. He and Bastos had met in the food plaza of the circus while the researcher was waiting for another participant who was late for her interview. Noticing the presence of the circus member in the plaza, the researcher introduced herself to him and described the aims of her research. Next, she asked if he would like to participate, and he spontaneously agreed. The interview started immediately, in lieu of talking with the other participant who by now had informed the researcher that she would not be able to make it that day.

The picture taken by the clown of the miniature model of the circus (see Figure 15.2) and his comment, which follows, expresses the close affective bond between the researcher and the participant, which contributed to their partnership.

Figure 15.2 Picture of the miniature model taken by the circus artist.

Excerpt 3 (40-Year-Old Circus Member From Chile):

> Here is the miniature. It is the most beautiful thing in the circus, it is the most beautiful thing we have.... The most beautiful side of the circus is everything. You cannot be sad when you see it. Each time I look at this miniature, I become happy.... I smile with my eyes, enjoy it. Because of this, it was the first thing I wanted to show you, the miniature. You also became excited, right? This is the most beautiful thing. And at the time of the spectacle, everyone is enchanted looking at it. Me too. Every time I pass here, I need to look at it, it looks like a toy for children. Beautiful! I love seeing it.

The way the participant talked about the miniature model of the circus expressed an overwhelming joy that spread to the researcher. He tried successfully to elate her by saying that the miniature was the first thing he wanted to show her. He even emphasized empathic aspects of their relationship, making the affective bond with the researcher stronger by claiming that she was excited as well. As a circus artist, he approached her as a former colleague, who would understand. His emphatic movement makes reference to the body expression of the researcher, looking into her "smiling eyes" and interpreting her feelings. He makes that moment of intersubjective sharing unique, because the researcher tacitly knew that he was expressing a joyful feeling only those who have had the concrete experience of being a circus artist could experience.

Such an emphatic experience of affective sharing also disquieted Bastos, who was not expecting this sort of feeling in her work as a field researcher. From the aseptic, distant, neutral perspective of field research, she was supposed to remain "professional" and concern herself only with investigative issues, but the incident presented here caused an overwhelming nostalgic feeling.

These incidents, presented as part of the field research, show the tensions that are inherent to self–other relationships (Simão, 2010). Participants in any study are individuals with life trajectories of their own that are usually very distinct from the path of the researcher. However, the life trajectories of the researcher and the participants can be similar in many aspects. Both approximations and distancing can produce rupturing experiences for researcher and participants alike. The outcomes of such lived experiences also allow or restrict the possibilities of interactions between the researcher and the participants.

From a semiotic-constructivist perspective in cultural psychology, the elaboration of the meanings emerging in such situations is an important task in the investigative process. It constitutes a triadic unity for data analysis that articulates the lived experience, the ruptured expectancies, and the possibility of comparing or reinterpreting them in light of other experiences and theoretical propositions. Therefore, keeping the academic aims in mind, the researcher actively intervenes in the relationship so as to minimize or understand the constraints imposed by the presence of the participants, who "express their opinions, approbation, reprobation, and all kinds of communicative actions" (Simão, 2004a, p. 30).

Therefore, the researcher-participant relationship is pervaded by tensions, conflicts, and potential involvement, all expressed in subtle or clear and evident ways, allowing or restricting the relevant partnership with the researcher. These tensions, conflicts, and potential involvements are therefore dynamic aspects of the researcher-participant relationship, aspects that depend on one's availability for sharing meaningful experiences (Simão, 2010).

Researchers need to be aware that they will face unexpected situations, and that they need to be able to cope with the anxiety provoked by uncertainty along the nebulous and irreversible path to the future (Valsiner & Connolly, 2005). In addition, it is important to consider how the participants are confronted with the researcher as someone who brings novel expectancies and uncertainty into their environment. Therefore, the partnership can only be constructed successfully if (a) the research becomes a meaningful task to the participants, who inevitably have nonacademic issues to solve in their daily lives, and (b) when both pay attention to the affective stream that permeates the relationship between them. An accurate interpretation of their emerging feelings allows for the co-construction of a respectful relationship, providing common ground for the exchange of experiences, and thus leading to valuable data for the investigation.

WHEN THE PHENOMENON-THEME IS THE MYTHICAL: MADRE ÑAME AMONG THE NONAM

In this section, we will discuss the notion of disquieting experiences that can occur when we meet with "the other," "the different," and "the strange." As an example, we will introduce the myth of Madre Ñame (Mother Yam) of the *Nonam* indigenous community. This tribe lives in Puerto Pizario next to the San Juan River, in the forest of the Colombian Pacific. Fish are the main source of food for the Nonam, who live in a territory with dense tropical forests as well as unforested areas closer to the settlements. Their land is also an important reserve of animal, vegetal, and mineral resources, including gold and silver (Sánchez & Malaga, 2005). The present report is the result of field research conducted by Hernán Sanchéz Rios.

The language spoken by the Nonam is Wounaam, which belongs to the linguistic group *Choco*. The language itself is a marker of their indigenous identity. With the introduction of schools into some of their settlements, Nonam children were given the opportunity to learn Spanish and to participate in diverse economic and educational activities in different parts of Colombia. Nevertheless, until the 1980s, only a few people spoke Spanish. For the most part, these were men who used it to establish permanent commercial ties with other communities, or to obtain basic products that were not available to the Nonam (e.g., manufactured goods; Simão & Sánchez, 2015).

The researcher first met the participants when he tried to recover cultural practices for the education of children in the indigenous reserve of Puerto Pizario (Sánchez & Malaga, 2005). Also at this time, he first heard about the myth of Madre Ñame.

We will now present a dialogue between a communal mother (CM) from Puerto Pizario and a Nonam girl, Bellanira (B), age 6 years. The dialogue was in Wounaam and was later translated into Spanish by Nonam teachers from the indigenous community.

CM: Bellanira, do you know the story of Madre Ñame?
B: I don't know it.
CM: What do you think the story will be about?
B: I don't know.
CM: I'm going to tell it to you: In ancient times, some men lived up the little river, and every day, they went to the hills to go hunting and to cultivate the land. Sometimes, the mothers

went to work with their husbands and left the children alone at home. At one of those times, an old woman came from behind a house with a hamper full of yams on her back. When she arrived, she told the children to chop firewood for cooking. The children obeyed and chopped the log to light the stove. Then, the old woman cooked the yams in a pot made of clay. When the yams were cooked, she peeled them and gave them to the children to eat. This is how Madre Ñame entered our community. In ancient times, the adults cut the leaves of banana trees to put the yams inside them and then gave them to the children as food. The old woman did the same: "You can eat this," she said. It was the first time the Nonam ate yam. After having eaten many yams, the children didn't want any more, because they were full. The old woman became furious and trod on the throat of a child until the child was dead. Afterwards, she returned to her house on the hill. The next day, she came back again, to give yams to the children and to kill another child from the community.

[The CM asks the child for feedback about the story.]

B: It is the story of Nonam children.

CM: Can you explain it some more? Can you tell me in your own words? [The child does not give an answer and the communal mother talks to the researcher in Spanish:]

CM: It looks as if she didn't take anything from the story. I'll tell it again.

[Again the communal mother speaks in Wounaam to the child:]

CM: In the past, the people worked far away from their homes, leaving the children alone. An old woman arrived with a hamper full of yams. Then, she cooked the yams in a clay pot for the children to eat. That was the first time the children ate yams and they liked this new food. However, after they didn't want it any more, the old woman killed a child by kicking it in the throat.

[Immediately, the child says something in Wounaam to the communal mother:]

B: She was an old woman that arrived from the hill and appeared from behind a house bringing many yams. The old woman cooked the yams to give them to the children to eat. That was the first time they ate yam. They didn't want to eat it any more. So, she trod on their throats and killed the children. Afterwards, she went back to the hills.

[The communal mother tells the following to the researcher:]

CM: That was what the child said: In the past, the people worked a lot and left children alone at their houses. After they had left, an old woman came from behind the house bringing along a hamper full of yams. Bellanira was telling this. Moreover, when the old woman arrived at the house, she cooked the yams in a pot of clay. After cooking them, she fed the children. That was what Bellanira said. Then, the old woman went back to the hills. That was what Bellanira said.

[The communal mother speaks in Wounaam to the child:]

CM: Now, I would like to invite you to draw something from the story of Madre Ñame. For instance, you can draw an old indigenous woman and the yam.

[The child draws the old woman.]

B: Now, can I draw a pot of clay and the head of yam?
CM: Yes.

[The child draws the pot of clay.]

CM: Are you drawing the yam?
B: Yes.
CM: Now, the ring of the clay pot.

[The mother talks in Wounaam to a group of children who are looking at Bellanira's drawings:]

CM: We do not need children here. We are only with the child that is drawing.

[After some minutes, the communal mother says something in Wounaam to Bellanira:]

CM: Did you finish?
B: Yes.
CM: Thank you Bellanira, very good.

Nonam children from the HC-ICBF (in English, Communitarian Houses of the Colombian Institute for the Familiar Welfare)5 hear the Madre Ñame myth through their communal mother, during the process of recovering cultural practices in the education of children of the indigenous reserve of Puerto Pizario (Sánchez & Malaga, 2005). The communal mothers, as educative agents, have a direct relationship with the children in their daily lives within the HC-ICBF, and are members of the community. Their task is to protect the children, in order to preserve the new generations of the Nonam people.

The mothers as well as the children construct an autonomous network of meanings, but the dialogue that emerges in the process shows the dynamic relationships between the diverse meanings that coexist. Therefore, our analysis does not isolate each member of the interaction; on the contrary, we think that the myth generates tension and disquiets the participants of a community, triggering symbolic articulations that keep alive and actualize the cultural identity of the Nonam (Simão & Sánchez, 2015).

Thus, we looked at the dialogues that emerged while we were considering the polyphony of voices6 in Bakhtinian terms: Within the expressions of the communal mother emerged the voice of Mr. Perdiz,7 who, in 2005, had narrated the myth to the community in a retelling that was anchored in the ancestral versions that belong to the Nonam people. Simultaneously, the mother's own interpretation of the myth was presented to the children. The children were also given their own voices while being confronted with the story. Additionally, the researcher was a participant in the setting, although he remained silent. We consider it a dialogical silence, because it is likely that his presence alone influenced the intersubjective stream that flowed in the conversation about the myth within the HC-ICBF.

Looking at the conversation between the communal mother, the child, and the researcher about the myth of Madre Ñame, it is possible to identify a set of social representations. They are related to the meaning of the myth among the Nonam:

1. The conversation concerns the origin of what constitutes one of the most fundamental things about the Nonam, emphasizing their existence alongside and within nature. This is because Madre Ñame is the Nonam myth explaining the origin of the yam.
2. It is also about the triumph of the Nonam over the perils brought by others, by a stranger. Madre Ñame does indeed kill the children, but when she dies, she becomes a yam.
3. It is about generational protection within families and communities, a function that needs to be fulfilled by adults together with children, because the adults need to work and Madre Ñame supposedly comes to take care of the children, but kills them instead.
4. Finally, some social representations implicitly permeate the mythic story, representing tensions in the self-other-world relationships, brought by the other, the stranger (Simão, 2007; Simão & Sánchez, 2015).

The dialogue between the communal mother and the child carries a double implication for the self–other–world relationship. First, she tells the myth in Wounaam to the child, because they speak in the language of Nonam all the time. She speaks Spanish to the researcher, because it is the language that allows her to communicate with him. The languages—i.e., Wounaam and Spanish—are frontiers in the dialogues between the interlocutors (Boesch, 1991). These frontiers constitute the cultural space in which each person acts. Within a concrete situation, the initial communicative aims demand the construction of strategies in order to achieve what was previously desired. In the effort to surpass the barriers or cross the frontiers, the person diversifies his or her actions (Simão, 2002a; 2002b).

Spanish is a frontier between the communal mother and the researcher, because it requires constant translation and active adaptation. The language of the researcher, although it is a necessity, ruptures the daily life of the Wounaam-speaking community. Spanish is used to make contact with the exterior world, the world that the researcher belongs to. Boesch (1991) proposes that the notion of a frontier is related to the binary opposition of the "here" and "there." The here is related to the known, the feeling of being secure. In the conversation between Bellanira and the communal mother, the here is the narration of the familiar myth. The there represents something unknown and less transparent, promoting insecurity and anxiety, but also curiosity and excitement because of the novelty. In the presented case, the communal mother might notice some uneasiness due to the presence of the researcher and his possible concerns regarding her educational practices. Simultaneously, the Wounaam language emerges as a barrier for the researcher. In a way, Wounaam also preserves the secrets of the Nonam.

These languages—Wounaam and Spanish—have a second implication in terms of frontiers and barriers. Both the mother and the child know Wounaam well. They exchange and negotiate the myth in this language. Nevertheless, to the children, Spanish is a barrier for communication. Each time the communal mother speaks Spanish to the researcher, the child does not understand, but understands that the speech is related to what he or she said: Something is being exchanged about her narrative, without her being able to follow along, but that "something" is obviously of interest to the other interlocutors.

Dialogues imply being in contact with the other, someone partially known and partially unknown, imagined, beloved, hated, or all these things at once, considering that human feelings are ambivalent (Simão, 2010). In the dialogue concerning the myth, the figure of the other became central to the constructive dialogical process, because the interlocutors had to build a setting for mutual coordination and sharing. Nevertheless, the two differing versions of the myth told by the communal mother and the child suggest that mutual coordination does not equal agreement or communality of objectives. The mother intends to leave some trace of the myth in the mind of the child: "[S]he didn't take anything from the story, so I will tell it again." In contrast, the child tries to show that she remembers parts of what she was told. The dialogue involves the construction of suppositions about the other, articulating personal ideas about the discussed topic, and the interaction during the course of this interchange. In the dialogues about the myth, each actor tells the story from a particular perspective, which is his or her own personal viewpoint. In so doing, all of them (communal mother, child, and researcher) are coordinating the situation, creating suppositions, and reconstructing them, aware of the impossibility of their own absolute or complete understanding. This inability is the expression of the constant tension that produces potential changes in the dialogical process (Marková, 2003).

The tension in the dialogue is a necessary requirement, because the dialogue produces friction and demands affective–cognitive reconstructions by the interlocutors. They can continue or stop talking about a certain topic, generating novel tensions in the process (Simão, 2004a). All utterances in a dialogue are, to some extent, a contribution to sharing information with others and making them understand (Simão, 2004b). So, in the dialogue about the myth, comprehensions and misunderstandings are related to different levels of intersubjectivity, collectively embraced and generated. Therefore, the emerging divergences in the dialogue depend on the interpretative possibilities of each participant with regards to the topic and the relationships between the actors during the dialogical process. Mutual trust is, thus, essential for human communication.

RESEARCHER–PARTICIPANT RELATIONSHIP AND KNOWLEDGE CONSTRUCTION WITHIN A SEMIOTIC-CULTURAL CONSTRUCTIVIST FRAMEWORK: CONTEMPORARY REFLECTIONS

The three studies presented here show how disquieting experiences, when meeting with the other, can be a constitutive dimension in the researcher-participant relationship. Focusing on self-other interdependence in the three research settings discussed—the experimental investigation on cultural transmission, the field research at the circus, and in an interethnic situation—allowed us to observe that the knowledge constructed in the realm of cultural psychology emerges in idiographic and irreversible situations. These situations can facilitate the co-construction of respectful relationships, and generate valuable data for the investigation, due to the attention paid to positive feelings of mutual understanding that may arise in the process of research.

Theoretical and methodological reflections within the framework of semiotic–cultural constructivism in psychology (Simão, 2010, 2012) are concerned with qualitative research that represents a rupture, as opposed to the conventional monologic and foundational theories of psychological development. Semiotic-cultural constructivism addresses the diversity, the difference, and the multiplicity of perspectives in the core of dialogical cultural psychology (Guimarães, 2012). It opens up a novel understanding of the research participant, whom the researcher may observe as a complex whole: a person with diverse and multilayered symbolic actions concerning affective, cognitive, and situational dimensions (Simão, 2002a; 2010). From this perspective, the researcher-participant relationship can be approached by a qualitative analysis of the experimental situation as well as through field research featuring open discourse as well as interviews. In the settings under discussion, the analyzed and interpreted data emerged from dialogical relationships that permeated the discourses and the actions of the interlocutors, giving meaning to the triadic unit of self-other-world, as proposed by Simão (2003, 2004b).

Therefore, there is always a mutual effort on the part of the researcher and the participants during the process of knowledge construction. Participants usually possess privileged information about the investigated issue; for instance, their own thoughts and feelings. Researchers, on the other hand, usually have privileged strategies on how to summarize and interpret the collected information, focusing on the objectives of the research. A central role of the researcher is to make explicit, through analysis and hermeneutic interpretation of the whole, the implicit aspects that led to the emergence of the concrete investigated results.

Out of concern for such complexity, Bibace et al. (1999) proposed a model to better comprehend, interpret, and investigate phenomena in behavioral sciences, stressing the relevance of reframing the researcher-participant relationship as a partnership in which the interdependence of self-other-world is not neglected.

Conceptualizing the researcher-participant relationship as a partnership does not presuppose that the researcher and participant are fused, or that they think and feel the same way. On the contrary, it allows us to pay attention to the dialogical gap between the researcher and the participant, their distinctions as interested subjects in the investigative setting, and their efforts to create a convergent situation for establishing a productive relationship in which exchanges become meaningful.

The partnership issue in its semiotic-constructivist frame, as studied by Bibace et al. (1999), is therefore one of the main concerns of cultural psychology. The partnership theory views the self-other-world relationship in its multiple intersubjective and intrasubjective dimensions. We argue that researcher and participant are both coparticipants, dialogically embraced within the cultural process of knowledge construction as a triadic unit: self-culture-other (Simão, 2012).

NOTES

1. This section should be understood as a synthetic retrospective report by the first author about selected aspects of her doctoral research, in the context of the present chapter. For purposes of stylistic consistency, it is written in the third person.
2. The focused theme was elected by the participant, according to her demands as determined by her relationships with the students' parents, and was discussed in weekly meetings. Each meeting was tape-recorded and transcribed, and what was talked about was organized by the researcher into content categories, which she assembled to form a notebook. At each meeting, the teacher had access to what was discussed in the previous sessions according to the notebook's organization; she could then modify her previous statements and correct the researcher's understanding of them. (For more details of this procedure, see Simão 1986; 1988).
3. The same teacher from the former master's research now asked for more meetings to talk about her relationship with the parents of some of her students.
4. From the original, in Portuguese, as required by the book editors: *O relato verbal é sempre dirigido ao experimentador enquanto experimentador, e não a outra pessoa* (Engelmann, 1985, p. 3).
5. The acronym HC-ICBF refers to the *Hogares Comunitarios del Instituto Colombiano de Bien estar Familiar* (Communitarian Houses of the Colombian Institute for the Familiar Welfare). The HC-ICBF is a program from the Colombian State coordinated by women from communities that assume educative and protective practices with 15 children between 0 and 6 years of age. In Puerto Pizario, the activities of HC-ICBF start at 8 a.m. and finish at 4 p.m. During this period, the communitarian mother dialogues, prepares food, plays, narrates stories, accompanies sleep, and pays attention to forest dangers.
6. See, for instance, Bakhtin (1986); Holquist (1990); Todorov (1981).
7. In the community, regular meetings with Mr. Juan Perdiz (spiritual leader and councilman of the community) and the children in the HC-ICBF took place, so that he could share his experiences and ancestral knowledge of the Nonam culture with them.

REFERENCES

Bakhtin, M. M. (1986). *Speech genres & other late essays.* Austin, TX: University of Texas Press.

Bastos, S. (2013). *O circo e suas construções de sentido: um olhar para a perspectiva do circense sobre seu cotidiano* [The circus and its construction of meaning:

Addressing the circus artist's perspective on his own daily life]. (Master's thesis). University of São Paulo, São Paulo, Brazil.

Bastos, S., & Guimarães, D. S. (2014). Cultural-affective bonds in field-research: Towards a semiotic-constructivist understanding of circus daily life. *Psychology and Society, 6*(2), 1–19.

Bibace, R., Young, S., Herrenkehl, L., & Wiley, A. (1999). An introduction to partnership in research: Changing the researcher-participant relationship. In R. Bibace, J. J. Dillon, & B. Dowds (Eds.), *Partnerships in research, clinical and educational settings* (pp. 3–14). Norwood, NJ: Ablex.

Boesch, E. (1991). *Symbolic action theory and cultural psychology.* Berlin, Germany: Springer Verlag.

Engelmann, A. (1985). Comportamento verbal e relato verbal [Verbal behavior and verbal report]. *Psicologia, 11*(1), 1–5.

Freitas, D. F. C. L. (2013). *Um estudo sobre o processo de transmissão cultural* [A study of the cultural transmission process]. (Master's thesis). University of São Paulo, São Paulo, Brazil. Retrieved December 2014 from http://www.teses.usp.br/teses/disponiveis/47/47132/tde-08102013-151447/

Freitas, D. F. C. L., & Guimarães, D. S. (2013). An experimental study about the cultural transmission process. *Psychology & Society, 5*(1), 67–86.

Guimarães, D. S. (2010). Symbolic objects as sediments of the intersubjective stream of feelings. *Integrative Psychological & Behavioral Science, 44*, 208–216.

Guimarães, D. S. (2012). Desdobramentos de um possível diálogo entre psicologia cultural e antropologia americanista [Ramifications of a possible dialogue between cultural psychology and American anthropology]. In S. M. P. Vichietti (Ed.). *Psicologia social e imaginário. Leituras introdutórias* [Social psychology and imaginary. Introductory readings] (pp. 153–167). São Paulo, Brazil: Zagodoni.

Holquist, M. (1990). *Bakhtin and his world.* London, England: Routledge.

Marková, I. (2003). *Dialogicality and social representations: The dynamics of mind.* Cambridge, England: Cambridge University Press.

Neiva-Silva, L. N., & Koller, S. H. (2002). O uso da fotografia na pesquisa e psicologia [The use of photography in research and psychology]. *Estudos de Psicologia,* 7(2), 237–250.

Sánchez, H., & Málaga, M. (2005). *Recuperación de practicas culturales de la comunidad indígena Nonam para la educación de los niños* [Recovery of cultural practices of the indigenous Nonam community for the education of children]. (Working paper). Cali, Colombia: Center for Research in Psychology, Cognition, and Culture of the Universidad del Valle.

Simão, L. M. (1986). *Relações professor-aluno (estudo descritivo através de relatos verbais do professor)* [Teacher–student relations (descriptive study through verbal teacher reports)]. São Paulo, Brazil: Editora Ática.

Simão, L. M. (1988). *Interação verbal e construção de conhecimento* [Verbal interaction and knowledge construction]. (Doctoral thesis). University of São Paulo, São Paulo, Brazil.

Simão, L. M. (1989). Interação Pesquisador-Sujeito: A perspectiva de ação social na construção de conhecimento [Researcher–subject interaction: The perspective of social action in the construction of knowledge]. *Ciência e Cultura, 41*(12), 1195–1202.

Simão, L. M. (1992). Interação verbal e construção de conhecimento: Aspectos do diálogo pesquisador-sujeito [Verbal interaction and knowledge construction: Aspects of the researcher–subject dialogue]. *Psicologia Teoria e Pesquisa, 8*(2), 219–229.

Simão, L. M. (2002a). O significado da interação verbal para os processos de construção de conhecimento: Proposta a partir da óptica Boeschiana [The meaning of verbal interaction for knowledge construction processes: A proposal from the Boeschian perspective]. In S. A. S. Leite (Ed.), *Cultura, cognição e afetividade: A sociedade em movimento* [Culture, cognition and affection: Society in motion] (pp. 85–102). São Paulo, Brazil: Casa do Psicólogo.

Simão, L. M. (2002b). A noção de objeto e a concepção de sujeito em Boesch [Boesch's notion of object and the conception of subject]. In L. M. Simão, M. T. C. C. de Souza, & N. E. Coelho Júnior, *Noção de objeto, concepção de sujeito: Freud, Piaget e Boesch* [Notion of object, conception of subject: Freud, Piaget and Boesch] (pp. 87–96). São Paulo, Brazil: Casa do Psicólogo.

Simão, L. M. (2003). Beside rupture—disquiet; Beyond the other—alterity. *Culture and Psychology, 9*, 449–459.

Simão, L. M. (2004a). Alteridade no diálogo e construção de conhecimento [Otherness in dialogue and knowledge-building]. In L. M. Simão & A. Mitjáns-Martinez (Eds.), *O outro no desenvolvimento humano: diálogos para a pesquisa e a prática profissional em psicologia* [The other in human development: Dialogues in research and professional practice in psychology] (pp. 29–39). São Paulo, Brazil: Pioneira–Thomson Learning.

Simão, L. M. (2004b). Semiose e diálogo: Para onde aponta o construtivismo semiótico-cultural? [Semiosis and dialogue: Where does it lead in semiotic cultural constructivism?] In M. T. C. C. de Souza (Ed.), *Ossentidos de construção: o si mesmo e o mundo* [The meanings of construction: The self and the world] (pp. 13–24). São Paulo, Brazil: Casa do Psicólogo.

Simão, L. M. (2007). Why otherness in the research domain of semiotic-cultural constructivism? In L. M. Simão & J. Valsiner (Eds.), *Otherness in question: Labyrinths of the self* (pp. 11–35). Charlotte, NC: Information Age.

Simão, L. M. (2010). Ensaios Dialógicos: Compartilhamento e diferençanas relações eu–outro [Investigating dialogues: The shared and non-shared in I-Other relationships]. São Pablo, Brazil: Editora Hucitec.

Simão, L. M. (2012). The other in the self: A triadic unit. In J. Valsiner (Ed.), *The Oxford handbook of culture and psychology* (pp. 403–420). New York, NY: Oxford University Press.

Simão, L. M. & Sánchez, H. (2015). Madre Ñame and the Nonam: One and another. In D. S. Guimarães (Ed.), *Amerindian paths: Guiding dialogues with psychology.* Charlotte, NC: Information Age.

Todorov, T. (1981). Mikhaïl Bakhtine–le principe dialogique suivi de Écrits du Cercle de Bakhtine [Mikhail Bakhtin–The dialogical principle, followed by writings of the Bakhtin circle]. Paris, France: Éditions du Seuil.

Valsiner, J. (1998). *The guided mind: A sociogenetic approach to personality.* Cambridge, MA: Harvard University Press.

Valsiner, J. (2007). *Culture in minds and societies: Foundations of cultural psychology.* New Delhi, India: Sage.

Valsiner, J., & Connolly, K. J. (2005). The nature of development: The continuing dialogue of processes and outcomes. In J. Valsiner & K. J. Conolly (Eds.), *Handbook of developmental psychology* (pp. ix-xviii). London, England: Sage.

Wertsch, J. V. (1991). *Voices of the mind: A sociocultural approach to mediated action.* Cambridge, MA: Harvard University Press.

SECTION V

THE FRIEND AND MENTOR: MEETING ROGER BIBACE AND THE AUTHORS

This book is dedicated to Roger Bibace, professor emeritus of psychology, Clark University, Worcester, Massachusetts. From Egypt, Roger Bibace journeyed to Vancouver, Canada, in order to receive his BA in 1949. Being a true globetrotter, he then travelled to the East Coast of the United States for the purpose of pursuing his PhD, which he completed in 1956 (see Figure V.1 for his PhD photograph displayed at Clark University, Worcester, MA). Following this accomplishment, he stayed in academia at Clark University and functioned as lecturer, assistant and associate professor, the director of the Psychological Services Center as well as of the Clinical Training Program, and from 1970 on, as professor of psychology. Dr. Bibace retired from his professorship at Clark University in 2006, but he is still a highly valued and very active member of the academic community, joining lab meetings, discussing research ideas, and contributing to academic writings.

Alongside his academic career, Dr. Bibace was also highly interested in applying his knowledge practically. His professional career as a psychoanalytically oriented clinician started in 1957 by working as a consultant at several different institutions, such as Montreal Children's Hospital, Worcester State Hospital, Worcester Public Schools, and the University of Massachusetts Medical Center (UMASS). As a clinical psychologist, he treated patients for up to three or four times a week, sometimes over a number of years. At UMASS, he also served as an adjunct professor of psychiatry,

Particulars and Universals in Clinical and Developmental Psychology, pages 271–272

Figure V.1 Roger Bibace's PhD photo as displayed at Clark University, Worcester, MA.

the director of behavioral sciences in the Department of Family and Community Medicine, and as a professor of family medicine and community health. Here, he worked together closely with faculty family physicians and residents, and his work included observing faculty and residents as they interacted with patients and their families. This led to his current research focus on partnerships in clinical, educational, and research contexts that, in his opinion, require a decrease of authority and power and a greater symmetry in the relationships between authorities and their partners.

His two interests of psychology and medicine are evident by him having worked as a researcher as well as a clinician. He even chaired the committee for the American Psychological Association that created an entirely new degree; a degree that also put emphasis on clinical skills and training, rather than solely focusing on empirical science.

Constantly being an incredible source of interesting ideas and new directions and providing valuable guidance, Dr. Bibace greatly contributed to today's research. For his outstanding performance, he received many awards and honors, this volume being one of them.

CHAPTER 16

NOT A MIND READER

Jaan Valsiner
Aalborg University

Roger Bibace is a very young man—even at the age of 89. When I arrived for my job interview at Clark University in 1995, he was the person most eager to talk with me and not about trivialities—we discussed interesting ideas about which he was passionate. I felt at home in a context like this—looking for intellectually rich academic surroundings was a find one could appreciate 20 years ago in Jonas Clark Hall.

The first encounter was only the beginning. During all my years at that small university with big traditions in psychology of the United States, I could enjoy Roger's support, appreciation for the ambience of our collective searches for new solutions in the "kitchen seminars,"[2] and even taking care of my personal welfare.[2] Roger is a deeply caring human being who is humble about his own contributions to psychology. Now—in 2015—he is perhaps more frail in health, but as youthful in his curiosity about the human mind as he was two decades ago. Age for sure takes its toll on the body, but the inquisitive mind stays.

Over his long stay at Clark—spanning six decades (he arrived as a doctoral student in September 1950, and has stayed away from home ever since)—Roger Bibace has not become a prominent "star" in American psychology. In his humility he would not have liked such Hollywood-type roles toward

Particulars and Universals in Clinical and Developmental Psychology, pages 273–276

which many contemporary psychologists strive. Instead, his work over the last half century can be best described by the metaphor of a bridge. He has been the bridge over the troubled waters of American clinical psychology—reminding our contemporary colleagues and students in that area that clinical practice is by far more than following a sequence of socially prescribed steps of some manual in treating a patient. Not everybody has listened to his message there—clinical psychology in the United States has become a business enterprise governed by the legal prescriptions of insurance companies. But some students have taken his message—to doctors and psychologists—into their hearts: talk to the "patient" who is a fellow human being, and find out the person's perspective! Roger Bibace's Partnership Model is not merely a perspective for treatment, or for research—it is a categorical imperative for the profession of psychology in all of its facets.

Roger Bibace is also the bridge between the past—the present—and, hopefully, the future, of psychology as science. A dedicated student of Heinz Werner, he has always considered his mentor's ideas with high respect—not as orthodoxy, but as guidelines for thinking. Werner brought to America—and to Clark University where he relocated in 1947—the developmental perspective of the *Naturphilosophie* of J. W. Goethe, elaborated by the "Hamburg tradition" of the 1920s and early 1930s[3]—Roger has been a constant reminder all over his years of the relevance of taking a developmental perspective. The proliferation of Werner's ideas in the post-World-War-II United States was extensive through the 1950s, but then gradually faded over the following decades. America has not been welcoming to developmental ideas in science, letting them immigrate at times and easily transforming them into one or another version of static ontological accounts (Cairns, 1998). Roger has been keeping the original ideas alive, and bringing new generations into contact with Werner's ideas through his own look at relevant psychological phenomena.

Finally, Roger is the bridge between psychological science and human psychological phenomena. The latter have been constantly in danger of being lost in the huge science manufacturing factory of American psychology (Cairns, 1986). Human beings have been treated—even symbolically—at different times of psychology's history as "observers," "subjects," or "research participants" (Bibace, Clegg, & Valsiner, 2009). Roger has emphasized the need of respect for the persons—both researchers and the researchees in any study are joint "participants" in the research encounter. And he keeps reminding all of us—proud to be researchers—that our understanding is always limited. On innumerable occasions we have all encountered his slamming his hand on the table in front of him, with a loud dramatic outcry,

"I Am Not a Mind Reader!"

And, of course, once the dramatic moment is over, he usually proceeds to provide a sensible and deep analysis of the *psyche.* Yet this analysis is not pretending to take the place of the assumed mind-position of the person analyzed. The focus on the partnership of the researcher and the researchee, and of the doctor and the patient entails understanding the Other *through* communication *with* the Other, but not the assumption that one *has become* the Other. One needs to presume intersubjectivity in order to construct it (Rommetveit, 1985), but inter*subjectivity* it stays. A person feels into the Other, and through that feeling-in (*Einfühlung*; Lipps, 1906) develops one's own deeply subjective understanding of oneself (and of the world). All objectivity is subjectively lived through.[4]

The present book has two functions. First, it celebrates Roger Bibace's long life in academia, and highlights his contributions for the worldwide audience to appreciate. And appreciate they will—all the friends he has made through his work with family doctors in the United States and within the Kitchen Network will have in the form of this book a rich material reminder of how Wernerian ideas and practices have grown through the activities of a humble nonreader of human minds. He is, and will be, warmly remembered in Brazil, Japan, Australia, Europe, and, of course, in the United States.

Secondly, the book will build a bridge of its own between developmental theoretical ideas of venerable history and the future of psychology at large and cultural psychology in particular. What Roger Bibace has done for decades is what needs to be central to psychology as science—close partnership between researchers, clinical practitioners, and "participants" ("clients," "subjects," etc.) establishing the knowledge base of psychology not only extensive in "data," but integrative in its human and humane focus. This is the basic message that stays as a guide to the future. Psychology needs it.

NOTES

1. These seminars—established in 1997 as I arrived to start my position at Clark—were located in the public area in the Psychology Department known as "the kitchen" (hence the name). These seminars operate on the principle of freedom of participation and equality—all participants come and go as they wish or need, say or not say something (except for discussing trivialities such as politics, in science or society), defy rules of polite talk in their eagerness to discuss the constructive possibilities for new understandings. Weekly texts to be discussed are sent to the network of scholars all over the world—once a "kitchener" one stays as such until one decides to leave. There are about 250 participants in this network (as of 2015, when the "kitchen" has relocated to Aalborg University in Denmark—www.ccp.aau.dk). The present

book is a concrete result of the "kitchen network" as it honors the contributions of Roger Bibace to our intellectually adventurous lives.

2. For example, as I arrived to take residence in Worcester, Massachusetts, he set me up with a very trustable and thinking personal care physician—an important resource for staying healthy in the complex medical care system of the United States. His fatherly care about my wearing appropriate shoes in the middle of Massachusetts ice storms was always heart-warming.
3. For a full overview of the roots of the ideas of Heinz Werner and their transposition from Europe to America see Valsiner (2005).
4. This is a basic philosophical point about any statement *about* something not being that something. The world "out there" may be "objective", but *any statement by me that it is so,* is necessarily subjective. It is mine—not that of the world—yet it is possible through my relation with the world. I am in a partnership—rather than ownership—relation with my world.

REFERENCES

Bibace, R., Clegg, J., & Valsiner, J. (2009). What is in a name? Understanding the implications of participant terminology. *Integrative Psychological & Behavioral Science, 43,* 1, 67–77.

Cairns, R. B. (1986). Phenomena lost: Issues in the study of development. In J. Valsiner (Ed.), *The individual subject and scientific psychology* (pp. 97–111). New York, NY: Plenum.

Cairns, R. B. (1998). The making of developmental psychology. In W. Damon & R. Lerner (Eds.), *Handbook of child psychology: Theoretical models of human development* (5th edition) (Vol. 1; pp. 25–105). New York, NY: Wiley.

Lipps, T. (1906). *Die* ästetische *Betrachtung und die bildende Kunst* [The aesthetic consideration and the fine arts]. Hamburg, Germany: Leopold Voss.

Rommetveit, R. (1985). Language acquisition as increasing linguistic structuring of experience and symbolic behavior control. In J. Wertsch (Ed.), *Culture, communication, and cognition: Vygotskian perspectives* (pp. 183–204). Cambridge, England: Cambridge University Press.

Valsiner, J. (Ed.). (2005). *Heinz Werner and developmental science.* New York, NY: Kluwer Scientific/Plenum.

CHAPTER 17

ENCOUNTERS WITH IMPACT

Every secret of a writer's soul, every experience of his life, every quality of his mind is written large in his works.
—Virginia Woolf

If Virginia Woolf is right, you can learn a lot about authors by reading their texts. In this book we have included quite a few articles, chapters, and talks Roger Bibace has written. In so doing we have not only introduced his ideas, but also given the reader an idea of the person he is. Nevertheless, we would like to add one more perspective. While writing this book, we asked friends, students, and colleagues of Roger to write short stories or anecdotes that would help others, who did not (yet) have the privilege to meet him, understand what kind of person he is on a more personal level. This is what they said:

Roger is different. For those who know him, he is not the status quo. The courses he taught took students on unexpected journeys, and Ideographic Science was my personal favorite. Rather than reducing human experience, he pushed us to take the long view. It was about life in context. It was about the choices one makes. And it was about realizing that there are many paths to the same destination. Indeed, Roger found a way to make the heroic human. This is most clear in his partnership approach to medicine and education. For both, the point is to co-construct, not dominate with power, whether teacher or student, physician or patient. This spirit traces back to Socrates, who to his death insisted on referring to his pupils as "friends," never "students." Roger is friend, teacher, and student in the truest sense.

Particulars and Universals in Clinical and Developmental Psychology, pages 277–286

His life-long learning inspires others to follow in kind. He makes you look where you'd least expect. He asks you to take the road less traveled, and only once you have do you realize the value of the unexpected journey.

Andrew C. Shurtleff
BA and MS, Clark University, from 2005–2010
Now EdD candidate at Columbia University

When we first met Roger on a very snowy afternoon in Worcester, sometime in February 2012, he immediately expressed his excitement about our upcoming project and swept us away with him. We were about to restart a research project he had initiated more than 30 years ago. Yet, its topic is still relevant to this day.

Not only has he been an incredible source of fascinating ideas and constantly provided guidance and valuable feedback on our research (he called it a "smorgasbord of thoughts"—and that it was!), but he also became a good friend. The most precious moments we shared were not discussing our research; it was those moments when we experienced Roger on a more personal level. We still joyfully remember his invitations to lunch or dinner, where he would entertain us with stories about his interesting and fulfilled life as clinician, researcher, husband, and father. It is not just that we have learned a lot about psychological research from Roger, but also about personal qualities, such as commitment, endurance, and passion. We are honored to have met and worked with him, and we are looking forward to future collaborations!

Alina Kriebel and Saskia Stöckigt
Visited Clark University in 2012 for writing their bachelor theses

"What are you interested in? What is it that you are trying to understand?" Dr. Bibace asked while directing me to take a seat. This was my first real meeting with Roger (see Figure 17.1 for a picture taken during discussion at the Kitchen Seminars). As a doctoral student, I was constantly faced with such questions. I had come to think of the process as facing waves while wading through a stream—you have to react appropriately in order to keep them from throwing you off balance.

I replied to Roger's question without hesitation and delivered what I thought to be a convincing answer built on recent "insider-only" discussions in the field. After I was done, Roger gently posed the question once again—"Yes, but what are *you* really interested in?" Thinking that he wanted to know what my personal contribution to the field would be, my response sounded like the "general discussion" section at the end of an academic article. After affirming how, yes indeed, truly interesting that would be, Roger asked me a third time—"But what is it that you are really trying to understand? Why

Figure 17.1 Roger Bibace during a Kitchen Seminar at Clark University, Worcester, MA.

are you doing all this?" His persistence alone indicated clearly enough that I had not answered the question. At the same time, in what I would learn is typical Roger fashion, his sincerity and warmth encouraged me to further search for an honest answer. I realized that he did not want me to respond to the standard "waves" that one encounters in such discussions, or to even place myself within a wider academic current. Rather, he wanted to know why I was walking through the stream in the first place. He wanted to know where I wanted to go and what I hoped awaited me on the other side. While the answer to this question was precisely that which had sent me off on this journey in the first place, I found it surprisingly difficult to respond. The deeply personal side to my work had somehow come to feel foreign and out of place in even my own thinking about the field.

I asked Roger if he would be willing to meet with me again, and he graciously agreed. Expecting the standard well intended but ultimately hollow offer to help, I was surprised the following week to hear Roger's voice on the other end of the phone. Before I knew what was going on, we had agreed to meet at his house later that week. Over the course of the next few days, I received several different voicemails from Roger. He asked me to bring a file from his office, a Dictaphone, a book from the library, and his mail from the department. On the day before our meeting, I spoke with Roger once again. After telling him that everything was ready, he asked me to bring along something more—"the two visiting German students." I agreed, but started to wonder what I had gotten myself into, and if I had not inadvertently turned myself into an errand boy.

The next day, I picked up the two Germans (after first figuring out who they were), and together we set off to Roger's house. As part of the ice-breaker in the car, all of us awkwardly confessed to not knowing what we were getting ourselves into. That shared apprehension immediately vanished upon the sight of Roger waiting for us in the doorway. We were all equally moved by the warm welcome that we received and by his obvious excitement at the meeting. Over the course of the next two hours, Roger asked us questions about our research in a way that gently encouraged us to merge our own personal convictions and interests with the language of the field. After posing such questions, Roger then explained our answers back to us, as he had understood them. Through this back and forth process we saw, in the most personal way possible, that much can get lost in translation, not only between speaker and listener, but also between our own personal goals and the professional language into which we must convert them. At the same time however, we also saw how, with hard work, concentration, and persistence, it is possible to meaningfully overcome these divides.

During our conversation, I learned that Roger had asked me to bring the library book as it contained a chapter he thought I might want to read. The file I brought from his office contained an outline that illustrated how one can approach such constructive conversations. The Dictaphone was there for our own use, so that later we could go back to earlier parts of the discussion to check where we were consistent and where we had changed our own stories. The German students were in the process of conducting similar interviews, and Roger had wanted to give them the chance to observe and participate in just such a discussion. He also wanted to include them, so that they might feel welcome and at home in their new academic environment.

I had underestimated the sincerity and depth of Roger's engagement with his students and with those around him in general. Beyond the particulars of our various subsequent conversations, I have learned a great deal from Roger. I have learned about my own relationship to the field, about mentoring, about interpersonal communication within academia, about how to be true to myself while acting within the limiting, but also helpful, confines of the social sciences. I learned that questions can be sincere, even within the university. I learned that when a professor asks a student to deliver books or files, a Dictaphone or even two visiting German students, it need not speak to a difference in power. For these lessons and many others, I am very grateful. However, I still can't figure out how delivering his mail fits in.

Lucas B. Mazur
Received his PhD from Clark University, Worcester, Massachusetts

Roger was on the faculty at Clark when I was a graduate student in the 1980s. What I remember most about knowing and working with Roger are the many conversations we had. There was a dynamic back and forth, with one idea sparking another. Many years later, it is still a model I use as I work with students.

A favorite recollection is of an occasion in which I made a comment that reminded Roger of something Piaget had said. Quickly getting up from his chair, he searched among the many books in his office and found the one he wanted. Soon he had the pages he was looking for and gave me the book. Roger assumed more competence in me than was warranted: the book was in French; I handed it back, asking that he translate. As was often the case, Roger was gracious about my ignorance; he translated the passages of interest, furthering our conversation, my education, and my respect for him.

He and his wife, Ruth (see Figure 17.2), opened their home to me (as they did for others) for early morning supervisions, in my case when I was working with family practice residents at UMASS Medical School. There, in the comfort

Figure 17.2 Roger Bibace and is wife Ruth in 2014.

of their beautiful home, Roger and I also talked about our respective children and his grandchildren, bringing a personal perspective to developmental theory and to our relationship. I am grateful to Roger for the many ways he enriched my life.

Barbara Dowds
PhD student at Clark University, 1982–1987

My first sight of Roger was that of a sophisticated, continental gentleman wearing a tweed hacking jacket with two side vents, a bespoke shirt, a regimental tie, and a foreign accent I couldn't identify, smoking a pipe (Balkan Sobranie). I was duly impressed and determined to make his acquaintance. To my great delight, I learned he shared my enthusiasm for jazz (Coleman Hawkins), an unwavering affection for the Marx Brothers, and awed admiration for Ava Gardner. We have been close friends for more than 60 years, sharing the intellectual challenges of Dr. Werner, Dr. Wapner, and a long distinguished array of faculty and visiting celebrities through our graduate years (he must remember Vicki, the "talking chimp" who flew over Dr. Werner and Dr. Kurt Goldstein rather than engage them in conversation). Roger was a part of my family's happy times, crises, and tragedies, as I shared in the events in the lives of his children, siblings, nieces and nephews, and grandchildren. It was Roger who arranged my first date with my wife, and in a remarkable coincidence, he married a girl I had known since she and I were children. Roger has unquenchable zeal for learning; many times over the years, I have been struck by his insights into otherwise challenging ideas, and his originality as a therapist, researcher, and communicator. His delight in discovering new ideas, new projects, and new challenges has not wavered even as an "octogenarian." I'm certain he would reject my referring to him by that term, it might suggest his intellectual energy might be waning. Not a chance! I hope this conveys the depth of my friendship for Roger.

Irving Hurwitz
Received his PhD in clinical psychology at Clark University
Retired as associate professor emeritus from Boston College
(School of Education).

The Brazilian poet Vinicius de Moraes, who wrote the lyrics to "The Girl from Ipanema"—Roger Bibace's favorite song—once called life the "art of encounter." I could not find a better expression with which to begin writing about my academic and personal encounter with Roger. Yet, meeting Roger Bibace was an academic and personal experience far beyond the scope of the particular research project we built together. My first memories of him are from the first time that I attended the so called "kitchen seminars," where amazing scholars from all over the world meet, disagree, discuss creatively, and work together to build bridges and horizons, setting a real dialogical domain for the fragmented field of contemporary psychology. Roger was a core participant in that enterprise, and Jaan Valsiner was right when he told me that Roger, being the eldest, was possibly the youngest, most refreshing mind among his peers at the kitchen and at Clark University.

Over the course of our weekly meetings at the kitchen seminars and for the research project, I was fascinated by Roger's openness to diversity and his warm concern about those foreign scholars and their foreign worlds. His ability to move through diverse fields in the area, opening possibilities of integration and convergence, is striking. I could also see Roger Bibace as humanist, truly interested in the personal drama and social experience in this troubled contemporary world, translating Jean Piaget when visiting American universities, being colleague and friend to scholars like Jerome Bruner, Irving Sigel, Heinz Werner, and Jaan Valsiner. While researching at Clark, I gained insight into Roger's place in the history of psychology in the USA. I would describe him as a very active scholar, eye-witness to its crossroads and perplexities, recollecting essential parameters and directions, open to the actual psychological dynamics of human living, free of small questions and power games. This is the Roger Bibace I encountered, as is also pointed out in our general introduction for the book *Cultural Dynamics in Women's Lives*, a nook that was born before sunrise and inspired by him, during the 6:30 a.m. Clark meetings. There, we editors comment on how Roger had expanded the horizons of the whole editorial project, through his "dream of building something more authentic than a mere set of medical and psychological questions on procreation" (Bastos, Uriko, & Valsiner, 2011, p. x):

> Women's lives are subjective, dedicated, playful, problematic, and resilient—each in their own way. And Roger—who always makes the emphatic claim "I am not a mind-reader!"—understands the intricacies of the human mind better than any professional mind reader ever could. From his perspective—which exists thanks to the legacy of Heinz Werner in developmental science—it is the full psychological dynamics of living that need to be carefully scrutinized to understand the intricacies of pregnancy and childbirth. (p. x)

I finish this brief, personal note evoking a memory of March 2006, when Roger, accompanied by his beloved wife Ruth, visited Brazil. This visit was a confirmation of every dimension of Roger Bibace I had glimpsed during my stay at Clark. During his lectures at the Federal University of Bahia and the workshops with researchers and students—including a visit to an educational center for children and adolescents in a poor neighborhood—Roger impressed all of us, writing extensive notes and suggestions concerning every research project he had discussed. It was his generosity and desire to bring everything he could from his knowledge and experience to the professors, researchers, students, and practitioners from Bahia.

For the last days of Roger and Ruth's visit, my husband and I travelled to Rio de Janeiro with them. Rio, because of soccer and, especially Bossa Nova, was part of their dream of Brazil. One morning, we went to see a fair in the neighborhood of Ipanema. Very much to Roger and Ruth's delight, a band beautifully played Roger's favorite song, "Garota de Ipanema," in the middle of the garden, creating a magical atmosphere—which they fully enjoyed—for their farewell from Brazil. The song mentions how the world can be transformed by a special encounter between human beings, even if it is only a fleeting moment.[1] Roger's encounter with me and my Brazilian colleagues[2] and students was not fleeting, but remains in time and contributes to our perspectives in psychology as a disciplinary field, in its theoretical and practical sides, and to the reframing of the dialogical interplay of identity-alterity in research settings.

Ana Cecília de Sousa Bastos
Professor at Federal University of Bahia
and Catholic University of Salvador, Brazil

It was October 10, 2007, my first kitchen seminar. I had arrived in Worcester some days before, just to be immediately swept away by the turmoil of the kitchen-group at Clark University. I remember that I walked along Clark's third floor corridor with a sense of hesitation. It took awhile for that environment to become more familiar to me and, eventually, it turned into an important part of my biography. But on the first day, I was quite anxious and worried because of my poor English skills and because I had no idea of the "usual routine." I entered the kitchen room, holding the draft in my hands, and Roger smiled at me saying "Buongiorno Signorina" in Italian. I was surprised that someone spoke Italian and we immediately started talking about my country and why he knew some Italian words as well as songs and movies.

The short exchange at the beginning of my first K-seminar helped to break the ice. I could enter the physical and symbolic space of the K-seminar more easily and relaxed. From that day on, the red leaves of the Clark trees became even more colourful and beloved to my eyes. For the following seven years, Roger kept welcoming me with a Buongiorno whenever I entered the room in the morning.

I experienced him as a fervent scholar. Many times, I saw him pounding on the table, screaming: "Perception! Perception!" Always linked with the topic under discussion, this was his way (among others) to drive our attention towards what are the very basics of mental functioning—aside of any speculation. In addition, Roger has always been ready to provide references to people discussing their work at K-seminar. During my last K-dinner in

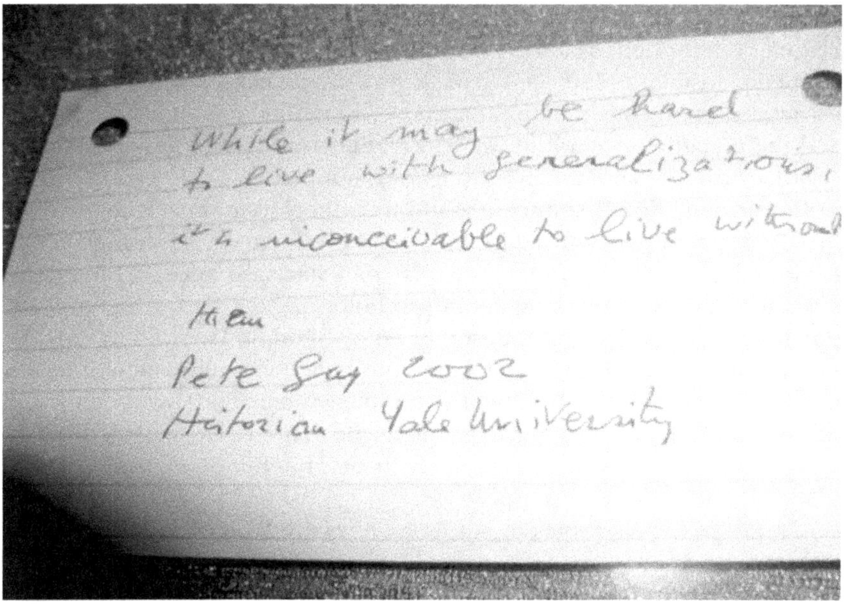

Figure 17.3 Reference note written by Roger Bibace.

2011, he got up from his chair at the end of the long table in the Vietnamese restaurant and came to me with a piece of paper (see Figure 17.3) he had brought from home.

It was a reference he had written down related to what I was and am still studying. I was very grateful, not only for the academic suggestion, but also for him thinking of me and spending time searching for that reference. His generosity always became visible in these small acts making him such a special human being. He had me on his mind when he searched for this reference; with this fond memory, he now is on my mind whenever I think of my time at Clark University.

Giuseppina Marsico
Assistant professor in developmental and Educational Psychology
University of Salerno, Italy

I first met Roger when I came to Clark to interview for a job. I had interviewed at a few other places, and the faculty were always very encouraging, almost as if they were trying to recruit me, not test me. At Clark, things were different. I had trained as a community mental health clinician, working on practical programs to intervene in communities and cultures. The Clark faculty interviewers didn't seem very impressed, but the biggest challenge came from Roger. Within the first minute of my interview with him, he asked me for the theoretical basis for our interventions. I had no theory. Hadn't even thought of the possibility. All I knew was that the interventions seemed plausible, and seemed to work. So I was panicked. When I stumbled through some feeble attempt at a theory, he grilled me about the details, and the meta-theory, and the ways to evaluate my ideas, and all the other "Clarkie" things I should have thought of, but hadn't.

Considering how that interview and the others went, I have no idea why the Department decided to hire me, but they did, as a community mental health clinician. The problem was that they had also opened my eyes to a whole new way of thinking about psychology, about theorizing, and the potential contributions of philosophy. So by the time I arrived to start the new academic year, I no longer wanted to be a community mental health person, or even a clinician. Roger (with the assistance of Mort Wiener and Bernie Kaplan) had managed to persuade me to not be the person they had hired me to be. For which I have always been grateful.

James D. Laird
Professor at Clark University, Worcester, Massachusets
Department of Psychology

NOTES

1. "Ah, se ela soubesse/Que quando ela passa/O mundo inteirinho se enche de graça". ["Ah, if she knew/ That when she goes by/The whole world fills with joy".] (Vinicius de Moraes & Antonio Carlos Jobim)
2. Especially Lívia Simão and Alvaro Duran, University of São Paulo; Virginia Dazzani and Waldomiro Silva, Federal University of Bahia.

ABOUT THE CONTRIBUTORS

Michael Bamberg has been a professor of psychology at Clark University, Worcester, Massachusetts, since 1986; and since spring 2013, Yunshan Chair Professor at Guangdong University of Foreign Studies in China. In 1975, Bamberg completed his Staatsexamen (master's equivalent) in German linguistics and literature, education, and theology at the University of Marburg, Germany. In 1978, he received an MPhil from the University of York, England, and later in 1985 his PhD in psychology from the University of California, Berkeley. In 1981, Bamberg took a lectureship in sociology at the Free University of Berlin where he worked on Martin Kohli's project on retirement, using biographic methods. In 1985, while still working on his dissertation, he went to Shanghai, China, to teach German and learn Chinese, before returning to the United States and taking a tenure track position at Clark University. Today, he is the editor of the journal *Narrative Inquiry* through which he supports and encourages theorizing and research into narrative from interdisciplinary perspectives. In addition, he is the series editor of *Studies in Narrative*, consisting of edited volumes and monographs at the cutting edge of narrative research. In his research he investigates the use of narratives in how people construct a sense of who they are in interaction with others. He is a proponent of positioning analysis and has developed a particular method of how to analyze interlocutors' identity navigation in real-life situations. Email: mbamberg@clarku.edu

Particulars and Universals in Clinical and Developmental Psychology, pages 287–295

Ana Cecilia de Sousa Bastos is a professor at Federal University of Bahia and Catholic University of Salvador, Brazil. From 2000 to 2015, she worked as a researcher for the National Research Council (CNPQ). For two decades, she has been studying the cultural organization of Brazilian families living in poverty, at times of intense social change, focusing on parental ideas and child-rearing practices. Currently, she is interested in the analysis of meaning-making processes that women from different generations build around childbirth (taken as a marker for understanding developmental transitions). Through their narratives, Dr. Bastos explores the changes in the meaning of parenthood across the life span. She also investigated developmental transitions, adopting collaborative autoethnography as a methodological tool. She is the author of *Modos de Partilhar: A Criança e o Cotidiano da família (Ways of Sharing: The Child and the Family in Everyday Life)*, editor of *Living in Poverty: Developmental Poetics of Cultural Realities* with Elaine Rabinovich, and editor of *Cultural Dynamics of Women's Lives* with Jaan Valsiner and Kristiina Uriko. With Giuseppina Marsico, Virgínia Dazzani and Marilena Ristum, she edited *Educational Contexts and Borders through a Cultural Lens.* The most recent work of her and of the group she coordinates was just published in the first volume of *Annals of Cultural Psychology: Making Meaning, Making Motherhood* (edited by Kenneth Cabell, Giuseppina Marsico, Carlos Cornejo and Jaan Valsiner). Email: anaceciliabastos@gmail.com

Suara Bastos is a professor of psychology at Group Unifox MBA in São Paulo, Brazil. She received her bachelor's degree in psychology in 2007 and her master's degree in 2013. Since then, she has been a PhD student at the Institute at the Institute of Psychology of the University of São Paulo. She is a researcher for the Coordination of the Improvement of Higher Education Personnel (CAPES). In addition, she is a member of the Research Group on Cultural Psychology (GPPC/USP) at the Laboratory of the Verbal Interaction and Knowledge Construction (LIVCC/USP). Currently, she is conducting research within the theorétical framework of semiotic cultural constructivism from a dialogical perspective focusing on the circus universe. Her main topics of interest are the cultural construction of meaning, intersubjectivity, affectivity and conviviality. Among her more representative works is the article "Cultural-Affective Bonds in Field-Research: Towards a Semiotic-Constructivist Understanding of Circus Daily Life" (2014) that she wrote together with Danilo Silva Guimarães. The article was published in *Psychology and Society*. Emails: suara@usp.br and suarabastos@uol.com.br.

Roger Bibace is introduced in the beginning of Section V (pp. 271–272).

Nancy Budwig is a professor of psychology at Clark University, Worcester, Massachusetts. Nancy Budwig received her BA from Vassar College in 1979

and her PhD from the University of California, Berkeley in 1986. Currently Budwig is associate provost and dean of research at Clark University where she also is a professor of psychology. Building on her prior research on language development and language socialization, which has examined the ways participation in language practices support the construction of language and personhood, Budwig's newer research examines the relationship between the development of knowledge and practice within knowledge building communities, especially institutions of higher education. She is particularly interested in how participation in communities of practice contributes to the gradual construction of meaning systems. Budwig is the editor of a book series entitled *Interdisciplinary Perspectives on the Study of Knowledge and Development* published by Cambridge University Press, an associate editor of the *British Journal of Developmental Psychology,* and is an editorial board member of several other journals in the area of human development. In addition to serving on the board of directors, Budwig is a past president of the *Jean Piaget Society for the Interdisciplinary Study of Knowledge and Development.* Email: NBudwig@clarku.edu

Ronald J. Comer has been a professor in Princeton University's Department of Psychology for the past 40 years, serving also as director of clinical psychology studies, and currently as chair of the university's institutional review board. Professor Comer has received the President's Award for Distinguished Teaching at the university. He is also a practicing clinical psychologist and a consultant to Eden Autism Services and to hospitals and family practice residency programs throughout New Jersey. He is author of the textbook *Abnormal Psychology* (nine editions) and the textbook *Fundamentals of Abnormal Psychology* (seven editions); coauthor of the introductory psychology textbook *Psychology Around Us* (two editions); and coauthor of *Case Studies in Abnormal Psychology* (two editions). He is the producer of numerous videos for courses in psychology and other fields of education, including *The Higher Education Video Library Series, Video Anthology for Abnormal Psychology, Video Segments in Neuroscience, Introduction to Psychology Video Clipboard,* and *Developmental Psychology Video Clipboard.* He also has published journal articles in clinical psychology, social psychology, and family medicine. Professor Comer completed his undergraduate studies at the University of Pennsylvania and his graduate work at Clark University. He lives in Lawrenceville, New Jersey, with his wife, Marlene. Email: comer@ princeton.edu

Carolyn E. Cotsonas has been the senior director of Primary Care & Family Medicine at Cambridge Health Alliance since 2012. Before, she was the director for strategic planning at the Boston Medical Center being responsible for the institution-wide clinical services, clinical service line development and implementation, new clinical technologies assessment, as well as acquisition. From 1993 until 2012, she was an associate professor (health law) at the Boston University School of Public Health. She was also the associate director of the Generalist Physician Initiative at the Boston University School of Medicine (1993–2000). Right after graduating from Harvard Law School (JD), she became associate professor and special projects director at the University of Massachusetts Medical School where she planned and implemented medical practice management and medical-legal curricula, and taught health law courses in the joint UMass-Clark University MHA program. She holds a BA in sociology from Tufts University.

Djalma Francisco Costa Lisboa de Freitas graduated in psychology from the Padre Anchieta University (2010), Brazil, and received his master's of science at the Experimental Psychology Department of the University of São Paulo in 2013. He is a doctoral student (Graduate Program of Experimental Psychology, IPUSP, Brazil), psychologist working at the Psychoeducacional Institute Bela Vista, Jundiaí, São Paulo, Brazil, and a researcher working for the Coordination for the Improvement of Higher Education Personnel (CAPES), Brazil. His main focus of investigation is the cultural transmission process in experimental studies in cultural psychology. Among his more representative works is the article "An Experimental Study about Cultural Transmission Process" that he wrote together with Danilo Silva Guimarães that was published in *Psychology & Society* in 2013. Email: djamlaffreitas@usp.br

Danilo Silva Guimarães, PhD, is a professor at the Institute of Psychology of the University of São Paulo, Brazil, where he coordinates a researcher group on cultural psychology. He is also a sponsored researcher of the Brazilian National Council for Scientific and Technological Development. His main focus of investigation is the process of symbolic elaborations out of tensional boundaries between cultural identities and alterities, psychology, and Amerindian peoples. Among his more representative works are the articles "Symbolic Objects as Sediments of the Intersubjective Stream of Feelings," which was published in *Integrative Psychological and Behavioral Science* in 2010; and "Amerindian Anthropology and Cultural Psychology: Crossing Boundaries and Meeting Otherness' Worlds" (2011), as well as "Scientific Concepts and Public Policies: Semiotic-Cultural Obstacles Concerning Intergroup and Intercultural Relationships" (2012), both published in *Culture & Psychology*. His most recent work is the book *Temporality: Culture in the Flow of Human Experience* (2015) that he edited together with Lívia Mathias Simão and Jaan Valsiner. Email: danilosg@usp.br

Leslie Rupert Herrenkohl is a professor at the University of Washington, Seattle, Washington, in learning sciences and human development. She received a BA in psychology from Lafayette College in 1988 and a MA (1991) and PhD (1995) in developmental psychology from Clark University. She completed a postdoctoral fellowship at the University of Michigan from 1995–1997 supported by the James S. McDonnell Foundation Cognitive Studies for Educational Practice Program. Currently, she is also affiliated with the elementary teacher education and museology programs at the University of Washington. Her research seeks to understand the contextual and social features of learning environments and their impact on participants' learning and development. Her early work focused on cognitive and social dimensions of learning. In more recent work, she combines understanding of the conceptual and social nature of learning with the affective and motivational dimensions to provide a more holistic account of learning. Her research program involves three interrelated strands: (a) research on the conceptual, social, and discursive dimensions of science learning; (b) understanding learning as a holistic process of developing people while expanding their knowledge and skills; and (c) bridging research and practice through partnerships in formal and informal settings. She has received funding from the James S. McDonnell Foundation, the Spencer Foundation, the National Science Foundation, the National Library of Medicine, and the state of Washington. She is currently an editor for the section "Science Learning in Everyday Life" for the journal *Science Education.* Email: leslieh@uw.edu

AeJa Jung is a full-time professor for clinical psychology at the medical school of Jeonbuk National University in Jeonju City, South Korea. As a second job, she helps people suffering from a variety of health problems using mindfulness-based stress reduction (MBSR), a program combining meditation practices and yoga. Email: jungaeja@jbnu.ac.kr

Aleksandra Kaszowska graduated in 2012 from Clark University in Worcester, Massachusetts, with a bachelor's degree in psychology. She worked as a research assistant at the Nathan S. Kline Institute for Psychiatric Research in Orangeburg, New York, and at the Department of Communication and Psychology at Aalborg University in Denmark. She is currently pursuing her doctoral degree in cognitive science at Tufts University in Medford, Massachusetts. Email: aleksandra.kaszowska@tufts.edu

Nikita A. Kharlamov is an associate professor at the Department of Communication and Psychology, Aalborg University, Denmark, where his focus of research is urban psychology and natural setting perception, under the auspices of the Niels Bohr Professorship Centre for Cultural Psychology. Email: nikita@hum.aau.dk

Sven Hroar Klempe is an associate professor at the Department of Psychology, Norwegian University of Science and Technology (NTNU), Trondheim, Norway. In the past, he has held positions such as a full professorship in musicology, an associate professorship in media studies, and he has worked as a teacher and journalist. His research is cross-disciplinary with an emphasis on the history of psychology, culture and psychology, theory of science, communication, and music psychology. Email: hroar.klempe@svt.ntnu.no

Alina Kriebel is a graduate student in cross-cultural psychology at Osnabrück University in Germany. Through traveling, living, and working abroad, she was able to get a deeper insight into differing societies and cultures from an early age. She discovered several distinct behavioral, cognitive, and emotional differences, which led to her specific interest in culture as it relates to psychology. Reflecting her passion for understanding cultural diversity, she has previously conducted research at the Cross-Cultural Research Centre in Wellington, New Zealand, at Clark University in Worcester, Massachusetts, and at the Kokoro Research Center at Kyoto University, Japan. Currently she is working on a project at the University of British Columbia in Canada investigating how culturally dependent self-concepts influence disidentification processes from in-groups. Email: alina.kriebel@gmail.com

James D. Laird is a professor at Clark University, Worcester, Massachusetts, Department of Psychology. He received a BA from Middlebury College in 1962 and a PhD from the University of Rochester in 1966. He has been working at Clark since that time. In his research, he explores feelings: how they arise, affect behavior, and may be controlled and organized. He uses a self-perception approach to emotional problems, including the premenstrual syndrome and the panic and posttraumatic stress disorder. Other ongoing research explores personality factors that predict medical outcomes and adherence to medical advice. Email: jlaird@clarku.edu

Hernán Sánchez Rios is a professor at the Universidad del Valle, Colombia and a researcher at the Centro de Investigaciones en Psicología, Cognición y Cultura (Cali, Colombia). At the moment, he is a doctoral student at Instituto de Psicologia da Universidade de São Paulo, Brazil (graduate program of psychology). His research focuses on the cultural process of children's development from the perspective of semiotic-cultural constructivism. Among his more representative works are the chapter "Cognitive Development and Interaction Context" (2009, with M. Orozco & A. Perinat) that was part of Bastos and Prabinovich's book *Living in Poverty: Developmental Poetics of Cultural Realities,* and the chapter "Madre Ñame and the *Nonam*: One and Another" (2015, with L. Simão) that was part of Guimarães' book *Amerindian Paths: Guiding Dialogues with Psychology.* Email: hersanch@usp.br

Philip J. Rosenbaum, PhD, is a clinical psychologist and the director of Haverford Universities' Counseling and Psychological Services (CAPS). He completed his psychoanalytic training at the William Alanson White Institute. His interests are in studying the commonalities between contemporary interpersonal analytic practice and cultural psychology, particularly as it is connected to understanding meaning-making processes as they occur in interpersonal situations. Email: prosenba@haverford.edu

Lívia Mathias Simão, PhD, is an associated professor at the Institute of Psychology of the University of São Paulo, Brazil, where she coordinates the Laboratory of Verbal Interaction and Knowledge Construction. She is also a sponsored researcher of the Brazilian National Council for Scientific and Technological Development. Her main research interests concern issues embracing the ontological construction of human subjectivity in I-Culture-Other relationships from the perspective of the semiotic-cultural constructivism in psychology with emphasis on the notions of alterity, temporality, and disquieting experience. Among her more representative works are "Bildung, Culture and Self: A Possible Dialogue with Gadamer, Boesch and Valsiner?" which was published in *Theory & Psychology* in 2005; *Otherness in Question: Labyrinths of the Self* (2007), which she edited together with Jaan Valsiner; and her chapter "The Other in the Self: A Triadic Unit," which was published in Valsiner's *Oxford Handbook of Culture and Psychology* in 2012. Among her most recent works are the book *Temporality: Culture in the Flow of Human Experience* (2015) that she edited together with Danilo Guimarães and Jaan Valsiner, and the article Culture as a Moving Symbolic Border (2015) published in the *Journal Integrative Psychological and Behavioral Science.* Email: limsimao@usp.br

Saskia Celina Stöckigt is a graduate student in psychology at the University of Hamburg, Germany. Her main fields of interest are cross-cultural differences and clinical psychology. During her stay at Clark University in Worcester, Massachusetts, she was able to combine these in a research project on cross-cultural differences in ethics and morals in healing professions. Her current research includes projects on cultural differences in the stigmatization of schizophrenia and unwanted effects and side effects of psychotherapy. Email: saskia.stoeckigt@gmail.com

Jaan Valsiner is the Niels Bohr Professor of Cultural Psychology at Aalborg University, Denmark (since 2013). He received his higher education in Estonia, where he graduated from Tartu University in 1976 and completed his postgraduate work in 1979. He has been working at Clark University, Worcester, Massachusetts, since 1997 in the field of theoretical and cultural psychology. He won the Alexander von Humboldt Research Prize in Germany in 1995 and is affiliated with research groups all over the world (e.g., Brazil, the Netherlands, Japan, and Estonia). His extended CV can be downloaded from: http://personprofil.aau.dk/130747 Email: jvalsiner@hum.aau.dk

Mary E. Walsh is Daniel Kearns Professor of Urban Education and Innovative Leadership in the Department of Counseling and Developmental Psychology, Boston College. She is also the Director of the Boston College Center for Optimized Student Support and the Executive Director of City Connects. Dr. Walsh received her MA and PhD in Clinical-Developmental Psychology from Clark University working under the direction of Professor Roger Bibace. Her current research focuses on school–community support for schoolchildren and their families. In this context, Dr. Walsh launched "City Connects," an evidence-based practice which provides a systemic approach for schools to address out-of-school challenges students living in poverty. Email: walshhur@bc.edu

Meike Watzlawik is a professor at Sigmund Freud University, Berlin, Germany, and the International School of Management, Hamburg, Germany; Privatdozentin at the Technical University of Braunschweig, Department of Developmental, Personality, & Forensic Psychology (since 2008); and the CEO of a private career counseling institute in Bremen, Germany (since 2010). From 2011 to 2014, she was a visiting professor at the University of Osnabrück, Department of Development and Culture, and from 2008 to 2009, she was a visiting scholar (Feodor-Lynen Awardee of the Humboldt Foundation) at Clark University, Worcester, Massachusetts, working in the field of theoretical and cultural psychology. Examining different aspects of identity has been the focus of her research: In depth, she examined the sexual identity development of adolescents in Germany and the United States (Watzlawik, 2004; Watzlawik & Heine, 2009) and the impact of sibling relationships on identity development (Watzlawik, 2008, 2009). The combination of different methodologies was her preferred approach when examining adolescents' identity development in American traditional and non-traditional families. She discussed the benefit of such combinations in several papers (e.g., Watzlawik, 2011). In addition, she critically reflects on constructs like "identity," "cultural identity," "sexual identity," and "gender identity" in several of her publications stressing the need for clear definitions and transparency in science (e.g., Watzlawik, 2012; Watzlawik, Schachter, & Cunha, 2015). As part of an international network, Watzlawik has worked with scholars from all over the world, has presented the collaborative work at conferences, or in recognized publications like the *Oxford Handbook of Culture and Psychology* (Watzlawik & Valsiner, 2012). She is part of the editorial board of *Culture & Psychology*. Email: m.watzlawik@tu-bs.de

Angela Wiley is a professor of family studies and an extension specialist at the Department of Human and Community Development, University of Illinois. Dr. Wiley received her BA in psychology and women's studies from Miami University, Ohio, and her MA and PhD in developmental psychology from Clark University, Massachusetts. She completed a post-doctoral fellowship at the University of Illinois in developmental psychology and joined the faculty in 1999. Dr. Wiley's research focuses on resilience among families with a special interest in immigrant and minority populations and programs designed to support resilience. In this context, Dr. Wiley has developed a health promotion program called Abriendo Caminos to help Latino families prevent childhood obesity and improve family well-being. Email: awiley@illinois.edu

Stephen "Skip" Dine Young is a professor of psychology at Hanover College in Indiana where he has taught for 17 years. He received his BA from Miami University and his PhD in clinical psychology from Clark University in Worcester, Massachusetts in 1997. At Clark, he studied development, therapy, symbolism, stories, and movies. He is currently a licensed psychologist with interests in identity, college advising, and psychological assessment. Since his senior thesis, Skip has been combining his personal passion for popular cultural (particularly movies and music) with his scholarship. He believes that movies can be "equipment for living," they can take on personal meanings for viewers that impact our everyday lives (hopefully for the better). He is author of the book, *Psychology at the Movies* (Wiley). Email: youngst@hanover.edu

www.ingramcontent.com/pod-product-compliance
Lightning Source LLC
LaVergne TN
LVHW052253200926
848481LV00002B/358
* 9 7 8 1 6 8 1 2 3 3 5 9 8 *